Queering Governance and International Law

Oxford Studies in Gender and International Relations

Series editors: Rahul Rao, University of St Andrews, and Laura Sjoberg, Royal Holloway University of London

Windows of Opportunity: How Women Seize Peace Negotiations for Political Change
Miriam J. Anderson

Women as Foreign Policy Leaders: National Security and Gender Politics in Superpower America
Sylvia Bashevkin

Gendered Citizenship: Understanding Gendered Violence in Democratic India
Natasha Behl

Queering Governance and International Law: The Case of the International Criminal Tribunal for the Former Yugoslavia
Caitlin Biddolph

Gender, Religion, Extremism: Finding Women in Anti-Radicalization
Katherine E. Brown

Enlisting Masculinity: The Construction of Gender in U.S. Military Recruiting Advertising during the All-Volunteer Force
Melissa T. Brown

The Politics of Gender Justice at the International Criminal Court: Legacies and Legitimacy
Louise Chappell

The Other #MeToos
Iqra Shagufta Cheema

Cosmopolitan Sex Workers: Women and Migration in a Global City
Christine B. N. Chin

Intelligent Compassion: Feminist Critical Methodology in the Women's International League for Peace and Freedom
Catia Cecilia Confortini

Hidden Wars: Gendered Political Violence in Asia's Civil Conflicts
Sara E. Davies and Jacqui True

Complicit Sisters: Gender and Women's Issues across North-South Divides
Sara de Jong

Gender and Private Security in Global Politics
Maya Eichler

This American Moment: A Feminist Christian Realist Intervention
Caron E. Gentry

Troubling Motherhood: Maternality in Global Politics
Lucy B. Hall, Anna L. Weissman, and Laura J. Shepherd

Breaking the Binaries in Security Studies: A Gendered Analysis of Women in Combat
Ayelet Harel-Shalev and Shir Daphna-Tekoah

Fixing Gender: The Paradoxical Politics of Training Peacekeepers
Aiko Holvikivi

Scandalous Economics: Gender and the Politics of Financial Crises
Aida A. Hozić and Jacqui True

Building Peace, Rebuilding Patriarchy: The Failure of Gender Interventions in Timor-Leste
Melissa Johnston

Rewriting the Victim: Dramatization as Research in Thailand's Anti-Trafficking Movement
Erin M. Kamler

Equal Opportunity Peacekeeping: Women, Peace, and Security in Post-Conflict States
Sabrina Karim and Kyle Beardsley

Gender, Sex, and the Postnational Defense: Militarism and Peacekeeping
Annica Kronsell

Good Victims: The Political as a Feminist Question
Roxani Krystalli

The Beauty Trade: Youth, Gender, and Fashion Globalization
Angela B. V. McCracken

Global Norms and Local Action: The Campaigns against Gender-Based Violence in Africa
Peace A. Medie

Rape Loot Pillage: The Political Economy of Sexual Violence in Armed Conflict
Sara Meger

Critical Perspectives on Cybersecurity: Feminist and Postcolonial Interventions
Anwar Mhajne and Alexis Henshaw

Support the Troops: Military Obligation, Gender, and the Making of Political Community
Katharine M. Millar

From Global to Grassroots: The European Union, Transnational Advocacy, and Combating Violence against Women
Celeste Montoya

Who Is Worthy of Protection? Gender-Based Asylum and US Immigration Politics
Meghana Nayak

Revisiting Gendered States: Feminist Imaginings of the State in International Relations
Swati Parashar, J. Ann Tickner, and Jacqui True

Out of Time: The Queer Politics of Postcoloniality
Rahul Rao

Critical Feminist Justpeace: Grounding Theory in Grassroots Praxis
Karie Cross Riddle

Gender, UN Peacebuilding, and the Politics of Space: Locating Legitimacy
Laura J. Shepherd

Narrating the Women, Peace and Security Agenda: Logics of Global Governance
Laura J. Shepherd

Capitalism's Sexual History
Nicola J. Smith

The Global Politics of Sexual and Reproductive Health
Maria Tanyag

A Feminist Voyage through International Relations
J. Ann Tickner

The Political Economy of Violence against Women
Jacqui True

Queer International Relations: Sovereignty, Sexuality and the Will to Knowledge
Cynthia Weber

Feminist Global Health Security
Clare Wenham

Bodies of Violence: Theorizing Embodied Subjects in International Relations
Lauren B. Wilcox

Queering Governance and International Law

The Case of the International Criminal Tribunal for the Former Yugoslavia

CAITLIN BIDDOLPH

OXFORD
UNIVERSITY PRESS

Oxford University Press is a department of the University of Oxford.
It furthers the University's objective of excellence in research, scholarship,
and education by publishing worldwide. Oxford is a registered trade mark of
Oxford University Press in the UK and in certain other countries.

Published in the United States of America by Oxford University Press
198 Madison Avenue, New York, NY 10016, United States of America.

© Oxford University Press 2025

All rights reserved. No part of this publication may be reproduced, stored in a retrieval system, transmitted, used for text and data mining, or used for training artificial intelligence, in any form or by any means, without the prior permission in writing of Oxford University Press, or as expressly permitted by law, by license or under terms agreed with the appropriate reprographics rights organization. Inquiries concerning reproduction outside the scope of the above should be sent to the Rights Department, Oxford University Press, at the address above.

You must not circulate this work in any other form
and you must impose this same condition on any acquirer.

Library of Congress Cataloging-in-Publication Data
Names: Biddolph, Caitlin, author.
Title: Queering governance and international law : the case of the
International Criminal Tribunal for the former Yugoslavia / Caitlin Biddolph.
Description: New York : Oxford University Press, 2025. |
Series: Oxford Studies in Gender and International Relations series |
Includes bibliographical references and index.|
Identifiers: LCCN 2024055399 (print) | LCCN 2024055400 (ebook) |
ISBN 9780197803141 (hardback) | ISBN 9780197803165 (epub) |
ISBN 9780197803172
Subjects: LCSH: International Tribunal for the Prosecution of Persons
Responsible for Serious Violations of International Humanitarian Law
Committed in the Territory of the Former Yugoslavia since 1991. |
Gender identity—Law and legislation—Former Yugoslav republics. |
Homosexuality—Law and legislation—Former Yugoslav republics. |
Yugoslav War Crime Trials, Hague, Netherlands, 1994- |
Yugoslav War, 1991-1995—Law and legislation.
Classification: LCC KZ1203.A2 B53 2025 (print) |
LCC KZ1203.A2 (ebook) | DDC 341.6/90268—dc23/eng/20241120
LC record available at https://lccn.loc.gov/2024055399
LC ebook record available at https://lccn.loc.gov/2024055400

DOI: 10.1093/9780197803172.001.0001

Printed by Marquis, Canada

Acknowledgments

This book is a product of the support, friendship, and inspiration that many people have generously provided. Thank you to Penny Griffin and Liz Thurbon, who supervised my doctoral thesis, on which this monograph is based. They are the most gracious, kind, and intelligent people, and I feel privileged to have received their wisdom over the years. With my work, they found promise where I found doubts, they pushed me to sit with the uncomfortable, to relinquish some control, and to surrender to the stories my research would tell. I am a better researcher because of them, and I thank them for their guidance and unwavering support. Enormous thanks must also go to Laura Sjoberg and Gina Heathcote, who were exceptional PhD examiners, and I still feel incredibly humbled that they read my work! My deep gratitude also extends to Laura Shepherd, who has been an amazing source of guidance and wisdom; the best person to have in your corner. The time spent as a postdoctoral research fellow at the University of Sydney with Laura was a gift and a privilege. It is an honor to have been mentored by Laura, and I'm quite sure this book would not be possible without her sage advice, insights, and encouragement. Thank you (again) to Laura Shepherd and Laura Sjoberg for providing extremely helpful feedback on some of the later versions of the chapters in this book.

While the early forms of this monograph were written during my time as a PhD student at the University of New South Wales (UNSW), Australia, much of the refining, revising, and additional writing were done during my time at the University of Sydney, Australia, as a Postdoctoral Research Fellow in Gender and Global Governance. I have made colleagues and friends that have been a great source of support. At UNSW, my thanks go to Nick Apoifis, Monika Barthwal-Datta, Deb Barros Leal Farias, Alba Boer Cueva, Will Clapton, Cait Hamilton, Andy Kaladelfos, Lucas Lixinski, Lenka Olejníková, Lana Tatour, and Sarah Williams. At the University of Sydney, special thanks to my feminist community: Doris Asante, Sulagna Basu, Charlotte Carney, Keshab Giri, Siân Perry, Jihyun Kim, Georgia Peters, Kate Scott, and Laura Shepherd. I have been fortunate to cultivate enduring friendships in academia that have sustained me and provided the motivation to complete this book, and to call many of these aforementioned people friends as well as colleagues. Big shout out to Caitlin Mollica and Q Manivannan as well, whom I've been lucky to find along the way. It is a joy to know all these people and call them my friends.

At Oxford University Press, I have been fortunate to work with Angela Chnapko, who has been incredibly patient and supportive, and has responded to my anxious emails with utmost grace. My thanks also my production editor, Andrea Smith, to the series editors, Laura Sjoberg and Rahul Rao, and the two anonymous readers for helpful comments and feedback at various stages of the project.

The research presented in this book was made possible by an Australian Government Research Training Scholarship, which offered invaluable financial support during my PhD, for which I am extremely grateful.

Data and analysis from Chapter 4 appeared elsewhere as follows: "Haunting Justice: Queer Bodies, Ghosts, and the International Criminal Tribunal for the former Yugoslavia," *International Feminist Journal of Politics* 26, no. 2 (2024): 216–239, https://www.tandfonline.com/doi/full/10.1080/14616742.2024.2333113 (Copyright: Taylor & Francis); "Queering (Un)Certainty in International Criminal Law: Reflections on the International Criminal Tribunal for the former Yugoslavia," in *Queer Engagements with International Law: Times, Spaces, Imaginings*, edited by Claerwen O'Hara and Tamsin Phillipa Paige (Routledge, forthcoming); "Queer Theories in/and Global Governance," in *Edward Elgar Handbook on Global Governance*, edited by Ruth Houghton, Aoife O'Donoghue, Yassin Brunger, and Cher Chen (Edward Elgar, forthcoming). I am grateful for permission to revise this material.

Thanks to my family, for supporting me through my never-ending educational pursuits, for listening to the highs and lows of this process and being my biggest cheerleaders. I am especially grateful to my parents for their love and for always believing in me. I am so grateful to Marios, for his love and support throughout. To my fur siblings, who I always said would feature in my acknowledgments: Jasper, Cooper, Jemima, and Sam.

This book was mostly written on the lands of the Darug and Guringai people, the traditional custodians of the land I call home. Each day I sat at my desk writing this book, the verdant green bushlands of Ku-ring-gai anchored me to this place. I am a settler living on this unceded land, and I thank Darug and Guringai elders, past and present for their custodianship of Country.

Finally, I would like to acknowledge the victims and survivors of the Bosnian conflict. Their pain, heartache, and hope are felt in the stories and testimonies they provided to the ICTY, and in the pages of this book.

Contents

List of Abbreviations	xii
Content Warning	xiii
1. International Law as a (Queer) Governance Mechanism	1
2. Queer Concepts and Methods	22
3. Logics of Governance and International Law at/of the International Criminal Tribunal for the Former Yugoslavia	49
4. Governing through Adjudication: Legal Violence at/of the International Criminal Tribunal for the Former Yugoslavia	72
5. Subverting International Law and Violence at/of the International Criminal Tribunal for the Former Yugoslavia	108
6. Queer Reckonings with International Law: Hope, Violence, and Critique	135
Appendix 1 ICTY Case Information	153
Appendix 2 List of ICTY Documents	154
Notes	170
References	172
Index	191

List of Abbreviations

EU	European Union
Former Yugoslavia	Bosnia and Herzegovina, Croatia, Kosovo,
former Yugoslav	Montenegro, North Macedonia, Serbia, Slovenia
territories or countries	
ICC	International Criminal Court
ICJ	International Court of Justice
ICTR	International Criminal Tribunal for Rwanda
ICTY or the Tribunal	International Criminal Tribunal for the former Yugoslavia
NATO	North Atlantic Treaty Organization
LGBTQIA+	Lesbian, gay, bisexual, trans, queer, intersex, asexual, aromantic, and other non-normative gender identities, sexual orientations, and practices
OtP	Office of the Prosecutor
PDA	Poststructural discourse analysis
QPDA	Queer poststructural discourse analysis
TWAIL	Third World Approaches to International Law
UN	United Nations
UNSC	United Nations Security Council
UK	United Kingdom
US	United States of America
WWII	World War II

Content Warning

Readers are advised that this book contains descriptions of graphic violence and traumatic material, including torture, sexual violence, killing, and genocide. The book also details instances of homophobia and ethnic slurs. Reader discretion is advised.

1
International Law as a (Queer) Governance Mechanism

[L]aw cannot *be* other-than-violence.

(Hamzić 2018, 84, emphasis in original)

Queering international law involves dreaming. It requires stepping outside the framing presumptions of "normal" law to reveal and challenge the heteronormative underpinnings of the hierarchies of power and value that the law sustains.

(Otto 2022b, 22)

This book is about the cis-heteronormative discourses and civilizational logics that animate governance and international law. It reveals the uncomfortable ways that international law is both violent *and* a site and agent of subversive possibilities, and that this simultaneity, this tension, constitutes international law as a (queer) governance mechanism. Using the case of the International Criminal Tribunal for the former Yugoslavia (ICTY or the Tribunal) as an illustrative example, the book illuminates the queer potential and resistances that infuse international law. This is even as law perpetuates cis-heteronormative discourses and civilizational logics of governance, violences that make possible the victimization, denunciation, and paternalism of racialized populations. The book *queers* governance and international law: it exposes gendered and sexualized meanings and critiques legal status quos so that more transformative, more liberatory, and queerer paths to justice might be dreamed and manifested within and beyond international law.

International law is composed by a multitude of contested perspectives, and this includes the various actors—such as international lawyers, State representatives, bureaucrats, and organizations—that propel its mandate. It offers legal accounts of violence and authorizes its various bodies (e.g., courts, tribunals, councils, etc.) as knowable (and knowing) sites of governance. But these juridical practices are unstable, constituted not by a fixed legal truth about violence, but by plural discourses and logics that shape how violent and violated bodies are known and governed. Such discursive practices are entangled with ideas about gender, sexuality, and violence, upholding the straight, cisgender legal subject as the common sense. What might it mean, then, to read international law as queer, even as it (re)installs exclusionary gendered, sexualized, and racialized configurations of (il)legality? And how might queer work complicate international law's exclusionary *and* subversive discourses of gender, sexuality, and violence?

International law is made known and permitted to judicially intervene in and through the invocation of gendered and sexualized discourses, as well as racial and civilizational logics about the world. Examples of these discourses abound in both the longer and recent histories of international law: the Hague Convention of 1899 spoke on behalf of "a community of civilized societies" to "extend [...] the empire [sic] of law" (quoted in Otto 2020, 23); the Geneva Convention of 1949 codified gendered constructions of civilians and combatants (Kinsella 2004); and, as demonstrated in this book, the ICTY positioned itself as "the only civilized alternative" to ethnic cleansing, rape, and atrocities in the former Yugoslavia (ICTY Annual Report 1994, para 15). In international law's demarcation of (il)legality, certain bodies and practices are criminalized through appeals to their hyper-heteromasculinity, others are infantilized and feminized as victims, while still others are authorized to denounce, condemn, imprison, and violate in the name of law and order. Just as international law is both constituted by and reinstalls violent, cis-heteronormative discourses and civilizational logics, stories of resistance, and of subverting juridical violence, also exist and shape law's governing practices.

The core argument of this book is that queering governance and international law reveals the coexistence of these seemingly contradictory things: that law is violent and violating, a site and agent that reduces complex lives and histories to "good" (lawful) and "bad" (criminal) bodies subject to protection, praise, or punishment; *and* that victims, survivors, and oppressed communities might find hope, resistance, and transgression within and outside international law's boundaries (see Chapter 6). By understanding international law as a (queer) governance mechanism, it is possible to envision the plurality and ambivalences that come with engaging the law as a form of justice and a response to injustice. It is to make visible the cis-heteronormative, civilizational common sense that undergirds legal discourse, and to trace how people navigate this violent governance mechanism in resistive and transgressive ways.

In this book, I am interested in how international law is a mechanism of and for governance (i.e., the technologies, structures, or practices through which people and things are governed), and that how international law governs depends on and (re)produces discourses of gender, sexuality, and violence. Drawing on the case of the ICTY, I trace how law's violence is shaped by and constructs legal subjects in cis-heteronormative ways. By cis-heteronormative, I refer to the institutionalized preference and normalization of cisgender identities (i.e., of individuals who accept their gender identity assigned at birth) and heterosexuality. Cis-heteronormative visions of gender and sexuality violently exclude non-normative identities and practices of gender and sexuality and depend on the devalorization of the queer and the feminine. My queer approach also reveals and revels in the plural, complicated, and entangled logics that animate international law. It is not just a question of how violence is reinstalled at/by the Tribunal (and through international law) in gendered and gendering ways but also that its governing practices also maintain the (queer) potential to subvert violence, and that *both* things are happening at the same time. Queering is about deconstructing gendered and sexualized meanings, *and* about revealing the plural, complicated, and entangled ways in which violence is constituted. Through my queer analysis of the ICTY, then, I expose and embrace the queer ambivalence, multiplicity, and potential of international law.

Feminist, Postcolonial, and Queer Approaches to International Law

My intervention contributes to an emerging body of scholarship queering international law, a research agenda that began in the early 2000s (see Morgan 2000; Buss 2007; Otto 2007) and has flourished in the proceeding years. It is important to trace its feminist connections and lineages, noting that much of the work queering international law (my own included) proceeds from a perspective that is both queer and feminist. Feminist international legal scholars were among the first to problematize the exclusionary foundations of international law (see Buss 1998; Charlesworth 1999; Charlesworth and Chinkin 2000; Smart 1990). They were increasingly troubled by the gendered structures that helped establish international law and how law "operates to reinforce gendered and sexed assumptions" (Charlesworth and Chinkin 2000, 18). Feminist analyses debunk the myth of an objective international law (Charlesworth 1999, 382). As Dianne Otto writes, this myth upholds "the power of law as a system of knowledge that sustains and celebrates masculinist and imperial versions of reality as universal, neutral, and rational, as ultimate/legal truth" (2022a, 396). These gendered binaries are sewn into the fabric of international law, making it difficult (although not impossible) to subvert the cis-heterosexist hierarchies of the field. As such, feminist analyses of international law recognize "the tension between . . . resistance and compliance," of "seeking change from within, versus working beyond the constraints of that system to completely reimagine international law" (Jones 2023, 11; see also Burgis-Kasthala and Sander 2024, 137–138). It is a tension and an (im)possibility I return to in Chapter 6, heeding feminist and queer suspicions of law's violence, while at the same time embracing their visions of justice beyond the law.

The queer approach I develop in this book shares much with these feminist analyses, but also extends, stretches, and tears at their boundaries by explicitly articulating not just the sexist but the cis-heteronormative common sense of international law (Otto 2013, 82). This is not to say that feminist analyses don't pay attention to binaries of cis-/trans and straight/queer *in addition to* masculine/feminine (see, e.g., Engle 2020; Heathcote 2019; Jones 2023), all of which are entangled. Rather, in articulating a queer analysis of governance and international law in this book, I work in dialogue with queer and feminist scholars to make explicit and critique the cis-heteronormativity of international law, and to embrace the contradictory, strange, and queer logics that make law a mechanism of both violence and resistance.

The queer analysis I develop in this book also owes much to postcolonial or Third World approaches to international law (TWAIL). These perspectives problematize the Eurocentric, colonial foundations of international law (Cetinkaya 2023, 18; Kapur 2015, 272; Rajagopal 2003, 172; Reynolds and Xavier 2016, 968; Watson 2014, 1), which is "entrenched in and perpetuates racialized hierarchies of humanity" (Ba 2021, 376). Postcolonial and TWAIL scholars argue that international criminal law "has reproduced colonial legacies more than it has challenged them" (Reynolds and Xavier 2016, 975), and that coloniality itself thrived and survives through the international criminal justice system (Ba 2021, 382, 385; see also Nesiah 2019). Much of this scholarship has focused on the International Criminal Court (ICC) as the embodiment of these "colonial durabilities" (Mertens et al. 2022), a court that "reproduce[s] racial blindness" (Edelbi 2020, 8), selectively prosecutes Global South crimes, and obfuscates Western ones (Ba et al. 2023, 9). As a result, it "continues to broadly associate the concepts of violence, criminality and dangerousness with the social construct of 'Blackness,' especially Black masculinity" (Ba 2021, 385; see also Clarke 2019, 88). This reflects the broader "role of political whiteness within international legal institutions" (Heathcote and Kula 2023, 9) and the difficulty of dislodging white coloniality as a function of international law.

Such critiques inform my own reading of international law. At the ICTY, civilizational logics about the former Yugoslavia construct "sadistic" perpetrators, feminized victims, and international saviors, with each subjected to different forms of legal treatment. Postcolonial and TWAIL scholarship reveal the multiple violences that are entrenched within, sustain, and stem from international law. These include the violence of reductive, civilizational, and racial logics of humanity, which denounce some populations as inherently violent and incapable of saving themselves or achieving justice. It also includes the perpetuation of "broader carceral colonial orders of modernity" (Ba et al. 2023, 2), taking criminal and carceral responses as the status quo and extending the "racism in domestic criminal justice systems" to the international (Grady 2021, 363–64; see also Rigney 2024).

In dialogue with feminist and postcolonial analyses of international law, queer perspectives have reimagined international human rights law (Duffy 2021; Kapur 2018; Lee 2021, 2022; Simm 2020); international criminal law (Biddolph 2020, 2021, 2024a, 2024b; Eichert 2021; Elander 2018b; Suhr 2022); neoliberal economic governance (O'Hara 2022; Zalnieriute 2018); colonial governance (Rao 2018, 2020); international security (Buss and Rutherford 2018; Hamzić 2018; Paige 2018); law and kinship (Gonzalez-Salzberg 2022; Sørlie 2018); and transitional justice (Bueno-Hansen 2018; Biddolph 2024c; Fobear 2014; Maier 2020). These queer approaches interrogate the gendered, sexualized, and racialized subjects and practices of international law (Ruskola 2010, 1478). Often, this manifests as scholars seek to amplify the rights and perspectives of lesbian, gay, bi, trans, queer, intersex, asexual, aromantic, and other non-normative sexualities and genders (LGBTQIA+). But most queer approaches to international law are committed to a broader critique and deconstruction of the structures of power that constitute law.

Queer orientations expose the violent, gendered, and racial (re)production of international law. Much of this scholarship is concerned with dismantling the cis-heteronormative, Eurocentric, and racist power relations that constitute the international legal project. Queer perspectives are therefore attentive not only to "how sexuality works as a fundamental organising principle in international law" (Otto 2018a, 6) but also to how it "remain[s] firmly anchored in militaristic, heteronormative, national imaginaries, in which other hierarchies of inequity are also securely sedimented" (Otto 2018b, 250). It is a research agenda committed to challenging "hierarchical global power inequalities based on intersecting structures such as heterosexism, transphobia, colonialism and capitalism" (Holzer et al. 2023, 6). Queering international law entails revealing, locating, and deconstructing the assemblages of gender, sexuality, and other analytical markers that constitute violence and construct legal subjects according to binaries of normal/perverse, victim/perpetrator, and legality/criminality. As an exercise in queering governance and international law, illustrated through the case of the ICTY, this book contributes to and extends these queer commitments.

International Law as a (Queer) Governance Mechanism

By embracing queer theory, I argue that international law is a (queer) governance mechanism, one that—as feminist, poststructural, and postcolonial scholars also recognize—is steeped in gendered and discursive power. At the same time, the legal actors who embody international law govern violence through these signifiers. Here, I introduce queer theories of governance, allowing me to develop an approach that embraces the plural, complicated, and constitutive power of international law. I understand "queer" to mean multiple things, both in terms of what it is and what it does. Through the case of the ICTY, I trace and embrace the messy and plural ways in which it genders, violates, and constitutes bodies at/of governance and international law. Queer also represents the gendered and sexualized dynamics (among others) that constitute our reality/ies. As I introduce in this chapter, and develop in Chapter 2, my approach to queer emphasizes the always already gendered and gendering logics that infuse mechanisms of governance. This is an orientation to queer theorizing that allows me to deconstruct, in Chapters 3–4, how the governance and adjudication of violence by international law depend on and (re)produce civilizational logics and cis-heteronormative discourses. Finally, although not wanting to foreclose the infinite possibilities this term offers, "queer" represents subversion, a resistance to the intimacies of violence woven through our discursive and material lives. A queer approach to governance and international law involves a commitment to disturbing the discourses of gender, sexuality, and violence that make law legible as a governance mechanism, including the legal-political possibilities they (dis)allow.

As a (queer) governance mechanism, international law is gendered and gendering, constitutive and agential, and violent and violating. Queer theory enables me to see the and/or of these characterizations, of the ways in which governance mechanisms can be both one thing *and/or* another (Weber 2016; see Chapter 2). I place "queer" in parentheses to indicate that governance mechanisms are always already queer (see Wilcox 2014). By attaching "queer" to "governance mechanism," I seek to make explicit the gendered and gendering, constitutive and agential, and violent and violating practices that always already underpin governance. Such an approach acknowledges that the ICTY, as an example of international law, can produce cis-heteronormative, gendered, and civilizational logics of governance and law *and* still be described as queer, because it is a mechanism also made meaningful through plurality, ambivalence, and resistance to these violences. Michael Bosia excellently captures this queer paradox in the context of human security, and argues:

> The queer in security is at once always present and impossible; security as it embraces the power of the state regulates sexual and gender behaviour, and therefore at the same time cannot be queer.... Ambivalently fluid, queer visions of human security, then, necessarily take into account both/and: *in* state discourses of human security, and in opposition to the normative constitution of sexualities and gender identities in/by statecraft. (Bosia 2018, 103, emphasis in original)

In my approach to international law as a (queer) governance mechanism, then, I am interested in the ways in which queer potential always already constitutes international law. This is even while it (re)installs violent cis-heteronormative discourses and civilizational logics of governance. This argument does not preclude an analysis of the law as "anti-queer to the extent that it is an instrument of a structure that operates by establishing, stabilising and normalising everything it regulates, including gender and sexuality"

(Ramos, quoted in Cunha 2023, 10). Rather, it acknowledges these violences *and* the queer potential to subvert them. The discussions of subverting and resisting violence in Chapter 5 take up this invitation to see queerness alongside the violence of the Tribunal. International law, conceptualized as a (queer) governance mechanism, "simultaneously embodies multiple, seemingly contradictory meanings that may confound and confuse" (Weber 2016, 19, quoted in Charrett 2019, 299). It is in this disruptive potential where I see my queer approach working at its best, illuminating the plural gendered and gendering meanings that constitute sites of governance.

The Gendered/ing Practices of Governance and International Law

International law is a (queer) mechanism of governance designed to adjudicate violence, and this is a process that is both gendered and gendering. International law is gendered; it is constituted by gendered bodies, discourses, and representations of violence committed across war and peace. It is gendering because its various legal actors (e.g., witnesses, judges, prosecutors, etc.) (re)produce discourses of gender, sexuality, and violence through the juridical decisions and grammars of the courtroom. Being attuned to gendered and gendering practices involves "paying attention to the discursive terrain of international institutions ... [which are] product/productive of a particular configuration of political authority and legitimacy that can, and should, be challenged" (Shepherd 2008b, 383).

Queer theorizing offers critical insight into the gendered and gendering practices of governance and international law, revealing how people are constructed by legal actors according to gendered discourses of victimhood and criminality. It exposes the heteronormative systems of governance that constitute our reality/ies, that is, the institutionalization of heterosexuality enforced in everyday spaces and practices (Ahmed 2014, 47; Berlant and Warner 1998). Heteronormativity assumes that heterosexuality is defined and made possible by the opposing concept of homosexuality (Namaste 1994, 222). Heterosexuality, therefore, is defined by what it is not. Queer theorizing exposes the violence of this "hetero/homo opposition" (Namaste 1994, 226; see also Sedgwick 1994, 11). Heteronormativity is insidious and made "invisible" (Heathcote 2019, 56), pervasive, and all-encompassing, delineating what gendered and sexualized practices, desires, and pleasures are acceptable, and sanctioning those that are not (see Sjoberg 2017a, 71).

An approach to international law as a (queer) governance mechanism alerts us to the gendered and sexualized discourses that (re)produce international law as a knowable thing with the power to affect bodies and the governance of violence. For example, as I show in Chapter 4, ICTY judges and prosecutors make sense of sexual violence against (cis-)men in the camps as a particularly shocking aberration.[1] Certainly, this violence (as with all practices of violence), should not be condoned. But in the moment that legal actors imply victim-survivors would or should feel embarrassed when soliciting testimony from them regarding sexual violence against (cis-)men, the ICTY reinforces cis-heteronormative discourses of gender, sexuality, and violence (Biddolph 2024b). By queering bodies and the social world, a queer approach can expose the institutionalization of heterosexuality as the norm.

Heteronormativity, as I have shown in this brief example, is also laced with gendered meaning, intersected by, and made possible through, cis-heterosexism, which privileges straight, cis-male subjectivities. I deploy the term "cis-heteronormativity," recognizing that international law reaffirms the cis-heterosexual subject. Queer theory that embraces trans-theorizing reveals how cis-heteronormativity institutionalizes heterosexuality and homophobia, as well as cisgender embodiment and transphobia (Shepherd and Sjoberg 2012; Sjoberg 2020, 80; Weerawardhana 2018). Cisgender, or cissexual, refers to "people who have only ever experienced their subconscious sex and physical sex as being aligned" (Serano 2007, 33; see also Shotwell and Sangrey 2008; Sjoberg 2012; Shepherd and Sjoberg 2012). It is this assumption that bodies are cisgender (as well as straight) that informs the treatment of legal subjects at the ICTY. Cis-normativity (as with heteronormativity) operates through logics of opposition, with "'trans-' ... framed as the aberration" in contrast to the privileging of cis-persons (Sjoberg 2012, 339). Queer theory seeks to untether these dichotomies through a critique of the gendered ways in which cissexism and heterosexuality are maintained and privileged. My queer approach to international law shows that the gendered and gendering practices rely on and prescribe cis-heteronormative discourses of gender, sexuality, and violence. As Gina Heathcote reminds us, "mainstream feminist approaches to international law are yet to incorporate queer and trans scholarship into feminist accounts," and so the straight, cisgender subject of law remains the common sense (2019, 21). A queer analysis is not uniquely qualified, but perhaps most effective at exposing the cis-heterosexist norms that constitute sites of governance (see, e.g., Clark 2019; Puar 2007; Weber 2016).

Queering international law involves a commitment to unsettling discourses of gender and sexuality and deconstructing cis-heteronormative systems of governance. The work of unsettling entails a curious, questioning, and disruptive methodology, one that makes explicit the violent cis-heteronormative assumptions embedded in and (re)produced by international law. In doing so, it seeks their dismantling and abolition (see Baars 2019). This is important work because it complicates the always already gendered and gendering practices that are so normalized within governance mechanisms that their violences are hidden from view. Queer offers "a way of pointing ahead, by rejecting restrictive contemporary arrangements, resisting homophobia and heterosexism and reimagining future politics, but one that never knows in advance, precisely at what or where to point" (Griffin 2013, 140).

Reading international law as a (queer) governance mechanism that does gendered and gendering work means acknowledging that gendered discourses are also plural and (at times) contradictory. For example, the ICTY court transcripts constructed perpetrators as simultaneously hypermasculine, heterosexual, homosexual, homophobic, dangerous, and perverse (see Chapter 4). While gendered discourses of hyper-heteromasculinity and homosexuality are different discourses that (re)produce distinct subject positions, they are nevertheless part of a discursive whole. In other words, both discourses reflect cis-heteronormative and sexist assumptions of the gendered body. These contradictory discourses exist together because of, rather than despite, their inconsistencies. This example demonstrates how binary logics of discourses depend on each other for their intelligibility. Discourses of gender and sexuality, then, are queer: strange, messy, and complicated representations that produce bodies, discourses, and practices of international law. Conceptualizing international law as a (queer) governance mechanism involves a commitment to exposing the gendered and gendering practices that constitute the legal regulation of violence.

The Constitutive, Agential, and Embodied Practices of Governance and International Law

International law is a (queer) governance mechanism that is also discursively constituted. Discourses of gender, sexuality, and violence (among others) are imbricated in and inform law's governing practices. International law is also agential, embodied, and authorial, as the bodies and (legal) actors who constitute international law wield power, enact violence, and (re)produce and/or subvert logics of governance. As Jonneke Koomen writes, "language work is central to the life of an international criminal court," and importantly, so too are the people "who mediate stories of violence and translate the vision of international criminal accountability across linguistic, geographic and social divides" (2014, 582). My approach to international law acknowledges both the constitutive or discursive, and agential capacity of governance mechanisms. International law is both things, and a queer approach best allows me to access this plural characterization of the Tribunal. For example, just as the ICTY is constituted by diverse and (often) contradictory discourses, people embody this mechanism. International law is therefore constituted by discourse, but also has the capacity—through the various people who act for, on behalf of, and within this mechanism—to install meaning. Put simply, law "is made of the bodies that inhabit it" (Elander 2018a, 107).

International law is discursive because it is constituted by and constitutive of discourses. Discourses are meaning-making practices, ways of knowing that organize our reality/ies. In this sense, nothing is external to discourse. Even as agential actors, we engage with, (re)produce, and are both known and knowable through the "citational network[s]" of discourse (Elander 2018a, 14). But discourses are not fixed, nor are they singular. International law is thus legible through unstable, messy, and multiple discursive articulations. There are various kinds of discourses that constitute international law, but I am specifically interested in how discourses of gender, sexuality, and violence make it knowable as a (queer) governance mechanism. Queering international law through the ICTY, these discourses (both overtly and tacitly) permeate the Tribunal, rendered intelligible through the legal decisions and practices that animate the courtroom. For example, cis-heteronormative discourses of gender, sexuality, and violence are (re)produced by prosecutors and judges who denounce the victimization of women, who abhor sexual violence against men, and who demonize perpetrators as deviant, sadistic criminals (see Chapter 4). In this way, my approach to international law as a (queer) governance mechanism is attuned to the discursive (re)production of international law; of the ways in which discourses of gender, sexuality, and violence constitute this site.

In queering governance and international law, I engage the ICTY as an illustrative case of law's agential capacity. The ICTY is composed of three organs, and all of these are made up of, and made meaningful by, people. First, the Chambers, consisting of three Trial Chambers and an Appeals Chamber, overseen by the president of the Tribunal. Second, the Office of the Prosecutor (OtP), containing a Prosecution Division, Immediate Office, and Appeals Division, directed by the ICTY prosecutor. Finally, the operational mandate of the Tribunal is underpinned by the Registry, led by the registrar and consisting of a Division of Judicial Support Services, Immediate Office, Chambers Legal Support Section, and Administration Division. Beyond this organizational structure and the various staff it comprises, defense attorneys, defendants, and witnesses all embody the ICTY. These various actors—from the judges, prosecutors, and defense teams, through to the defendants and witnesses, to the victim-survivors and perpetrators—are integral to the Tribunal's function and reason for being. In addition, the United Nations secretary-general, the States and State representatives constituting the United Nations Security Council (UNSC), the former Yugoslav countries, and the Yugoslav people are also embodied in the work of the Tribunal. I return to many of these actors in this book, with a predominant focus on discourses (re)produced in the Trial Chambers and the ICTY's foundational documents.

Throughout this book, I refer to the "ICTY" or "the Tribunal" as if it were a single, unitary mechanism. But as with international law more broadly, the ICTY is embodied by a multitude of contested and contradictory perspectives, and this includes the various actors that propel the ICTY's mandate. As a site of international law, then, the Tribunal is a (queer) governance mechanism that both represents and intervenes in discourses of gender, sexuality, and violence. As I have written elsewhere, "international criminal justice mechanisms are not passive translators of evidence but reproduce and contribute to gendered logics of war" (Biddolph 2024b, 229). This means that the Tribunal is a site of violence and engages in practices of violence itself. Thus, to speak of the Tribunal and international law as agential, is to position the actors who embody this mechanism as (variously) empowered to (re)produce and/or challenge gendered and sexualized discourses (see K. Campbell et al. 2019, 268).

In Chapters 4 and 5, I show how the ICTY presidents, judges, prosecutors, witnesses, and defendants perpetuate and/or subvert simplistic and cis-heteronormative discourses of gender, sexuality, and violence. For example, prosecutors reinforce the discourse of (cis-)women as victims in their questioning of witnesses when they ask every (cis-)woman witness if they experienced sexual violence, a line of questioning not maintained for (cis-) men witnesses (see Chapter 4). In other instances, witnesses challenge the power of judges, prosecutors, and defense lawyers by being "noisy" survivors who speak their trauma beyond what was asked of them (see Chapter 5). In these ways, the Tribunal is embodied by authoritative, compliant, subversive, and messy actors, all who have the power to (re)produce, resist, and reject discourses. These findings about the ICTY have broader implications for international law, reflecting plural and embodied legal practices, and of the potential to transform violent, exclusionary regimes of juridical governance. Thus, international law does not provide unified, coherent discourses of gender, sexuality, and violence, but is instead occupied by people who engage with and intervene in an assemblage of divergent sense-making practices.

The Violent and Violating Practices of Governance and International Law

International law is both violent and violating. But it maintains the potential to subvert violence. International postconflict tribunals exist because of violence, their mandates established in response to conflicts. They are thus inextricably bound to and characterized by violence. But international law is also violating, that is, it *does* violent things. Tribunals wield violence through law (see Heathcote 2011, 21). This is evident in the ways in which witness testimony is curtailed, or in the (re)production of civilizational logics that situate perpetrators as "sadistic" rapists from "uncivilized" lands (see Chapter 4). "Violence perverts, inverts or renders unintelligible certain ways of being in the world while endorsing others" (Shepherd and Sjoberg 2012, 19). For example, in Chapter 4, I reveal that through their judgments, lines of questioning, and categorization of gendered and ethnicized bodies, court officials engage in practices of juridical violence. While the (re)production of exclusionary discourses (e.g., cis-heteronormativity) is harmful in and of itself, these discursive practices also have violent effects, such as the incarceration of individuals, the denunciation or restriction of certain testimonies, and sometimes the legitimation of military intervention. But international law can subvert violence too, evident in how various juridical actors at/of the ICTY challenge governing logics that constitute violent acts and international law (see Chapter 5).

Queer postcolonial scholars have shown how Western and Global North countries invoke queer rights discourse in violent and imperialistic ways (see, e.g., Agathangelou 2013; Puar 2007; Rao 2010, 2020). These interventions represent important contributions to my own queer reading of violence in/of international law, including the ways in which international law (re)produces gendered, civilizational discourses and logics (see Chapters 3 and 4). For example, Jasbir Puar (2007) developed the term "homonationalism" to refer to actors (often states) that denounce the LGBTQIA+ rights record of Global South countries. This kind of violence is evident at the ICTY, where judges and prosecutors condemn the "patriarchal" and "intolerant" values of "Balkan" perpetrators who commit homophobic violence against detainees (see Chapter 4). It is therefore important that queer analyses recognize how "the project of establishing the civilized/barbaric binary has always been one that is rooted in sexuality and gender as well as racism, with these three dimensions often inseparable" (Vernon 2024, 5).

Other queer research, such as Nivi Manchanda's (2015) work queering the Pashtun, deconstructs how hypernationalist agendas materialized through the War on Terror in Afghanistan are made possible by gendered, sexualized, and racialized representations of the Other. In particular, Manchanda focuses on the figure of the "Talib"/"Afghan man"/"Pashtun male" through the Western gaze, arguing that such a subject-position "conjure[s] up a certain image, a pathologized figure, at once freakishly effeminate and monstrously misogynistic" (2015, 130). This figure comes to represent all Afghan men in War on Terror discourse, rendered intelligible through logics of monstrosity and sexual perversion, in turn constituted by "an Orientalist, specifically homo-nationalist, framework" (Manchanda 2015, 130, 143). Manchanda's research problematizes the violence of representational practices that hail these figures of sexual and racial aberration into being, an argument echoed in my own analysis of gendered discourses and Balkanist logics at/of the ICTY (see Chapter 4). Ahmad Qais Munhazim has revisited these queer constructions in the Afghan context, to explore how "queer and trans Afghan Muslims" are legible through discourses of white, Western saviorism, manifested through "imperial solidarity," which "advance[s] projects of homoempire, including Islamophobia, racism, and 'othering' of nonwhite sexualities and gender expressions" (2024, 1, 11). In addition, Patrick Vernon's research queering the coloniality of humanitarian intervention discourses in the UK context reveals how figures such as "'The ISIL Terrorist,' 'The Brutal Dictator,' and 'The British Self' are personified representations of a British worldview defined by racial hierarchies, hetero/homonormativity, . . . and the concurrent operation of colonialism and neoliberal governance" (2024, 128). Queer postcolonial research in IR has thus offered necessary analyses of "(extreme) racialised and queered cultural figures, understood as backwards or barbaric, against whom the commissioning of violence is deemed legitimate" (Vernon 2024, 160). It is telling that similar civilizational logics and discourses of "perverse" gender and sexuality manifest at the ICTY, and in international law more broadly.

As a site of governance and international law, the Tribunal is legible because it depends on the specific war-making practices and violence committed in the former Yugoslavia. But it also maintains authority through the violation of lives subjected to its legal gaze. My approach is guided by queer postcolonial scholars (see Manchanda 2015; Puar and Rai 2002) attuned to the global civilizational logics through which gender, sexuality, and violence are installed. Indeed, as Ratna Kapur argues:

Legal justice is an intervention—it is claimed from a structure that is already always in place, where power relations are already deeply embedded and normalised. It serves primarily as an intervention rather than something that is transformative or facilitative of the desire for freedom. Rather than an end goal, it is already encrusted by the weight of history and context and continues in its postcolonial afterlife to be structured by civilizational divides and sexual and gender normativities. (Kapur 2015, 273–74)

I return to Kapur's work and the question of whether international law can ever be queer (in the transformative sense) in the concluding chapter of the book. Her argument here exposes the violences of legal justice and the gendered, sexual, and civilizational hierarchies on which they rest. Even if and as oppressed groups are increasingly included within international law's fold (Burgis-Kasthala and Sander 2024, 139; see Chapter 6), Kapur cautions against celebrating this development, noting that "legal justice performs a normalizing function in the context of precarious desires" (2015, 272). In other words, even as people may subvert and resist the cis-heteronormative violences of international law from within, broader questions must be asked about the transformative potential of this work, and whether, as a (queer) governance mechanism, international law is even able to deliver radical and queerer forms of justice.

Queer critiques of international law similarly expose the violence of governance mechanisms. Otto argues that heteronormative tropes of gender and sexuality "have helped to institute, legitimate, authorise and sustain a neoliberal international legal order" (2018a, 6). Indeed, because international law is so steeped in Western or Eurocentric thought, the politics and queer lives of those "outside the west" are often obscured from mainstream academic and policy accounts of international law (Otto 2013, 87). Heathcote argues that the international legal project is not only one that reflects and (re)produces the "heteronormative status quo," but also perpetuates "racialised, able-bodied . . . and . . . economic hierarchies" (2019, 4). These queer approaches to international law are predicated on the broader argument that law itself is violent (Hamzić 2018; Heathcote 2005), "dividing that which is authorised from that which is regulated and outlawed" (Heathcote 2011, 23). Developing my own queer approach to international law in this book, I show how the ICTY violates through the categorization of bodies according to cis-heteronormative discourses and Balkanist logics. For example, as I argue in Chapter 4, perpetrators are constructed in the ICTY documents as gendered and civilizational deviants who will be punished via international law. In these discourses, "the 'enemy' is made out to be 'queer' in its dehumanizing sense, as variously unnatural, backward, effete/promiscuous, strange, underdeveloped, and uncontrollable" (Otto 2022b, 24).

Taking the violent and violating capacities of the ICTY seriously involves scrutinizing the modes through which gendered, sexualized, and ethnicized legal subjectivities are constructed and violently demarcate some lives as mattering, some as criminal, and some as not mattering at all. My queer reading of international law through the case of the Tribunal exposes how cis-heteronormative discourses and civilizational logics (re)produce international law as a (queer) governance mechanism authorized to designate innocence and guilt. International law thus regulates and sustains violence.

The Case of the ICTY

I undertake a queer analysis of the ICTY to problematize and complicate the governing practices of international law. In engaging the Tribunal as a case study, I acknowledge that as a site of analysis, it too is contested and unstable, dependent on and (re)producing multiple discursive articulations of law and violence. Both international law and the ICTY (as an example of the same), are plurally constituted and embodied. My queer intervention does not seek to reduce or contain governance and international law within the specific case of the Tribunal. Instead, I embrace the tensions and ambivalence between a case study that is both singular (as an example of international law) and plural (as a reflection of international law's multiplicity and contingency), and that the messy, complicated, and queer dynamics of international law will always exceed its manifestation in specific sites.

The ICTY was created in 1993 by the UNSC as a response to the conflicts that occurred in the former Yugoslavia during the 1990s (see Chapter 3 for an overview of the conflicts). The Tribunal was tasked with holding individuals criminally responsible for war crimes, grave breaches of the Geneva Conventions of 1949, crimes of genocide, and crimes against humanity committed in the former Yugoslav territories (United Nations Security Council 1993, para 2). As the first tribunal established in the late twentieth century (as part of the renewed, international criminal justice project, see Engle 2020, 81), the ICTY constitutes an important example of international law as a site of governance that intervenes in the lives and worlds of violent and violated bodies. This case study offers new opportunities to reimagine international law queerly, as I pay particular attention to how law's ability to govern depends on and reinforces discourses of gender, sexuality, and violence at/of the Tribunal.

My interest in the practices of violence that are represented, spoken, and written through international law (and at the ICTY) is entangled with a more specific concern with how discourses of gender, sexuality, and violence—both overt and tacit—intersect, prescribe, and proscribe legal-political possibilities. A "queer curiosity" (Weber 2016) led me to question how such cis-heteronormative discourses could be (re)produced by and constitute the ICTY as a mechanism of governance and international law. While the Tribunal is frequently heralded for its legacy and contribution to the broader international criminal justice project (Brammertz and Jarvis 2010, 96), these celebratory approaches take for granted that international law and its associated implications (e.g., denunciation, imprisonment) are "acceptable" responses for governing violence (Burgis-Kasthala and Sander 2024, 131). What is missing here is an interrogation of the political arrangements that govern violent and violated bodies through civilizational logics and discourses of gender and sexuality.

Critical feminist analyses of international law offer a welcome critique of these arrangements. Karen Engle's work (2015, 2016, 2017, 2020), for example, has been pivotal in exposing the carceral common sense of appeals to international law as a response to sexual violence in conflict. In a careful yet incisive critique, she argues that "as advocates increasingly turn to international criminal law to respond to issues ranging from economic injustice to genocide, they reinforce an individualized and decontextualized understanding of the harms they aim to address, even while relying on the state and forms of criminalization of which they have long been critical" (2015, 1071; see also Grady 2021, 367). It is not just through the overemphasis on "criminal law ... [as] the enforcement tool of choice" (Engle 2015, 1071) that other modes of justice (including community-based) are decentered. The criminal turn is inherently violent, advancing "military, carceral and security regimes" (Pinto 2021, 363) targeting racially, gendered, sexually, and socioeconomically marginalized populations. As Engle argues, and as evidenced in my own queer critique of the ICTY, "Criminalization is often done in a way that demonizes individual perpetrators ... has little justification beyond retribution, and makes little sense even to the victims (though it is generally done in their names)" (2017, 141; see also Chapter 4). In the case of the ICTY and its prosecution and imprisonment of perpetrators responsible for imprisoning victims in camps across Bosnia, Kate Grady's suspicion of these carceral logics is worth heeding, that is: "whether there might be a logical flaw in imagining that a problem of (unlawful) incarceration may be remedied by a solution of (lawful) incarceration" (2021, 367). This criminalizing and denunciatory violence of international law follows civilizational logics, a critique I develop in Chapters 3 and 4 (see also Buss 2007).

Using the case of the ICTY, I identify how international law depends on a range of civilizational logics, evident through the Tribunal's dependence on and reification of Balkanism as a civilizational logic about the former Yugoslavia. I trace how subject positions conjured by witnesses, defense, prosecution, and judges relied on Balkanist logics that organize discourses of gender, sexuality, and violence. Balkanism as a logic functions similarly to Orientalism (Said 1978), but refers specifically to the Balkan region (or southeast Europe). It denotes a set of pejorative knowledge practices that frame "the Balkans" as "backward," "violent," and "Other" to a "progressive," "peaceful" European "Self." Balkanism situates "the Balkans" as semi-Other, insofar as it maintains a sense of "semi-Europeanness," forming the bridge between "civilized" (western) Europe and the "uncivilized" Orient. Such a logic depends on and (re)produces assumptions about race, ethnicity, and religion, terms I understand as multiply signifying and entangled, social constructions that are marshaled in specific ways in ICTY discourse about the former Yugoslavia (see Chapter 3). My queer reading of international law through the ICTY reveals that the Tribunal's key foundational and legal texts both overtly and tacitly (re)produce Balkanist logics of the former Yugoslavia, which underpin cis-heteronormative discourses of gender, sexuality, and violence in the courtroom. As I show in Chapter 4, gendered, Balkanist logics legitimated the extraordinary power of the Tribunal to indict, sentence, and imprison individuals. The (re)production of Balkanist logics by legal actors at the ICTY was both tacit and explicit, connecting to broader gendered discourses of redeemers, victims, and criminals in global politics and international law, as well as more specific, historical discourses about "the Balkans" as a place and people in-between two worlds: the "civilized" West and the "uncivilized" Orient. The ICTY's (re)production of Balkanist logics is illustrative of the broader civilizational and racializing logics that constitute international law and its violences.

Through my queer poststructural discourse analysis (QPDA) of selected ICTY texts, I argue that the ICTY overwhelmingly (re)produces civilizational logics and cis-heteronormative discourses of gender, sexuality, and violence. The (re)production of these exclusionary discourses means, for example, that non-normative gender and sexual identities and practices are erased from the Tribunal's representation of violence in Bosnia (see Chapter 5). For example, in a personal communication with a former ICTY legal intern, I was told that there were lawyers working at the ICTY advocating for crimes against LGBTQIA+ people to be investigated and prosecuted. Indeed, queer victims had come forward to testify, but ended up withdrawing due to the high risks of testifying and the inadequate witness protection program in place. Despite this advocacy for recognition of violence against members of the LGBTQIA+ community, the ICTY was overwhelmingly silent on these matters (see Biddolph 2024b), a silence that reflects the cis-heteronormative status quo of international law.

The invocation of civilizational logics by judges and prosecutors in the courtroom and in the ICTY's foundational texts authorizes practices of denunciation (by demonizing hyper-heteromasculine Balkan perpetrators) and paternalism (by demarcating Bosnians as helpless victims). This is representative of, rather than anomalous to, international law more broadly, of its civilizational, racialized, and paternalist practices of governance. But when these dominant discourses of gender, sexuality, and violence are disrupted at the ICTY (by witnesses, perpetrators, prosecutors), they challenge the governing logics of the Tribunal, pushing back at how violent and violated bodies are expected to experience crimes in international law. Both kinds of practices constitute, and are wielded by, agentic actors at the ICTY. This simultaneity, of embodying plural subjectivities (Heathcote 2019), of being one thing and/or another (Weber 2016; see Chapter 2), constitutes international law as a (queer) governance mechanism.

Structure of Book

In this book, I analyze how discourses of gender, sexuality, and violence are both embedded within and invoked by textual practices of international law. I focus on the ICTY's various legal texts, including witness testimonies, trial judgments, indictments, annual reports, and completion strategies. I trace these discourses and their legal-political effects; that is, what they enable or authorize, and what they preclude or prohibit, which includes the perpetuation of cis-heteronormativity as the common sense within international law, and the designation of people according to civilizational logics justifying legal intervention and carceral responses. Queering governance and international law at/of the ICTY illuminates these violent, gendering practices. But it also exposes the plural and subversive potential of this mechanism (see Chapter 6). The discussions in this introductory chapter have formed the foundations for thinking through international law as a (queer) governance mechanism replete with multiple and contested discourses of gender, sexuality, and violence.

Chapter 2, "Queer Concepts and Method," establishes the queer methodological approach of this book. It centers the power and politics of discursive practices, (gendered) embodiment, and the methodological tools to deconstruct international law's (re)production of civilizational logics and the straight, cisgender legal subject as the common sense.

Chapter 3, "Logics of Governance and International Law," offers an account of the gendered discourses and racialized, civilizational logics that constitute international law, through mapping the ICTY's Balkanist logics and gendered discourses. I trace the ICTY's origin stories that organize and authorize the extraordinary powers of the Tribunal and critique these stories for the governing logics and global hierarchies they (re)produce. Discourses of gender, sexuality, and violence intersect and are made possible because of these governing logics that perpetuate gendered, civilizational accounts of international law.

Chapter 4, "Governing through Adjudication," queers international law through an analysis of the legal violence (re)produced and embodied at the ICTY. I show how the Tribunal, as an agent of violence, governs through adjudication and (re)produces Balkanist logics and cis-heteronormative discourses of gender, sexuality, and violence. The ICTY positions perpetrators as hyper-heteromasculine and perverse criminals, victims as passive and feminized, and those representing the ICTY (judges, prosecutors) as lawful adjudicators. The Tribunal constructs these subject positions through juridical practices of violence, including victimization, denunciation, and paternalism. These various discursive practices prescribe the indictment and punishment of individuals found guilty of atrocities, the reinforcement of legal subjects as straight and cisgender, and the designation of "the Balkans" as a site for (Western/European) intervention and transformation. This echoes and sustains broader practices within international law and the demarcation of gendered and racialized populations as legal subjects variously marked as worthy of protection or deserving of violence.

Chapter 5, "Subverting International Law and Violence," explores how people at/of the ICTY subvert violence. I focus on two examples of subverting violence at the Tribunal, exploring how "noisy" survivors and "complex" perpetrators in international law challenge a simplified vision of bodies subjected to, and (re)produced through, violence. In doing so, my queer analysis of international law reveals its gendered and gendering, constitutive and agential, violent and violating, *and* subversive capacities. The findings developed in this chapter about the ICTY's subversive potential reflect the queer potential always already stored in international law.

Finally, in Chapter 6, "Queer Reckonings with International Law," I conclude with some reflections about the implications of my queer analysis of international law. I return to some of the tensions and questions that have animated this book, namely, What can be made of the desire for international law by victims and survivors, the (cis-heteronormative, civilizational) violence of international law, the calls to work with(in) the law, and the provocation to move away from it entirely, to seek more liberatory and queerer forms of justice?

Law is built on and (re)produces assumptions about bodies in global politics, bodies that are seen and known according to cis-heteronormative discourses and civilizational logics, as well as ethnic and racial difference. By embracing queer in this book, I contribute to a broader project of deconstructing the taken-for-granted machinations of international law, and of showing how (gendered, sexualized, and civilizational) discourses matter and legitimate extraordinary interventions in global politics.

2
Queer Concepts and Methods

Queering international law involves tracing the intersecting discourses of gender, sexuality, and violence that both constitute and are (re)produced at/by this mechanism. In this chapter, I develop a queer methodology for the investigation presented in the chapters that follow. I do so following Noreen Giffney's argument that "[q]ueer theory is an exercise in discourse analysis," insofar as queer "exemplifies the contradictions nestling within [discourses], the way in which meanings proliferate and spill out of the terms the more we try to contain them" (2009, 6). I develop a discourse analysis that is informed by and (re)imagines existing discursive approaches within queer, feminist, postcolonial, and poststructural scholarship. As a new form of discourse analysis, queer poststructural discourse analysis (QPDA) both extends and departs from existing methodological approaches. It centers the queer logics of multiplicity and contradiction that infuse discourse. By developing this toolkit, I provide the methodological foundations that constitute this book, and that allow me to argue in the remaining chapters that civilizational logics constitute cis-heteronormative discourses of gender, sexuality, and violence in international law. QPDA offers new and insightful ways of tracing the plural, entangled, and contradictory discourses (re)produced by international legal actors. As a queer method, QPDA "challenge[s] monological ways of seeing, grasping, interpreting, and inhabiting our realities and the law" (Holzer et al. 2023, 6). Anchored in a hopeful queer reading—one that interrogates the violence of international law while recognizing the queer potential it holds (see Chapter 6)—the concepts and methods introduced in this chapter offer possibilities for both critiquing international law *and* seeking queerer, plural justice futures.

Chapter 2 begins by introducing poststructural methods and approaches to discourse. It then maps the elements of QPDA in detail, with an explicit focus on the gendered and sexualized power of discourse as embodied in international law as a (queer) governance mechanism. It outlines the queer

Queering Governance and International Law. Caitlin Biddolph, Oxford University Press. © Oxford University Press (2025). DOI: 10.1093/9780197803172.003.0002

reflexive ethic I adopt in the book, before charting the practical application of QPDA to my research, introducing the discursive tools that form my QPDA toolbox: presupposition, predication, subject positioning, deconstruction, and pre/proscription. The chapter develops a method of discourse analysis that aims to make strange, unsettle, and deconstruct the discourses of gender, sexuality, and violence that make international law meaningful as a mechanism governing violence.

Queering Discourse and Poststructural Methods

This book argues that international law is constituted by discourse. As established in Chapter 1, I emphasize the constitutive or discursive power of the international law as a (queer) governance mechanism. Discourses are central to my queer analysis of international law. It is through discourses that I read gender, sexuality, and violence, and how these discourses are (re)produced and destabilized in testimonies, judgments, and other international legal texts. It is discourse that renders (in)justice, violence, and governance legible in/through international law. In this section, I redeploy the poststructural concepts of discourse, representation, logics, performativity, and (re)productive power in queer ways.

Discourse and Representation

Discourses are systems of meaning that constitute our world, (re)producing bodies, things, knowledges, and practices. My interpretation of discourse is informed both by poststructural thinkers (Derrida 1978, 1988; Foucault 1976) and by feminist, queer, and postcolonial scholars drawing on and challenging these canonical readings of discourse (see, e.g., Butler 2014; Chow 2002; Griffin 2009; Richter-Montpetit 2017; Shepherd 2008a). Discourses are representational practices that attempt to make sense of and articulate meaning in a socially contingent world. A discourse or "discursive structure ... is an articulatory practice which constitutes and organises social relations" (Laclau and Mouffe 1985, 96, emphases in original). Discourses have a (re)productive effect, insofar as they render ourselves and our world/s meaningful, bringing multiple and contested realities into being.

Discourses are forms of representation that are informed and constructed by a plurality of past and existing discourses. Forming a foundational component of poststructural discourse analysis (PDA), scholars argue that "there is no point outside the world from which the world can be observed" (Edkins 2007, 88) because all subjects and objects are constituted by discourse. Integral to this argument is the inherent instability, mutability, and contingency of discourse. Discursive formations are not cemented expressions of meaning but fluid articulations of power that are only ever temporarily fixed (Berggren 2014, 237). PDA thus offers immense potential to resist, "make strange[,] and denaturalise" the assumed truth and stability of hegemonic discursive structures (D. Campbell 2007, 218). It seeks to expose the historically constructed and contingent nature of discourse and critique the modes of power that produce bodies and prescribe some forms of action at the expense of others.

Discourses are revealed and concealed through texts. Texts are representational practices of "social signification" (Gentry 2016, 37) that "work to create a 'reality'" (Doty 1993, 306). They reflect and are (re)productive of our world and the subjectivities within it, producing "specific and particular representation[s] of a situation" (McLeod 2016, 15–16). Examples of texts include "objects and artefacts such as words, images, and sounds" (Khalid 2017, 7–8), "speeches, reports, manifestos, historical events, interviews, policies, ideas, even organisations and institutions" (Howarth 2000, 10), as well as "bodies in space, spaces without bodies, and texts comprised of nonlinguistic semiotic systems" (Gannon and Davies 2012, 13). International law is also constituted by and constructs texts. At the International Criminal Tribunal for the former Yugoslavia, for example, texts may include official documents such as the Statute and reports; legal policies and frameworks; court transcripts and recordings; indictments, judgments, and decisions; the physical space of the Tribunal; and the people that are represented and constituted by the discursive site of the ICTY.

Representations are practices that constitute subjects, objects, things, and reality/ies (McLeod 2016, 15–16). Discourses do not reflect a fixed reality, insofar as "the real, or the what of our knowing, is inseparable from how it resides in our modes of representation" (Shapiro 1988, 8). This speaks to the contingent and fragmented (re)production of discourse. While discourses enable us to make sense of the world, these entanglements of meaning are always incomplete and open to contestation. Representations are always ambiguous, resulting in discursive articulations that are never fully fixed, even as they attempt to reiterate their dominance against other discourses in "the field of discursivity" (Laclau and Mouffe 1985, 112). Discourses, then, can be challenged, as there are multiple and competing systems of meaning that constitute our realm of intelligibility. As I examine in Chapter 4, governing logics such as Balkanism organize the dominant (cis-heteronormative) discourses of gender, sexuality, and violence in international law. But alternative and subversive discourses co-exist, such as the subject positions of "noisy" survivors and "complex" perpetrators seen in Chapter 5. In this way, discourses do not operate in isolation, but are formations, constellations, and assemblages of meaning that make sense only through their relational capacity with other discursive practices (see Wilcox 2015). This subversive potential, and the deconstructive practices it enables, are intrinsic to a queer project dedicated to unmooring the governing logics that underpin cis-heteronormative discourses of gender, sexuality, and violence in international law. If discourses are always partial and fleeting, bumping into and against other discursive articulations, then it is possible to subvert dominant knowledge claims with alternative discursive practices.

According to feminist poststructural scholars, discourses "maintain, construct and constitute, legitimise, resist, and suspend meaning" (Shepherd 2015, 893); "are social configurations of political space" (Griffin 2009, 24); delineate knowledge, truth, and reality (Gannon and Davies 2012, 15); produce identities (Khalid 2017, 5); and are "imbued with order, regularities and discipline" (Griffin 2009, 28). These perspectives illuminate how our reality/ies are discursively constructed, (re)produced, and (re)articulated through a multitude of representational practices. Reading discourse as partial and unstable enables us to "denaturalise what seems 'natural' and to interrupt essentialist thought" (Gannon and Davies 2012, 15). A queer approach allows me to identify and deconstruct the cis-heteronormative discourses of international law (see Chapters 4–5). For example, it becomes clear that perpetrators as well as legal actors (e.g., judges, prosecutors) hold the assumption that all bodies subjected to violence, as well as all bodies before the Tribunal are straight and cisgender. A queer reading exposes the instability of these discourses, alerting us to the plural ways in which people are embodied and made meaningful.

A queer approach to discourse is one attuned to the hierarchies of knowledge that perpetuate gendered and sexualized normativities, among others (see Chapter 1). I extend existing queer interrogations of discourse by maintaining an emphasis on the violent arrangements of gender and sexuality that configure discourses but do so by applying these ideas to the specific governing practices of the international law. As I explain later in this chapter, my QPDA illuminates the tensions that constitute discursive practices, or how our social realities are constituted by complex and unstable discourses of gender, sexuality, and violence. This approach to discourse is embedded across queer research, with scholars engaging with discourse analysis and queer theory not as separate approaches but as intrinsic to each other. It allows me to deconstruct the taken-for-granted cis-heteronormative discourses that make violence intelligible within international law. Queer approaches to discourse recognize that reality is socially constructed and that discourses both (re)produce and are (re)produced by bodies. Working from the idea that discourse matters, and that it is always partial, we open the possibility of denaturalizing the normative hold that discourses seek to fix. This is an epistemological goal that queer scholars maintain in their commitment to queering the systems and discourses that construct gendered and sexualized bodies.

Penny Griffin writes that queering power involves "expos[ing] the limitations, unstable foundations and power-laden assumptions of the 'straight' political, psychological, cultural and economic discourses that govern us ... but also [understanding] the ways in which bodies are actually and continually classified, organised and regulated" (2013, 139). This articulation of queer work demonstrates the potential for queer approaches to discourse in "seek[ing] to subvert the apparent naturalness of the authorities, hierarchies and discourses residing in the socio-economic systems that govern us" (Griffin 2009, 37). Queer theory embodied in PDA approaches reveals the instability of norms, regimes, and practices that constitute gender, sexuality, and violence. Queer thus functions as a form of "interruption" and disruption (Heathcote 2019). QPDA continues a poststructural awareness of the (re)productive power of discourse, embodied in its partial and contingent constitution. To engage in a queer analysis of governance and international law entails a commitment to exposing systems of power. As Nicola Smith and Donna Lee argue, "Power, is, in short, what queer theory is about" (Smith and Lee 2015, 55). Taking a queer approach to PDA allows me to "query and disrupt such familiar and reductive spatial, temporal and discursive moves; to open up space for multiple readings that are simultaneous; to recognise contingency and possibility" (Basham and Bulmer 2017, 68–69). A queer approach to discourse analysis, building on but distinct from a poststructural one, is also about illuminating how discourses themselves are gendered and sexualized. While discourses are temporally fixed to gain coherence, they nevertheless occupy a precarious existence, one that depends on (re)production and intertextual connections with other discourses. Thus, in seeking to queer discourse, we can engage in deconstructive practices that unsettle the seemingly stable foundations on which discourses of gender and sexuality rest (Freccero 2017, 132–33).

These poststructural commitments manifest in my development of QPDA. I queer discourses in/of international law by illuminating the plural ways that bodies are constructed through discourses of gender, sexuality, and violence. Ideas about who constitutes the proper subjects of law (i.e., who are the enemies, who need saving) and who should enforce the law (i.e., who are the authorized and lawful actors), all stem from discourses of governance constituting law and justice. Taking the history and politics of representation seriously, my QPDA destabilizes the assumed truth behind these and other discourses, exposing how discourses of gender, sexuality, and violence intersect, often in violent and exclusionary ways. As Patrick Vernon writes, "A queer deconstructive approach . . . explores how seemingly neutral and even benevolent norms can facilitate violence that is deeply racialised, gendered and sexualised" (2024, 31). I use QPDA to identify the points of tension and the logics that hold these discourses together. In doing so, I open the potential to locate alternative discourses of gender, sexuality, and violence that may challenge cis-heteronormative and civilizational understandings of governance (see Chapter 5).

Queer Logics

Discourses of gender, sexuality, and violence in international law are legible through their organizing logics. According to Laura Shepherd, "[l]ogics organise a discourse and produce, through signification, the overarching semblance of fixity that allows for the expression of the known/knowable" (2021, 32). They structure, organize, or hold discourses together, providing "coherence or authority . . . [to] certain possibilities, while precluding others" (Shepherd 2021, 32–33). Logics shape how we understand each other and what is expected of us as subjects endowed with certain attributes and characteristics (Shepherd 2013). As with discourses, logics are also plural, impermanent, and subject to change (Shepherd 2021, 16).

QPDA allows me to trace how discourses of gender, sexuality, and violence intersect in/through international law, and to identify the implications of these practices. By attending to these discourses, I am also closely analyzing the logics that constitute them. I introduce civilizational logics in Chapter 3 and show in Chapter 4 how cis-heteronormative discourses of gender, sexuality, and violence are (re)produced in the ICTY's legal texts (e.g., trial judgments) through their reliance on Balkanist (i.e., civilizational) logics; about the hypermasculine Balkan perpetrator, the passive Balkan victim, and the authorized legal actors who embody the Tribunal. In this way, gendered assumptions and subject positions are made possible through logics of civilization.

My queer methodology also deploys the concept of logics in relation to queer logics of *and/or*. *And/or* logics embrace the multiplicities, simultaneities, and contradictions that constitute international law. Queer logics of *and/or* show how international law can be "*both* one thing *and* another (plural/perverse) while *simultaneously* one thing *or* another (singular, normal)" (Weber 2016, 40, emphases in original). Using the ICTY as an example, *and/or* logics deconstruct how representations of gender, sexuality, and violence simultaneously (re)produce *and* subvert cis-heteronormative discourses and Balkanist logics. *And/or* logics also allow me to characterize international law plurally, as I have demonstrated in my conceptualization of international law as a (queer) governance mechanism that is gendered and gendering, constitutive and agential, and violent and violating (see Chapter 1). *And/or* logics embrace the plural discourses, logics, and practices that constitute international law, and that are constituted by legal actors. Thus, while, in Chapter 4, I address the dominant discourses of gender, sexuality, and violence, in Chapter 5 I reveal alternative, subversive representations that coexist within international law.

Rather than reinforcing the "stabilising 'slash' in . . . binaries," queer logics of *and/or* instead operate "as multiplying and complicating connections, figures, and orders rather than reducing and simplifying them" (Weber 2016, 43). Deploying *and/or* logics, I embrace the simultaneity that *and/or* signifies, acknowledging that such a conceptual intervention opens possibilities for the deconstruction of cis-heteronormative discourses of gender, sexuality, and violence. It also enables me to read international law as a (queer) governance mechanism (see Chapter 1), one that simultaneously engages in violent cis-heteronormative discursive practices *and* maintains the possibility of subversion and queerness. Employing this as a blueprint for my own analysis of international law as a (queer) governance mechanism this book reveals how—through the case of the ICTY—international law *simultaneously* destabilizes *and* (re)inscribes civilizational logics and cis-heteronormative discourses of gender, sexuality, and violence.

I adopt Cynthia Weber's (2016) queer approach to *and/or* logics in this book, supplemented by Gina Heathcote's analysis of the "split subject." Split subjects reject boundedness; "instead they are diverse, fractured connected, singular, and fluid all at once" (Heathcote 2019, 128). Within the context of international law, Heathcote argues that "the recognition of plural legal forms . . . disrupt[s] the very possibility of a singular notion of the legal subject in favour of diverse subjectivities" (2019, 81). This conceptualization effectively pairs with Weber's articulation of queer logics that are both plural and singular, relational, and always already constituting the discursive and embodied. Embracing queer logics of *and/or*, of the plural and the split, allows me to demonstrate how discourses of gender, sexuality, and violence intersect in ways that construct and (re)produce plural subject positions, ones that are at times contradictory but contribute to broader cis-heteronormative understandings of international law. As I describe here, Weber's queer logics and Heathcote's split subject also offer possibilities for revealing how queer theorizing complicates the work and practices of international law. Applied to the ICTY—as an example of international law—they destabilize the assumption of unitary and fixed legal subjectivities, thereby allowing more complex representations of real lives and bodies to emerge (see Chapter 5).

Attending to the discourses of gender, sex, and sexuality that constitute bodies, Weber argues that queer logics of *and/or* refuse to signify monolithically. This introduces the notion that subjectivities are made meaningful through plural and (often) contested signifiers. Instead of being legible through neat, singular, and dichotomized categories, people are complicated, messy, and queer. Bodies therefore occupy more than one subject position, while governance mechanisms, for example, (re)produce as well as destabilize certain norms and practices. As I show in Chapters 4 and 5, bodies are (re)presented differently by those wielding violence (i.e., perpetrators), those subjected to violence (i.e., victims, witnesses, survivors), and those adjudicating crimes (i.e., the judges, prosecutors). There is no singular subjectivity that constitutes international law, at the same time as there are multiple and competing discourses of gender, sexuality, and violence that constitute mechanisms governing violence. In this way, Weber's queer deployment of *and/or*, supplemented by Heathcote's split subject, is a valuable tool for queering governance and international law.

Performativity and (Re)productive Power

Discourses and the logics that organize them are not disembodied, but are dependent on and constitute subjectivities. Subjects, objects, and modes of being are "always *within* a world of signifying practices" (Howarth 2000, 8, emphasis in original). For example, at the ICTY, the governance of violence occurs in and through broader signifying arrangements about gender, sexuality, Balkanism, and war-making practices in the former Yugoslavia. This complex entanglement of subjectivity and meaning signifies the performative power of discourse, "that discursive practice that enacts or produces that which it names" (Butler 2014, 13). At the Tribunal, and for international law, this means, for example, that judgments pronouncing guilt performatively construct and bring into being the guilty subject. Thus, discourses not only constitute reality/ies through representational practices. The construction and intelligibility of bodies also depends on this performative process (see Wilcox 2015, 8). As a result, discourses are embodied, insofar as "'bodies' in discourse (organic and inorganic, textual, visual, material and immaterial) exist as 'objects' of discourse and are surfaces and scenes of discursive inscription" (Griffin 2015, 8). Attending to the performative power of discourses in/of international law allows me to reveal how gender, sexuality, and violence constitute bodies within governance mechanisms, whether that be witnesses, perpetrators, prosecutors, or judges.

Performativity is frequently deployed by feminist poststructuralists to understand how "the body becomes its gender through a series of acts which are renewed, revised, and consolidated over time" (Butler 1988, 523). As the "stylised repetition of acts" (Butler 1999, 179), performativity is always already occurring, manifested in daily rituals and practices that instill norms about the "proper" or "expected" embodiment of gender and sexuality (among other social signifiers such as race, ethnicity, class, ablebodiedness, etc.). Performativity is a useful concept for emphasizing both the historically embedded and contemporary reinvention and/or reiteration of norms. Discourses enact bodies through material and semiotic representations, and these are always made meaningful through gendered, sexed, and other analytical categories of identity and difference. Discourses of gender and sexuality figure bodies in violent and exclusionary ways. As Judith Butler argues, when analyzing and scrutinizing the power and implication of discourse, "it is not only a question of how discourse injures bodies, but how certain injuries establish certain bodies at the limits of available ontologies, available schemes of intelligibility" (2014, 224). These discursive practices are predicated on gendered and sexualized hierarchies and oppositions (Shepherd 2015, 899), and it is these configurations of power that manifest in/through international law.

The concept of performativity hinges on the idea that power is performative, generative, and dispersed throughout the social world. Performativity relies on Michel Foucault's notion of productive power, that far from solely being a force of repression, "relations of power ... have a directly productive role". (Foucault 1976, 93). For example, I show in Chapter 4 how the legal actors who constitute international law construct bodies as feminized, helpless victims, thereby needing saving and protection; and hypermasculine, sadistic perpetrators, thereby requiring prosecution and punishment. In these ways, performativity exposes the (re)productive power of governance and international law.

Attending to performativity and (re)productive power allows me to trace how discourses of gender, sexuality, and violence construct bodies in and through governance mechanisms, bodies that can be known and acted on. Discourses are reinforced and challenged over time, so that historical representations of violence and justice, for example, are embedded and altered in contemporary discursive practices. The invocation of civilizational logics in discourses of gender, sexuality, and violence at the ICTY, for instance, can be seen as a continuation of origin stories about the Tribunal, and (historical) Balkanist logics of governance (see Chapters 3 and 4). At the same time, these discourses are challenged by competing and contradictory discourses that position victims and perpetrators as far more complicated than conventional legal readings of them depict (see Chapter 5). Because judgments and legal proceedings at the ICTY are held as truth, the plural and messy nature of the Tribunal is concealed, precisely because "a performative 'works' to the extent that *it draws on and covers over* the constitutive conventions by which it is mobilised" (Butler 2014, 227, emphases in original). By embracing a performative approach to discourse in my QPDA, it is possible to expose the forces of erasure and foreclosure that constitute the ICTY and international law more broadly, as well as those discourses and practices that are erased and foreclosed.

My queer analysis of governance and international law relies on the concepts of performative and (re)productive power because I center the discursive, constitutive, and embodied practices of gender, sexuality, and violence. Such an approach continues feminist poststructural approaches to discourse. However, as the next section reveals, it is not enough to embrace the poststructural argument that discourses are contingent expressions of meaning that constitute the social world. Nor is it enough to situate oneself within this process of meaning-making developed in the reading and writing of texts. Rather, I argue that QPDA is best equipped to illuminate how cis-heteronormative assemblages of meaning—comprising discourses of gender, sexuality, and other discursive markers—organize bodies and worlds in complicated and contested ways. Redeploying PDA along queer lines, discourses of gender, sexuality, and violence in/of international law can be queered and disrupted, to illuminate the power relations constituting these representational practices. So rather than "functioning as 'straightening devices' . . . queer methods pluralise and disorientate the story of international law away from a single linear trajectory signalling progress" (Holzer et al. 2023, 7).

Gender, Sexuality, and Violence

Gender is a contested concept, both within and beyond feminist activism and scholarship. In contrast to gender essentialists and social constructivists, I deploy a feminist poststructural and queer approach to this concept. Gender essentialists assume that men and women have innate, but different, social characteristics predetermined by their biological sex (see critique of essentialism by Grosz 1995; Phillips 2010). Essentialist theorizing about gender and sex is evident in the cis-heteronormative discourses of international law. At the ICTY, biological essentialism directs the prosecutor's line of questioning witnesses, evident when the prosecutor asks every woman whether they have been raped, a question that assumes the innate rapability of women and of the witnesses' gender identity (see Chapter 4).

Gender essentialism, embodied in cis-heteronormative discourses, demarcates "proper" and "perverse" practices and identities of gender, sex, and sexuality.

Meanwhile, social constructivists maintain that gender is socially constructed and has no predetermined connection to biological sex (Haslanger 2000; see critique of approach by Carlson 2010; Sjoberg 2012, 338). Social constructivist approaches to gender have provided a much-needed critique of biological essentialism (de Beauvoir 2010 [1949]; Haslanger 1995; Mackinnon 2013). Indeed, such a perspective has enabled feminists "to debunk the claim that anatomy is destiny" in the determination of gender roles (Butler 1986, 35). Simone de Beauvoir's *The Second Sex* (2010 [1949]) paved the way for a social constructivist view of gender that liberates gender from the essentialized body, a foundational argument that poststructural feminists would later build on and take further. But both essentialist and social constructivist approaches to gender are at best limited, and at worst harmful, insofar as they perpetuate "the suturing of gender ... to bodies" (Zalewski 2017, 203) and assume the stability and truth of biological sex. Reflecting on de Beauvoir's work, Butler notes that the theorist "occasionally ascribes ontological meanings to anatomical sexual differentiation," but acknowledges that "her comments just as often suggest that anatomy alone has no inherent significance" (1986, 45). Indeed, Butler suggests that "de Beauvoir's theory seems implicitly to ask whether sex was not gender all along" (1986, 46). Social constructivist perspectives of gender thus frequently subscribe to notions of "sex as biological/stable" (Haslanger 1995, 98) and that sex and gender are entirely separate. But these perspectives also contain the seeds of a more poststructural theory of gender.

Social constructivist approaches to gender in international law similarly reject biologically deterministic articulations of gender. But they have also had a similar effect of assuming a binary and biological stability of the gendered subject (McNeilly 2019; Otto 2015). For example, the ICC's definition of gender cleaves to an essentialist perspective, where gender equals sex (male and female). But it also enables a social constructivist interpretation, where gender must be understood "within the context of society" (Rome Statute 1998). The "constructive ambiguity" of gender in the Rome Statute allows for both essentialist and social constructivist theories of gender, and in theory, allows for a broader view of sex, gender, *and* sexuality, if interpreted accordingly (Oosterveld 2005, 4). But in practice, this definition, along with feminist scholarship adhering to a social constructivist approach (see, e.g., Loenen 1994; Hernandez-Truyol 2011, cited in Otto 2015, 306), erases the fluidity and social construction of sex and sexuality, in addition to gender. In contrast, I follow feminist poststructural and queer ontologies that theorize the production and regulation of gender, sex, and sexuality as discursively enmeshed, performative, and socially meaningful (see Griffin 2007). I read gender and sexuality as discourses that give meaning to bodies and practices (see Peterson 1992, 9; 1999, 37). This allows for an approach to sex, gender, and sexuality that exceeds the biological stability and binaries promoted by essentialist and social constructivist approaches.

Gender and sexuality are legible through an assemblage of subjectivities, experiences, and tropes (Cohn 1993). Throughout this book, I speak of cis-heteronormative discourses of gender, sexuality, and violence, or else refer to the hyper-heteromasculinities, femininities, and (homo)sexualities that make violence legible. These concepts are intelligible by shifting representations of femininities, masculinities, sexualities, queerness, desires, fantasies, pleasures, and imaginaries that are discursively performed and (re)inscribed onto bodies. These concepts are not concrete and immovable, but inherently unstable, contested, and consistently subject to "movement, redefinition, and subversive performance" (Cohen 1997, 439; see also Ruskola 2010, 1484). A queer approach recognizes that gender and sexuality cannot be made "to signify monolithically" (Sedgwick 1993, 8). They are not discrete, unrelated entities, but mutually constituted analytical categories that are articulated in and through the discipline and regulation of bodies (de Lauretis 1997, 268). Gender and sexuality are infused with other forms of embodiment too, including race, ethnicity, class, caste, able-bodiedness, age, geography, Indigeneity, and (post- or settler-)coloniality (see Chowdhry and Ling 2017; Heathcote 2018b; Rao 2020). In international law, discourses of gender and sexuality are constituted by racial, ethnic, religious, and national signifiers, enabling the representation of violence and the (re)production of bodies. These assemblages of meaning are articulated through discourses. At the ICTY, for example, gender and sexuality cohere through civilizational logics, ethnicity, and religion, evident in the designation of Serbs and Mujahedin by the Tribunal as dangerously cis-heteromasculine (see Chapter 4). Gender and sexuality are therefore meaningful in relation to plural social assemblages, and this is reflected in the governance of international law.

But discourses of gender and sexuality are not "passively inscribed" onto bodies (Wilcox 2015, 44). Following the new materialist turn in feminism, bodies "cannot be ontologically separated from cultural or discursive forces" (Wilcox 2015, 45). Instead, "bodies have a capacity to push back against their inscription and formation in discursive practices" (Wilcox 2015, 45). By adopting this ontological approach that maintains discourse as performative and felt in and through bodies, it is possible to see gender and sexuality as discourses that are simultaneously imposed, embodied, and resisted (see Griffin 2016, 180). Acknowledging the complex entanglement of discourse with bodies offers opportunities for queer theorizing, evident in the ways that people can engage with or resist gendered and sexualized discourses. This argument is important for responding to the core questions that animate this book. I read the intersecting discourses of gender, sexuality, and violence with an eye to the variously embodied inscriptions and experiences of harm. Discourses constitute bodies, but they are also affected by them. As Laura Sjoberg argues, people live war and conflict sensorially; with "tastes, smells, sounds, sights, and feelings" some of the ways in which people experience violence (2015, 450). My analysis is attuned to how the materiality of real lives and bodies interacts with, and forms part of an assemblage with practices of legal violence. In addition, taking the embodied and resistive capacities of bodies seriously enables me to trace how discourses of violence materialize in ways whereby victim-survivors and perpetrators can subvert simplistic constructions of victimhood and criminality (see Chapter 5). I pay attention to the embodied, material, and resistive modes through which discourses and bodies are made intelligible because international law is filled with these bodies who are intimately connected and contribute to discourses of gender, sexuality, and violence.

Queer scholarship tackles questions of embodiment by blurring the (supposed) distinctions between subject positions and identities. Puar's (2005) concept of queer assemblages allows me to approach discourses and bodies in/of international law not as discrete entities, but as vibrant, complicated, and intimately entangled. For example, at the ICTY, it is the plural and simultaneous practices at play that enable legal actors to adjudicate violence in the former Yugoslavia. Extended to the concepts of gender and sexuality, assemblages "allow us to attune to intensities, emotions, energies, affectivities, textures as they inhabit events, spatiality, and corporealities"

(Puar 2005, 128). While Puar develops queer assemblages to read the formation of the "turbaned Sikh terrorist" in War on Terror discourse (2005, 122), it can be applied to other sites of global governance, including international law. Queer assemblages problematize the representation of bodies in/of international law as simple, readable objects and instead embrace the strangeness and uncertainty through which multiple and contingent subjectivities are constituted and embodied. For instance, in Chapter 5 I analyze an example from the ICTY court proceedings of a man who disobeyed the orders of a camp guard to perform the Serb three-finger salute, because he was missing a finger, and therefore could not do it. In this example, I show how bodily materiality can be a site of power and refusal, just as much as bodies are subjected to violence. Thus, the various actors that constitute international law have embodied and agential capacity.

Gender and sexuality, then, are both discursive (or constitutive) and agential (or embodied). Attentive to this dynamic, Shepherd argues that "how we make sense of gender is thoroughly imbricated in our understanding of sexual activity and sexual desire, they are co-constitutive" (2012, 5–6). This is because, as Sjoberg argues, sexuality is so embedded within our social and discursive realities, that we cannot make sense of these realities without the invocation and (re)production of sexual meanings and practices (2017a, 73). This relationship can be seen through the legal violences of international law. In Chapter 4, I show how victimization, denunciation, and paternalism are informed by interlinking discourses of gender and sexuality. Legal actors denouncing sexual violence against (cis-)men, for example, depends on the assumption that "homosexualizing" violence is particularly abhorrent and embarrassing. This is an assumption that rests on the cis-heteronormative tethering of heterosexuality, masculinity, and manliness and the denigration of homosexuality, femininity, and otherness. Gender and sexuality therefore work and gain meaning in tandem. How victims, survivors, and perpetrators are understood and legible within/by international law depends on a binary, cis-heteronormative status quo. It is through understanding gender, sex, and sexuality as discursively constructed categories that organize our world, that it then becomes possible to challenge these dominant discourses.

Gender and sexuality are inscribed onto bodies in ways that render them legible, but they can also legitimate acts of violence in international law. For example, the positioning of women as predominantly victims of sexual violence performs a form of legal victimization, where women are feminized, passive, and disempowered subjects of international law. Moreover, discourses of gender, sexuality, and ethnicity are invoked as justification for the modes through which legal violence is sanctioned. In this sense, denunciatory or paternalistic practices of international law, such as those (re)produced at the ICTY (see Chapter 4) reflect a desire to manage, regulate, and control unwieldy subjects. Bodies are complicated and difficult to read, and so international law classifies and governs bodies in ways that make them legible, including as hyper-heteromasculine, racially Othered perpetrators and as feminized Othered victims requiring the (juridical, carceral, military) intervention of lawful interveners. Thus, to regulate and control bodies, they must be simplified and classified according to their desirability or threat.

Through repetition and reproduction, discourses of gender and sexuality become knowable realities, thereby rendering bodies meaningful in violent and exclusionary ways. These are forms of violence, but they are also constitutive of violence. Violence is both material and discursive (see also violence as a language, Myrttinen 2018). That is, "acts of violence, broadly conceived, are productive of particular modes of being in the world, prescribing certain behaviours and proscribing others" (Shepherd 2012, 6; see also Ruskola 2010, 1529). This approach is informed by feminist poststructuralists who have been able to *gender* violence, as well as illuminate the "violent reproduction of gender" (Shepherd 2013, 17). In my QPDA of selected ICTY texts, I use discursive tools to trace how discourses of gender, sexuality, and violence are made legible in these documents. By deploying my QPDA toolbox to the violent and violating practices at/of the ICTY, I scrutinize how such legal violence depends on and (re)produces gendered and sexualized discourses and situate these effects within the broader project of international law.

As I described in Chapter 1, I argue that international law is a (queer) governance mechanism that is both violent and violating. This entails the recognition that legal discourses can be sources of violence, because they perpetuate cis-heteronormative and exclusionary logics of gendered embodiment and criminality. As both an analytical category and a discursive practice, violence constitutes our world. In Foucauldian terms, it is both repressive and (re)productive, insofar as it has generative power in the moment of violence, able to produce bodies in the process of violation (Wilcox 2015). It is in this way that discourses are violent (see de Lauretis

1997, 266). A queer analysis reveals the intimately violent machinations of discourse, of the ways that gender, sexuality, and violence have violent and violating capacities in the (re)production of subject positions and the pre/proscription of legal-political possibilities. Discourses of gender and sexuality are violent because they regulate bodies and determine those who are accepted and those who are rendered abnormal or perverse, or as not worth mattering at all. For example, in Chapter 4, I show how legal discourses violently impose cis-heteronormativity and civilizational logics of legal subjects in international law, configuring the straight, cisgender legal subject as the common sense and justifying carceral responses to conflict through gendered, civilizational logics.

In this book I adopt a queer approach to violence, which emphasizes its discursive articulation and its manifestation in and through all aspects of the social world. It allows me to locate violence in "everyday practices, representational discourses and multiple modalities of power" (Kantola 2007, 279; see also Parashar 2013), to reveal how discourses of gender and sexuality, evident in both overt and tacit practices, constitute (legal) violence. This departs from an exclusive focus on sexual violence as gendered, instead emphasizing how all forms of violence ("sexual" and "nonsexual") (re)produce and gain meaning in a "gendered/violent world" (Sjoberg 2017b, 138–39). This approach reveals the plural forms of violence, and the workings of legal violence, in sites of international law. Taken together, this queer understanding of gender, sexuality, and violence is deployed in the book to analyze how these discourses intersect and (re)produce bodies in/through international law.

Queer Reflexive Practice

My analysis of international law is shaped by my personal identities, experiences, and privileges. As an exercise in queering governance and international law, this book necessarily commits to a queer reflexive practice. I embrace a reflexive ethos that rejects a tick-box exercise of listing my identity categories and privileges (Gani and Khan 2024; Krystalli 2023), and instead explore how my work both recognizes and seeks to challenge these entangled markers and modes of being. Weber argues that identifying as cis- and/or straight should not preclude researchers from calling themselves queer scholars, so long as their research is committed to the radical potential the term offers. Being a white, Northern, straight, cisgender woman does not mean I "cannot be a queer IR scholar or cannot be an advocate on behalf of queer scholars and scholarship" (Weber 2017, 17; see also Griffin 2013, 142, on "straight" and "queer" research). While it is imperative that the privileges I hold by virtue of these identities be recognized and challenged, for many queer scholars, identifying as queer is about questions that go beyond personal gender and sexual identities, or essentialized notions of them.

While our personal subjectivities are always imbricated in our research agendas, queer scholars frequently situate themselves according to a queer intellectual identity because of their discomfort with the cis-heteronormative and patriarchal logics that govern the discipline and practice of world politics (see Griffin 2011, 546). As with other queer scholars, my work is queer because of the goals and ethics I commit to, because of a desire to move beyond the cis-heteropatriarchal discourses that animate sites of governance. A queer reflexive practice is one that is explicitly attentive to the cis-heteronormative regimes of power that organize our world. Within these regimes, individuals are constituted and can (re)produce and/or resist the governing discourses that situate bodies, places, and things as meaningful. Thus, as a gendered, sexed, and raced person, I am also constituted, and make sense of, the power relations that delineate meaning. It is critical then, as Weber urges us, to ask, "On whose behalf am I deploying this term ['queer'], and what are the practical political effects of my deployment?" (2017, 17). Maintaining this identity involves a commitment to the aims, politics, and implications of queering, something that is embodied in my QPDA and woven throughout the book.

My reflexive ethic is informed by feminist, postcolonial, and queer reflexive research (see, e.g., M. Henry 2003, 2007; Haritaworn 2008; Weber 2016). I am guided by Brooke Ackerly and Jacqui True's development of a feminist research ethic that allows me to consider the "power of knowledge ..., boundaries, marginalisation, and silences"; power relationships; and my "own situatedness" as a researcher (2008, 695; see also Kim et al. 2024). Maintaining this feminist reflexive practice is about taking an approach to research that "is a total corporeal/emotional/intellectual engagement" (Soreanu 2010, 391). My research is constituted through "my self" (Shepherd 2016), imbued and energized through the multiple subject positions and experiences that I embody (Deutsch 2004, 891). My affective responses (Åhall 2018); my identity as a white, Northern feminist; and my life experiences as an embodied subject all manifest in the production of a book that attempts to reveal and dismantle the gendered regimes of power that constitute governance mechanisms. At all times, a reflexive practice must work to deconstruct, as Heathcote writes, the "history of violence, gendered violence, raced violence, homophobic, able-bodied privileges, and anti-queer violence that constructs the places I call home" (2019, 193). As a white, settler Australian who calls so-called Australia my home, I must place my self/selves within the various violences that sustain my world/s, and how this translates into a need to "call[] out" the violence of international law (Heathcote 2019, 193).

A feminist and queer reflexive practice attempts to illuminate the multiple selves that constitute my work, my obligation to others, and to communities of learning and knowing. This entails a commitment to problematizing my positionality and privilege, to draw attention to the political work they do and the research possibilities they both elevate and foreclose. The goal of reflexivity is to expose these tensions, to demonstrate the "fractured mobility of the self, and of the ways in which the self attempts to hide from exposure that writing always threatens—the revelation of its imperfection, of its weakness, of its partiality, or its *wrongness*" (Dauphinée 2016, 54, emphasis in original). Even as these multiple subjectivities and positionalities cannot always be escaped, recognizing the privileges they afford and the implications they have on our research practices is a key part of a reflexive research ethic. This kind of reflexivity is both feminist and queer, insofar as both seek "to 'queer' the positions of researcher and researched themselves through a recognition that the relations between them are perpetually unstable" (Nash 2010, 141).

My positions and privileges change my research, affecting the kinds of knowledge I seek to analyze; the focus on gender, sexuality, and violence and on international law; and the desire to do this research queerly. My reading can only ever be partial, a product of my personal-political self/selves and the broader institutional and cultural regimes of power that I am constituted through. There are subjects and topics that I will miss, research agendas that will never come to life because my multiple subjectivities and the broader cultural forces of my being mean that only certain things may be interesting or revealed to me by virtue of my identities and the privileges they bestow. In adopting a queer reflexive practice, I must grapple with the fact that "I am building my career on the loss" of those subjected to violence in Bosnia (Dauphinée 2007, 1; see also Subotić 2021), and that no matter how attentive to power I can be, my writing will always be an exercise in violence (Dauphinée 2007, 11; see also M. Veličković 2024, 16).

My queer reflexive practice manifests as I seek to expose the unequal relations of power that constitute gender and sexuality by interrogating how they are represented and governed in/by international law. I show that governing logics constitute gender, sexuality, and violence at the Tribunal, and that these (re)produce gendered and sexualized hierarchies (see Chapters 3–4). I embrace queer with the goal of disrupting the normalization of gendered and sexualized discourses in/of international law. I do it with the hope of illuminating alternative representations of violence that are antinormative, transgressive, and challenge the dominant truths of crimes and their prosecution under international law (see Chapter 5). And I use the term "queer," cognizant of its contested history, of the power relations that render it intelligible in multiple contexts, and of the bodies, subjectivities, and practices that it performs. To deploy queer in my research is to make a statement about the types of gendered and sexualized discourses that construct international law, to trace how they are (re)produced and destabilized in the representations and practices of mechanisms governing violence. It is to recognize the violence driving the construction of gendered and sexualized bodies in international law, to illuminate how these queer configurations exist in a longer genealogy of governance, to prescribe some possibilities and preclude others.

A Toolbox for Queer Poststructural Discourse Analysis

This final section of the chapter articulates how my QPDA is applied to the ICTY texts in Chapters 4 and 5. An emphasis on discourses of gender, sexuality, and violence combine with these tools to produce a form of PDA that recognizes the queerly configured discourses constituting global governance and international law.

The concepts that make up my toolkit are commonly deployed in (feminist) poststructural research. However, I recognize the potential for them to be queered. This involves (re)deploying them in queer ways; to recognize the subversive ways they can be applied to read gender, sexuality, and violence in/of international law. In queering the ICTY texts, I use the tools of presupposition, predication, subject positioning, deconstruction, and pre/proscription. These tools are used across Chapters 4 and 5, although in each chapter I emphasize certain tools and concepts more than others.

Presupposition

Presupposition constitutes the "background knowledge" of a text (Doty 1993, 306). It is "an important textual mechanism ... [that] constructs a particular kind of world in which certain things are recognised as true" (Doty 1993, 306). Prior knowledge or information constitute discourse, but such textual context need not be explicitly articulated in a discourse for it to make sense. For example, representations of sexual violence in international legal texts involve presuppositional information, assumed knowledge that gives meaning to this discursive formation. At the ICTY, sexual violence is understood as a violation against (gendered and sexualized) bodies, based on the presuppositional practices of international criminal jurisprudence and the values and norms of Yugoslav society (see K. Campbell 2002, 155). This background knowledge is held to be true but is not always explicitly articulated in the reproduction of discourses about sexual violence.

As a key tool in my reading of these texts, presupposition allows me to trace the historical and contextual discourses that make international law possible. Deploying this analytical tool in my QPDA means that I must be aware of the cis-heteronormative and ethnonationalist configurations of violence that constitute crimes heard before the Tribunal and international law more broadly. To do so, I engage with a range of academic and nonconventional sources on the history and conflict in the former Yugoslavia, the (re)production of ethnic identities, and the gendered and sexed norms and values across the former Yugoslav territories. I also map the broader logics of governance and origin stories that constitute the ICTY (see Balkanism in Chapter 3). This background knowledge shapes my interpretation of ICTY texts and allows me to reveal the presuppositions that constitute discourses of gender, sexuality, and violence in international law.

Predication

Predication "involves the linking of certain qualities to particular subjects through the use of predicates and the adverbs and adjectives that modify them" (Doty 1993, 306). It is a descriptive tool that enables us to make sense of and "affirms a quality, attribute, or property of a person or thing" (Doty 1993, 306). Critically, predication "constructs worlds" and the subjects within them (Doty 1993, 306). Predication allows me to identify and problematize how gendered and sexualized bodies are constructed and attributed qualities in/by international law. This discursive practice is (re)productive. It ascribes, delimits, and (re)produces meaning through the attachment of predicates to social subjects and artifacts. Predication also alerts us to the ways in which inanimate objects, places, and geographies (e.g., the former Yugoslavia/Balkans) are described according to gendered, sexualized, and civilizational predicates.

I use this tool to identify and deconstruct discourses of gender, sexuality, and violence that constitute international law as a (queer) governance mechanism. For example, the subject position of the (cis-)woman as a victim of sexual violence in ICTY discourse assumes the predicates of a *feminized* and *passive* victimhood. Such predication works to make crimes of sexual violence against (cis-)women, while horrific, nevertheless intelligible in a context aimed at prosecuting crimes against humanity. The (cis-)woman as a victim of sexual violence subject position (re)produces the international legal discourse of victimized femininity and its utility in contemporary practices of international law.

Subject Positioning

Subject positioning depends on presuppositional and predicate practices that "work to create a 'reality' by linking particular subjects and objects to one another" (Doty 1993, 306). It demonstrates the relational nature of discourse and its inscription on bodies. In other words, discourses (and the subjects they construct) are made meaningful and are *positioned* in relation to other discourses and subjects (Doty 1993, 306; 1996, 11; Shepherd 2017, 26). Subject positions are "precarious, contradictory and in process" (Weedon 1997, 32), because discourses constituting subjectivity are always in flux, constituted by "moments of transition" (Edkins 1999, 8). They also maintain "the permanent possibility" of being reiterated, transformed, and resisted (Butler 1995, 46–47). This means that subject positions are discursive practices that temporarily establish meaning but are only possible through a complicated web of queer, contradictory, and plural signifying practices (see plural subjectivities and the split subject, Heathcote 2018a, 2019).

I use subject positioning in this book to highlight the (re)production of subject positions through the governing practices of international law (e.g., sadistic perpetrators, feminized victims, and "noisy" survivors, see Chapters 4 and 5). As a (queer) governance mechanism, international law is "a site for the production and reproduction of particular subjectivities and identities while others are simultaneously excluded" (Hansen 2006, 18–19). Subject positioning reflects how particular gendered, sexualized, and racialized bodies are constructed in relation to others; how *subjects are positioned* and juxtaposed in complex and multiple ways. Subject positioning not only produces bodies but also renders actions possible in sites of atrocity and in the legal discourse of the courtroom.

Deconstruction

Deconstruction seeks to identify hierarchical, binary discourses and undo them from within (Derrida 1978, 280–81). I use deconstruction to identify the various signifiers that constitute and are constituted by the legal actors that embody international law, and to disturb the assumption that these discourses are fixed and unchanging. Butler argues that "to deconstruct these terms ['the subject,' 'the body'] means ... to continue to use them, to repeat them, to repeat them subversively, and to displace them from the contexts in which they have been deployed as instruments of oppressive power" (1995, 51). As I demonstrate in Chapter 4, the ICTY itself is a site for, and an agent in, the (re)production of hierarchical categories, of those designated as "Balkan" criminals, or "hopeless" victims, versus lawful adjudicators. In international law, oppositions rely on essentialisms, and on an assumption that such ordering of bodies is natural and inescapable. Deconstruction reveals the mutability of these designations.

Deconstruction requires that we reverse the hierarchy between binary oppositions. This is achieved by revealing "first, how the hierarchies on which the binary depends are constructed and therefore not true and/or reliable, and second, how such oppositions can be betrayed into inverting themselves through their very need to hold themselves together" (Griffin 2013, 211). It also involves dislodging discourses from the systems in which they are articulated (Derrida 1988, 21), and offers opportunities for queer researchers to "open up" the realms of intelligibility that organize bodies according to binary oppositions, to reclaim and redeploy terms in ways that resist and transgress cis-heteronormative systems of governance (Butler 1995, 48). For example, in Chapter 5, I trace how various actors at/of the

ICTY engage subversive discourses of violence that unsettle the assumed stability of dominant discourses about victimhood and criminality in international law. Deconstruction therefore exposes the violence of discourses in international law, but also points to the instabilities, inconsistencies, and ways of refusing expectations about the "proper" legal subject.

Pre/proscription

Pre/proscription traces how presupposition, predication, and subject positioning permits some possibilities and prohibits others (Griffin 2009; Khalid 2017). It alerts us to the ways in which "discourses . . . actively and continually predicate, pre/proscribe and reproduce preordained 'realities' to which individuals must fit by redefining their behaviour" (Griffin 2009, 45). In other words, once particular "truths" and "realities" have been established through the discursive practices of presupposition, predication, and subject positioning, certain possibilities are pre/proscribed (see also Sjoberg's approach to proscription as "discursively impossible," 2017b, 54). Any actions following from "processes of pre/proscription" can thus "logically follow as acceptable" (Khalid 2017, 10).

I use pre/proscription to identify how discourses of gender, sexuality, and violence may authorize or prohibit actions in international law. I am interested in how these discourses, made meaningful through presuppositional practices, predicates, and subject positioning, (dis)allow legal-political possibilities at the Tribunal and in international law more broadly (see Dauphinée 2008, 50–51). International law can therefore be understood as a mechanism that pre/proscribes violence (Sjoberg and Gentry 2007, 11). Using the example of sexual violence from earlier, cis-heteronormative discourses of gender and sexuality at the ICTY predominantly articulate (cis-)women as victims in crimes of sexual violence. By reproducing the (cis-)woman victim as a subject of legal analysis, legal actors who constitute the Tribunal engage in practices of pre/proscription that enable the (re)production of this subjectivity in prosecutions related to sexual violence, but also preclude other discursive and embodied realities (e.g., LGBTQIA+ victims of sexual violence, (cis-)women as victims of "nonsexual" violence, etc.). In an international legal context, pre/proscription works to produce (cis-heteronormative) legal subjects, thereby authorizing relevant legal actions and possibilities (e.g., criminal charges, imprisonment), while also curtailing alternate experiences, articulations of justice, and realities of embodiment (see Philipose 2002, 164).

Taken together, these five discursive tools constitute my QPDA. They allow me to identify the textual practices that constitute discourses of gender, sexuality, and violence within international law and the legal-political implications of these practices. Discourses make "logical and proper certain policies by authorities and in the implementation of those policies" and alter "people's modes and conditions of living" (Milliken 1999, 236). This pre/proscriptive power of discourse is articulated through the ICTY texts, which reveal how international law is both constituted by and constitutive of civilizational logics and cis-heteronormative discourses of gender, sexuality, and violence.

The following chapters apply these tools to five ICTY cases, using them as examples of international law applied: *Brđanin* (IT-99-36); *Delić* (IT-04-83); *Kvočka* et al. (IT-98-30/1), *Mucić* et al. (IT-96-21), and *Tadić* (IT-94-1) (see Appendix 1). These cases were chosen because they consist of extensive material detailing "sexual" and "nonsexual" forms of violence heard at the ICTY and consist of an ethnically diverse range of victims and perpetrators. In undertaking my QPDA of these cases, I analyzed indictments, court transcripts, and trial judgments available on the ICTY website. To avoid duplicating texts, I focused on evidentiary aspects of the court transcripts, that is, those areas that deal with testimonies of witnesses and the defense. This is because the decisions made by the judge are largely detailed in the judgment documents. The court transcripts are the basis for much of the juridical authority invested in the trial judgments, and "include rich, experiential and situated/subjective accounts of the conflict" that do not always translate into the representation of crimes in the judgments (K. Campbell et al. 2019, 258). It was therefore important that I focus on these legal texts alongside my reading of the institutional documents and trial judgments, to engage with the real lives and stories that constitute violence (as much as one can through reading transcripts) (see Appendix 2).[1] My analysis of five ICTY cases is by no means a representation of all its cases, so future research in this area could both strengthen and contribute to findings developed in this book. Interesting insights could be gleaned from analyses that focus on other practices, sites, and theaters of violence investigated by the Tribunal. Moreover, while my research focuses on the ICTY's digital archives as an example of international legal texts, future research could encompass working with the Tribunal's physical archives, as well as engaging with court officials, civil society actors, and communities across Bosnia to enrich my analysis.

Concluding Thoughts on Queer Concepts and Methods

Queer theories, methods, and methodologies are diverse and do not provide a singular blueprint for doing research. It should go without saying that my queering of concepts and methods, and the development of my own queer methodology, is but one way of doing queer research. I have developed this approach with the hope that it might be useful to others curious about the queer discursive machinations of global governance, at the same time as it allows me to access these same dynamics in/of international law. In this chapter, I have offered QPDA as a way through which discourses of gender, sexuality, and violence can be traced and deconstructed. Informed by feminist, queer, postcolonial, and poststructural scholarship, I developed a queer discursive approach that is attentive to the gendered and gendering, constitutive and agential, and violent and violating practices I outlined in Chapter 1.

Discourses are central to this book, particularly as I seek to trace their intersections and effects in/through international law. My engagement of poststructural approaches to discourse in my queer methodology exposes the performative power of international law as a (queer) governance mechanism, insofar as it (re)produces subjects according to the gendered, sexualized, and civilizational meanings it imposes. A queer (re)imagining of PDA into QPDA emphasizes the imbrication of gender, sexuality, and violence with discourse. This method also comes with its own discursive toolbox, consisting of presupposition, predication, subject positioning, deconstruction, and pre/proscription. QPDA allows me to argue in later chapters that discourses of gender, sexuality, and violence—as represented in the practices of legal violence in the courtroom—predominantly reinforce cis-heteronormative discourses and civilizational logics of governance and international law. QPDA reveals how bodies are made legible in international law through gendered subject positions, ethnicized presuppositions, and civilizational logics, to name but a few of the discursive practices that constitute and are (re)produced by the various actors embodying the Tribunal. It identifies the plural, entangled, and contradictory discourses that make international law legible as a (queer) governance mechanism with the authority to delimit innocence from guilt, legality from criminality, and victim from perpetrator from lawful intervener.

These discourses of international law, manifested at/of the ICTY, operate in and through gendered, civilizational logics and origin stories. In the courtroom, legal actors such as judges and prosecutors engage these logics and represent victims and perpetrators according to civilizational logics. As a (queer) governance mechanism, international law depends on these logics of governance, logics that are integral to the legibility of law and justice through cis-heteronormative discourses. In the remainder of this book, I trace the legal-political work these logics and discourses do within international law, at the ICTY, and the implications of these practices for real lives and bodies subject to the violence and potential of international law.

3
Logics of Governance and International Law at/of the International Criminal Tribunal for the Former Yugoslavia

In 1993, the United Nations Security Council (UNSC) unanimously adopted Resolution 827, bringing the International Criminal Tribunal for the Former Yugoslavia (ICTY) into creation. The establishment of the Tribunal marked a renewed emphasis on the role of international law in governing and adjudicating violence in global politics, ushering in hope and possibility in the power of criminal justice to address atrocities. But such a turn to international law was not without its own violences. Indeed, pejorative discourses about the former Yugoslavia as a place of "savagery" and "backwardness" in the "backyard of Europe" requiring the "civilizing" hand of international law characterized much of the ICTY's foundational documents. Moreover, these discourses were gendered, sexualized, and racialized, constructing feminized helpless victims in need of protection from hyper-heteromasculine perpetrators, the former of whom were to be infantilized and disempowered before the courts, the latter of whom were to be castigated, denounced, and incarcerated on the world stage. The gendered discourses and civilizational logics that constituted the ICTY continued earlier racial logics of international law. They also formed the foundations for subsequent international legal mechanisms like the International Criminal Court (ICC) to justify international criminal justice on the basis of "saving" feminized and racialized victims from hyper-heteromasculinized, racialized criminals. These governing logics and discourses are not only sources of violence in themselves. They also enable legally sanctioned violence in the form of international criminal justice, a governance mechanism that commits its own forms of victimizing, denunciatory, and paternalistic harms. International law then, is violent and violating, and the gendered, racialized, and civilizational discourses and logics it (re)produces suggest little possibility for a queerer, liberatory law. However, even against the violence of these discursive and legal practices, there always already holds the potential for subverting these violences, within and beyond international law (see Chapters 5 and 6). This is only possible once these violences are exposed and deconstructed, to reveal that they are changeable and impermanent, and that global justice can be thought and conceived otherwise.

Chapter 3 traces and identifies logics of governance and international law through the case of the ICTY. It engages in discussions about the gendered discourses and civilizational logics through which international law is authorized to govern and regulate people and populations. In this chapter, I am concerned with the governing logics of the ICTY, and what they can tell us about international law more broadly. My queer reading of international law through the case of the ICTY must interrogate the broader cultural forces and discourses through which its authorization and operation was made possible. I am also interested then, in how the ICTY is conjured in its foundational texts, and how academic and media discourses contribute to stories about the ICTY's origins and purpose. This chapter establishes the ICTY as a knowable and powerful site of international law that stems from, and (re)produces, broader geopolitical logics of (legal) governance. These logics do not exist in isolation, but are made possible by, reinforce, and/or challenge broader logics of governance and international law.

Throughout this chapter, I argue that as a (queer) governance mechanism, international law both engages with and (re)produces logics of governance that continue a longer history of Eurocentric representations of the world. These logics depend on historical discourses of mass atrocity, inaction and (non)interventions, and Orientalist accounts of populations. At the ICTY, this manifests through Balkanism: the representation of the former Yugoslavia as violent and premodern, and thus different from, and inferior to, the peaceful cosmopolitanism of "proper" Europe. I also reveal the ways in which logics of governance and international law constitute the Tribunal and perpetuate gendered and sexualized discourses of global politics. For example, frequent justifications for the creation of the ICTY point to "authors of ... barbarous acts" who "massacre and burn children, women and elderly people ... with diabolical regularity" (ICTY Annual Report 1994, 18; UN Doc S/PV/3217 1993, 21). The foundational texts of the ICTY draw on Balkanist logics to construct a former Yugoslavia that is populated with hyper-heteromasculine criminals and feminized victims (see Chapter 4). These Balkanist logics constitute the presuppositional knowledge of the Tribunal. Balkanism therefore functions as a kind of "legal Orientalism," "a set of usually unarticulated cultural assumptions about that which is not law, and about those who do not have it" (Ruskola 2013, 23). Such legal Balkanism, to adapt Teemu Ruskola's concept, similarly constructs a "world of legal modernity" that requires "an unlegal, despotic Orient to summon it into existence" (2013, 23).

To this end, I use this chapter as a backdrop for my QPDA of selected ICTY texts, to trace how discourses of gender, sexuality, and violence intersect in/through international law, and their effects (see Chapters 4 and 5). In this chapter, I identify and deconstruct the problematic Balkanist logics and origin stories that anchor these discourses. I also reveal some of the legal-political implications of these representations, such as the pejorative classification of "uncivilized" populations and the sanctioning of (military, legal, political, economic) interventions. As a result, this chapter offers vital insights into logics of governance and international law at/of the ICTY, and the ways in which discourses of gender, sexuality, and violence intersect in international law (see Chapters 4 and 5). Crucially, it evidences the violence of international law as a (queer) governance mechanism. In doing so, it paves the way for an analysis in later chapters that considers how international law is both violent and a site through which subversion, ambivalence, and queerness operate.

The ICTY's Origin Stories

My queer analysis of the ICTY texts depends on the presuppositional logics that give meaning to the Tribunal as a site of international law. The ICTY was not created in a vacuum. Rather, the Tribunal's establishment was made possible by broader historical and geopolitical logics about the former Yugoslavia, mass atrocities, and international law.[1] In this first section, I present four origin stories through which logics of governance and international law are at work. There is no singular voice or actor who (re)tells these stories, but rather a plurality of academic, policy, and popular discursive positions that lend weight to these representations. In identifying these four stories, it is not my intention to foreclose a range of other (origin) stories about the ICTY, or international law more broadly. Rather, I discuss these four stories because they situate the Tribunal as an example of international law and its dependence on civilizational logics. *Origin Story I* casts back to the end of World War II and the creation of the war crimes tribunals in Nuremberg and Tokyo, informed by the memory of the Holocaust and pleas for "Never Again." *Origin Story II* is intimately connected to the first origin story, anchored in (Western) media, policy, and academic discourses of outrage about the camps in Bosnia. The camps are compared to the Nazi concentration camps, and in this origin story, they are the ultimate motivation for the Tribunal's creation. *Origin Story III* shifts to the immediate post–Cold War context that preceded the ICTY's creation. Failed (and lack of) interventions by Western-led forces set the scene for the Tribunal's historic inception by the UN. Finally, *Origin Story IV* sees the ICTY as the promise of international law. By tracing these origin stories, I problematize some of the (gendered, civilizational) violences that constitute international law as a (queer) governance mechanism. In doing so, I deconstruct these violent discourses and show them to be fluid, changeable, and just some of the discursive possibilities that characterize international law.

Origin Story I: "Never Again" and the War Crimes Tribunals

The ICTY's origins can be traced to the end of World War II. This origin story establishes the Tribunal as clearly connected to the collective guilt (and trauma) of the Holocaust and the failure to prevent the genocide of at least six million Jews, a quarter of a million each of Roma and people with disabilities, nearly 2,000 Jehovah's Witnesses, and thousands of homosexuals as well as the millions of Polish, Soviet, and Serb civilians, and political opponents in Germany (United States Holocaust Memorial Museum 2019). In the aftermath of the genocide, the newly formed UN vowed that mass atrocities such as those committed during the Holocaust would *never again* occur (Rosenfeld 2009, 136–37). This rallying call produced the UN as a knowable subject: a moral, civilized, and outraged group of (State) members who would simply not allow genocide to happen again.

Part of the postwar process of healing, retribution, and instilling of the "Never Again" rhetoric involved the creation of war crimes tribunals in Nuremberg (to prosecute Nazi war criminals) and Tokyo (to prosecute Japanese war criminals). Each of these mechanisms marked a turning point in how mass atrocity was understood in global politics. While both tribunals are marked with flaws—including the critique that they were forms of victor's justice (Schabas 2012)—they offered a new way of responding to mass atrocities, one situated within international law. This postwar discourse advanced justice that favored Western, Eurocentric norms and values and continued to perpetuate (neo)colonial and imperialist practices in the Global South. Indeed, despite the mass atrocities and conflicts occurring outside of Europe (and often at the hands of these colonial powers), the "Never Again" rhetoric was about preventing another genocide *in Europe*.

It is from this call for "Never Again" that *Origin Story I* begins. According to this discourse, the ICTY was established because of Europe's failure to prevent another genocide from occurring on "European soil" (Askin 2003, 12). Less than fifty years later, the mass atrocities taking place across the former Yugoslav territories (especially in Bosnia) reminded Western and European countries of Nazi crimes and the Holocaust (Steinweis 2005, 278). Journalists and international leaders alike saw, in the Omarska prison camp, flashbacks to the ghettos and concentration camps of World War II, invoking "the 'mythic' power of sites like Auschwitz" in discourses on Bosnia (D. Campbell 2002b, 153). Witnesses who testified at the ICTY likened the camps to Auschwitz, and for one witness, even Hitler's crimes could not match the atrocities taking place in Bosnia (*Brdanin* 2002, Trial hearing 27 February; 2002, Trial hearing 3 June).

The 1995 genocide of over 8,000 Bosnian Muslim men and boys in Srebrenica was the ultimate reminder of the failed promise of "Never Again." It is no surprise then, that once the ICTY was established, the Srebrenica genocide was a key investigation for prosecutors. The ICTY's relationship to Nuremberg and the Holocaust sustains what Kamari Clarke calls "a legacy and set of sentimental commitments against mass atrocity," one that reinforced Eurocentric visions of international law (Clarke 2019, xxi). In the early 1990s, the years in which the ICTY was established, "the Holocaust was more firmly established in Anglo-American culture than at any other time" (Patrick 2016, 148). This broader Eurocentric and Western attachment to Holocaust memory served as the context through which the war in Bosnia, and the subsequent creation of the ICTY, occurred.

From this origin story, it is interesting that Bosnia is considered European. As I discuss later in this chapter, Balkanist logics construct the former Yugoslavia as both European and non-European, and this is evident in the coding of the ICTY's origin stories. Reference to the detention camps "in the heart of Europe" (Robison 2004, 379), the "tragic conflict in the European 'backyard'" (Engle 2020, 39), or simply labeling "the Balkans" "as one of Europe's danger spots" (Norris 2006, 101–2) positioned the conflict as distinctly European. As I show in the final discussions of this chapter, however, Balkanist logics also cast the former Yugoslavia outside of

Europe; a place on the border of "civilized" Europe and "uncivilized" Orient (M. Todorova 1997, 188). These logics are not unique to the Tribunal, or to the former Yugoslavia; they manifest in other civilizational and racial logics in international law (see Clarke 2019; Sagan 2010). In this sense, while *Origin Story I* frames the Yugoslav conflicts as crimes taking place on the European continent, thereby harking back to memories of the Holocaust, it simultaneously cast "the Balkans" out as Other, as a sort of quasi-European region anchored in historical enmities and timeless violence.

The ICTY's establishment reinforced this distinction between the "moral" and "peaceful" (western) Europe and the "ancient hatreds" of more distant, (non-)European lands. It was clear that international responses to the Yugoslav conflicts of the 1990s were driven by a "moral cause" to address the "evil" of "the Balkans" (Mehler 2017, 611). In this way, *Origin Story I* renders the ICTY intelligible as a site through which the UN (through international law) can right the wrongs of the past, of the collective failure to prevent another genocide from occurring. This origin story is also dependent on gendered discourses of intervention, with the creation of the ICTY justified through the need to save infantilized, feminized populations from the "barbarous acts" of violence endemic to the region (ICTY Annual Report 1994, 18; see also Un Doc S/PV/3217 1993, 21), in addition to direct comparisons with victims of the Holocaust (Kovačević 2008, 159–60). The Tribunal therefore represented a moral cause, to appease the guilt of breaking the promise of "Never Again." At the same time, the ICTY represented an opportunity to condemn "the Balkans" as so exceptionally bad and violent that it required the first ad hoc criminal tribunal of the late twentieth century. These Balkanist logics that permeate *Origin Story I* and its invocation of Holocaust memory stem from the comparisons made between the camps in Bosnia and the Nazi concentration camps. *Origin Story I* therefore depends on, and is intimately entangled with, *Origin Story II*, which situates the existence of camps in Bosnia as one of the core reasons for the ICTY's creation.

Origin Story II: Camps in Bosnia

In August 1992, Western media were granted access to the prison camps in Bosnia (Patrick 2016, 146). At the Omarska and Trnopolje camps, journalists photographed "emaciated detainees imprisoned behind barbed-wire fences" (Askin 2003, 12–14). It was the existence of these "concentration camps in Europe" (Power 2002, 269) that would later justify the UN's decision to establish the ICTY, thus forming *Origin Story II*. This origin story is constituted by and (re)produces Balkanist logics of the former Yugoslavia, which I discuss later in this chapter. Especially in media discourse, the violence and existence of the camps were described in ways that, as with the quote from Kelly Askin above, would cast Bosnians as helpless, hopeless victims of atrocities that could only be explained by "the 'traditional' Balkan propensity to violence" (Jiggins 2018, 39). Importantly, it was this Balkanist logic (which cast the former Yugoslavia as both Europe and not-Europe) that made comparisons between the camps in Bosnia and the Nazi camps possible. When images of the Omarska and Trnopolje camps crossed Western newspapers and television screens, audiences were reminded of the concentration camps of the Holocaust, a historical period of atrocity that remained central in "the Western psyche" (Patrick 2016, 148). The re-emergence of camps in Europe—fifty years after the promise of "Never Again" was made—played a powerful role in the turn to international law through the creation of the first ad hoc criminal tribunal since Nuremberg and Tokyo.

The photographs taken at Omarska and Trnopolje would almost instantly turn into "icon[s] of contemporary atrocity" (D. Campbell 2002a, 6). Others describe the "discovery" of these camps as "a symbol of the horrors of the war in Bosnia" (Askin 2003, 12–14), one that "inflamed public outrage . . . like no [other] postwar genocide" (Power 2002, 276). It was this outrage that led to the investigation of atrocities in the former Yugoslavia and was "one of the catalysts" for the creation of the ICTY to prosecute these crimes (Askin 2003, 12–14). In the Tribunal's formative documents, media documentation of the violence committed in the camps prompted the UNSC to quickly establish the ICTY (Popovksi 2002, 56). In ICTY texts, reference was made to the existence of "concentration camps" in Bosnia (UN Doc S/PV/3217 1993, 42) and "the notorious Bosnian Serb camp at Omarska" (ICTY Annual Report 1995, 18).

Furthermore, both ICTY documents and academic, policy, and media discourse expressed outrage over reports of "rape camps" in Bosnia (Stanley 1999). Calls for the creation of the ICTY therefore also took a gender justice approach, with various feminists seeing in the Tribunal the promise of international law to hold (mainly) Serb men accountable for raping Bosnian Muslim women (Askin 1997; Batinic 2001; Mackinnon 1994). These radical feminist perspectives shined a much-needed spotlight on gender-based crimes committed against women, and their legal activism would later see a commitment to gender justice enshrined in the ICC's Rome Statute

(Copelon 2000; Mackinnon 2013). The ICTY Statute made explicit reference to sexual violence against Bosnian Muslim women, emphasizing not only the crimes committed in Bosnia but also the "organised and systematic detention and rape of women" and "Muslim women" in particular (ICTY Statute 2009, 15, 17). Thus, *Origin Story II* invokes gendered, ethnicized, and Balkanist subject positions in its framing of the camps in Bosnia. Calls for the ICTY gained traction through radical feminists' scripting of Bosnian Muslim women as helpless victims and Serb men as hyper-heteromasculine perpetrators in discourses about the camps (e.g., Askin 1997; Batinic 2001; MacKinnon 1994; Quindlen 1993, cited in Engle 2020, 55).[2] As I argue later in this chapter, these discourses depended on problematic, gendered, Balkanist logics and were later echoed in the legal violences of the ICTY (see Chapter 4).

The camps in Bosnia played a prominent role in the ICTY's creation and mandate, justifying the role of international law in prosecuting individuals associated with crimes related to them. The placement of the camps within the ICTY's origin stories has implications for how the Tribunal engages in violence. The camps feature as knowable realities for legal actors to make sense of and govern violence. The camps hold presuppositional knowledge through their comparison to the Nazi concentration camps, and it is this historical and cultural connection to European memories of atrocity that position the camps in Bosnia as a legitimate site to investigate. As I argue in Chapter 4, legal discourses construct detainees, guards, victim-survivors, witnesses, and perpetrators in and through the context of an already mythologized violence the camps are seen to embody. This manifests in other examples of international law. At the ICC, notable crimes or atrocities also figure as iconic and pivotal cases for prosecution (e.g., *Prosecutor v. Al Mahdi* and the destruction of religious monuments in Timbuktu; *Prosecutor v. Abd-Al-Rahman* and the rapes committed by the Janjaweed militia). Forming the foundations for prosecution, these crimes are narrated and gain iconic status in international law, invoking gendered discourses and racialized logics and informing the kinds of justice responses adopted.

Back to the ICTY, David Patrick notes that "Not even the organised massacre at Srebrenica . . . could match the intense level of press interest sparked by Omarska, Manjaca and others" (Patrick 2016, 146–47). While Srebrenica became a focal point in the ICTY's investigations, with 20 individuals indicted for crimes related to the Srebrenica genocide, many more were indicted for crimes that occurred within the camps across Bosnia.

Indeed, my QPDA of the ICTY texts involves an analysis of just 5 of the at least 22 cases (many of them consisting of multiple accused) that investigated detention camps and facilities in Bosnia. It is telling that the landing page for the film *Crimes before the ICTY: Prijedor*, an ICTY documentary that focuses on the camps, introduces the film with the statement: "The discovery that set international criminal justice into motion" (ICTY 2013). The camps in Bosnia are therefore integral to the creation and operation of the ICTY.

Origin Story II provides the presuppositional knowledge needed to engage in a queer critique of (legal) violence in the following chapter. But *Origin Story II* only exists in relation to other origin stories about the Tribunal, including comparisons between the Holocaust and the postwar tribunals. The existence of the camps also features in broader debates on humanitarian intervention, discussions that fueled the discourses operating in the third origin story of the Tribunal.

Origin Story III: (Non)interventions in the Post–Cold War Period

Origin Story III situates the ICTY within the wider geopolitical context of the post–Cold War period. Paying attention to how the ICTY's creation and mandate was authorized amid a context and discourse of humanitarian and military intervention is crucial for tracing the ways in which the Tribunal, as an example of international law and agent of global violence, (re)produces gendered, Balkanist subjectivities to be saved or condemned through criminal, carceral responses.

The late 1980s and early 1990s witnessed several conflicts and military interventions. Various US administrations deployed force as part of its democratization mission. In this new post–Cold War context, the United States and other Western countries launched and participated in a string of military interventions (Buchan 2015, 326). For example, the United States intervened when Iraq invaded Kuwait, and led the infamous mission in Somalia that resulted in the withdrawal of US troops after the failed Battle of Mogadishu (see Baker 2018b, 128–29). These military interventions—often justified by and steeped in humanitarian discourse—deeply influenced US and Western foreign policy in the 1990s (see Schwöbel-Patel 2021, 78–82). After the failed intervention in Somalia, there was a hesitance to engage in foreign conflicts if it meant risking the lives of US soldiers (see Belloni 2007, 462). This is part of the reason why the UN and its Member States were slow to respond to ethnic cleansing and genocide in the former Yugoslavia and Rwanda (see Baker 2018b, 128–29).[3] My aim here is not to assess the efficacy or the (neo)imperial politics of humanitarian intervention (see, e.g., Mahdavi 2015; Vernon 2024). Rather, I point to these conflicts in the 1990s as they were the backdrop against which the ICTY (and the International Criminal Tribunal for Rwanda [ICTR]) was created through appeals to international law rather than military force.

The conflicts in the former Yugoslavia had been occurring for at least two years before the Tribunal was established by the UN, although discussions were taking place as early as 1992, with some journalists calling for a tribunal as early as May of 1991 (Nelaeva 2011). By the time of its establishment in 1993, mass atrocities had already been taking place across Bosnia, in villages, urban centers, and detention camps. Neu argues that the creation of the ICTY could in part be attributed to guilt at not having intervened to stop genocide, that the Tribunal was merely a "cynical ploy to save the world's conscience in the face of almost complete inaction" (Neu 2012, 77). According to this explanation, the ICTY represented an opportunity for redemption and a way of promoting peace, justice, and accountability. Indeed, the ICTY is often posited in annual reports as proof that the "international community . . . was not sitting back idly while thousands were being brutally abused or massacred" (ICTY Annual Report 1994, 10). In this origin story, international law represents a remedy to conflict in the former Yugoslavia. Stressing the need to "alleviat[e] their suffering and anguish," encourage the "development of stable, constructive and healthy relations among ethnic groups," and "promote . . . a return to normality" (ICTY Annual Report 1994, 12), the annual reports (re)produce what Vanessa Pupavac (2004) describes as a discourse of therapeutic governance. In this sense, Balkanist logics in the ICTY texts depict the former Yugoslavia as a place and people of abnormality and perversion. Entangled in this discourse, these subjects of international law are those beyond the "essence of civilised conscience," in places where "those responsible for [grave violations] have escaped the hand of justice, such as the Khmer Rouge in Cambodia, and the warlords in Somalia, Sudan, Iraq and Haiti" (UN Doc S/PV/3217 1993, 7). This curated list of "distant" lands beset by violence conjures racist and Orientalist dichotomies between a "civilized" West/Europe and "uncivilized" and "lawless" geographies (see also Vernon 2024, 58–59). Indeed, the Tribunal's annual reports cast the Yugoslav region or "the Balkans" as a place of "madness," "hatred," and "brutality" (ICTY Annual Reports 1998, 66; 1994, 12). The ICTY's institutional texts craft a discourse that tethers the fate of the former Yugoslavia (and "civilization") to the ability of concerned Member States to address the violence through international law. It is through this paternalistic, Balkanist logic that the UNSC established the ICTY, to save an infantilized Balkans from its own harm (see V. Veličković 2012, 168).

In this origin story, the Tribunal and international law is posited as "the only civilised alternative" to the former Yugoslavia's "penchant" for violence (ICTY Annual Report 1994, 12, see Chapter 4), driven by the UN's "moral" and "peaceful" motives. This discourse (re)produces dichotomies between a civilized West/Europe and a violent, backward Other, one that is similarly echoed in other examples of international law, including at the ICC (Ba et al. 2023) and in other UNSC fora such as Arria Formula meetings (Hamzić 2018). These discourses and practices of humanitarian intervention depend on "the unspoken construction of feminine vulnerability and a narrative of masculine rescue" (Heathcote 2017, 201). Gendered meanings underpin *Origin Story III*, making possible the assumption that the ICTY is a moral necessity. The Tribunal has been established because "other" countries lack the rule of law, peace, and justice that characterizes the "civilized" Western world.

In this third origin story, the ICTY is positioned as just one arm or approach to "the Balkans." The Tribunal advances the project of international law, one that relies on not just retributive and carceral modes of governance but also practices of military intervention meant to achieve peace and justice. In this way, the ICTY's ability to adjudicate violence is enabled by logics of governance and international law that criminalize Balkan violence but legitimate (Western) intervention, placing the legal actors who embody the ICTY as authorized, paternal interveners (Biddolph 2024a, 6; see Chapter 4). While North Atlantic Treaty Organization (NATO) interventions in the former Yugoslavia did not occur until later in the conflict (specifically in relation to the conflict in Kosovo), the kind of transitional justice approach taken involved both physical force and criminal justice. Boas argues that "since the NATO bombing of Serbia in 1999, an interesting development is the growing prevalence of the use of force by the 'international community' as a 'tool' of international justice," with the airstrikes and intervention in Kosovo "justified in part by rhetoric of justice" which eventually led to the arrest and prosecution of key leaders and participants in the conflict (2012, 22–23). In this sense, the post–Cold War context gave rise to a new kind of military-carceral governance, one that deployed international law in tandem with military force (see Engle 2015, 1076, 1112). Elizabeth Philipose argues that few scholars, policymakers, and media sources "question the complicity of war crimes tribunals in sustaining the right of states to wage war or the meaning of 'humanitarianism' in an international context" (Philipose 2002, 160). It became clear that in the face of mass inaction during much of the Yugoslav conflict (as well as in other conflict contexts such as Rwanda), hawkish liberals and conservatives alike supported the NATO military intervention in Kosovo and Serbia, and in general supported the use of intervening forces to capture fugitives and send them to the Hague (Philipose 2002, 160).

International law is discursively powerful. It reinscribes hierarchies of violence which inform exceptional actions such as military intervention or the creation of an international criminal tribunal. For the ICTY, both actions occurred and were mutually reinforcing. The Tribunal thus embodied a collective "international effort" to categorize geographies of violence "outside of the boundary of acceptable society" (Sagan 2010, 15), by establishing a governance mechanism in the image of Western, European democratic peace.

Origin Story IV: The Promise of International Law

Origin Story IV scripts the Tribunal as an arbiter of justice. International law is seen as a beacon of hope and an achievable goal in response to violations of international humanitarian law. As an instrument of international law, the ICTY authorizes the prosecution of individuals responsible for crimes of genocide, war crimes, and crimes against humanity. The ICTY was created and invoked under Chapter VII of the UN Charter because the conflicts in the former Yugoslavia (occurring since at least 1991) were "characterised by such terrible and widespread atrocities... [that] lasting peace and reconciliation were impossible without some form of accountability for the ordering and commission of such crimes" (Kerr 2007, 374). The unanimous decision by members of the UNSC to establish the Tribunal was informed by preceding calls for action to be taken in response to the conflicts (both within the former Yugoslavia, by victim-survivors, and from other countries, see Nelaeva 2011). This culminated in the UN secretary-general commissioning and presenting "a report on the question of creating an international tribunal to try those most responsible for violating international humanitarian law on the territory of the former Yugoslavia" (Nelaeva 2011, 105). Once established under UNSC Resolution 827, the ICTY's mandate allowed for temporal and territorial jurisdiction for crimes committed after January 1, 1991, in the former Yugoslav territories (ICTY Statute 2009, Art. 8).

Over the course of its 24-year mandate (ending in December 2017), the ICTY has been hailed for its contribution to the broader project of international law. For example, the annual reports depict the ICTY as marking a "turning-point," setting "a momentous precedent" and "a novel and experimental institution—a momentous advance in the world community" (ICTY Annual Report 1994, 49). Being the first ad hoc tribunal since the postwar tribunals of Nuremberg and Tokyo, the ICTY is presented as an achievement in and of itself, but also a stepping stone to "a new path towards the realisation of true international justice, and hence of peace, in the world community" (ICTY Annual Report 1994, 50). The ICTY is therefore frequently discussed in relation to its predecessors (at Nuremberg and Tokyo),[4] its contemporaries (the ICTR), and current and emerging mechanisms of international criminal justice (e.g., the ICC).

According to this origin story, the kind of international law the ICTY embodies is central to the new forms of governance in the aftermath of the Cold War. As the first international criminal tribunal of the late twentieth century, the ICTY represented a significant milestone for the progression of an international legal and political society based on the pillars of law, justice, and democracy. This legal-political significance is reflected in the Tribunal's symbolism as "an instrument of transitional justice . . . [that] go[es] hand in hand with and [is] supportive of democratisation" (Spoerri and Freyberg-Inan 2008, 351–52). More than just a procedural criminal mechanism that prosecuted individuals, the ICTY had normative significance, insofar as it was "an institution of the United Nations, a subsidiary organ of the Security Council, a transmitter of norms, an interpreter of law [and] a progenitor of contemporary international criminal law institutions" (Kaye 2014, 393). In *Origin Story IV*, then, the ICTY is a symbol of success. Here, the ICTY is something to be celebrated, in contrast to *Origin Stories I, II*, and *III*, where success is steeped in historical and contemporary echoes of guilt.

Judges, presidents, prosecutors, lawyers, and administrators represented the Tribunal as uniquely equipped to impose law and order on nations still beset by their "uncivilized" and "violent" ways (see Chapter 4). As I discuss in the next section of this chapter, logics of governance that animate this origin story are both gendered and Balkanist. For example, these logics frequently invoke the Bosnian or Balkan woman as the Other in need of rescue, "that it was the West's task to bring 'freedom' and 'democracy' to 'isolated' and 'underdeveloped' easterners" (Gal and Kligman 2000, in Owczarzak 2009, 9–10). While *Origin Story IV* celebrates the ICTY and international law, it nevertheless depends on these civilizational logics of feminized victims, hyper-heteromasculine perpetrators, and the paternal intervention of legal actors to adjudicate (see Chapter 4). While those who embody the ICTY are cognizant of its shortcomings (see, e.g., in its annual reports and completion strategies), overall, the ICTY texts paint a picture of success at having held individuals accountable for violations of international humanitarian law. The larger moral project of the ICTY, though, and of international law, mostly goes unquestioned.

Taken together, the four origin stories I have identified offer an image of the moral, political, and humanitarian justifications for the ICTY's creation, revealing how the Tribunal depends on logics of governance and international law. Seen from this perspective, the ICTY—and the broader international legal project—cannot be understood without acknowledging the moralizing goals of bringing peace, law, and order to the former Yugoslavia and the world. This logic depends on the construction of "the Balkans" or Global South countries through Othering discourses. Furthermore, none of these discursive moves are devoid of gendered politics. Rather, as I turn to the next section of this chapter, I argue that gendered, civilizational logics are vital to reading the ICTY as a response to the Yugoslav conflict. These four origin stories provide the presuppositional or background knowledge for my QPDA of the ICTY texts in the remaining chapters of this book. My analysis of governance and international law, through the case of the ICTY, must acknowledge the civilizational (read: Balkanist) logics that underpin the Tribunal's creation. This is particularly important, given these civilizational and moralizing discourses inform how violence is represented and governed through broader practices of international law.

The ICTY's Civilizational Logics

International law is both constituted by and (re)produces various discourses of gender, sexuality, and violence. Logics, are the "centre ... of the discourse that hold together certain possibilities, while precluding others" (Shepherd

2021, 32), and they organize these discourses of international law at the Tribunal. As I argued in Chapter 2, logics help to signify or make discourses meaningful. In international law, cis-heteronormative discourses of gender, sexuality, and violence depend on logics of governance, including civilizational logics. In this section, I craft an image of the logics of governance and international law at/of the Tribunal. I focus on the civilizational (i.e., Balkanist) logics of governance that animate the ICTY. The ICTY sits within a broader history of gendered, Balkanist depictions of the former Yugoslavia and within broader racial and civilizational logics of international law. Balkanism is a pejorative logic, one that engages gendered discourses of civilization to distinguish between a "superior" Europe and an "inferior" Balkans.

As I introduce in this chapter (and show in Chapter 4), practices of legal violence at the ICTY perpetuate Balkanist logics. It is necessary to problematize the governing logics that constitute the ICTY because they help to construct the legal subjects—that is, the survivors, witnesses, and perpetrators of violence—as gendered and sexualized Balkan bodies. As an example of international law, the Tribunal engages in discursive practices that (re)produce feminized victims to be saved and hyper-heteromasculine "uncivilized" perpetrators to be prosecuted (see Chapter 4). I argue that the ICTY—in both its creation and operation—is Balkanist; dependent on harmful discourses that categorize the people of the former Yugoslavia as backward, innately violent, and in need of protection and/or condemnation. This is illustrative of the broader racist and civilizational logics and hierarchies of international law. This argument reflects the violent and violating capacities of international law as a (queer) governance mechanism, capacities that can and must be critiqued and deconstructed to allow subversive and queer possibilities to emerge.

International law is predicated on civilizational logics of governance. These discursive practices help to justify and legitimate extraordinary actions, such as the international jurisdiction of the Tribunal and its ability to condemn and punish individuals. Logics of governance and international law continue a longer legacy of civilizational posturing that place Western and European nations as moral superiors and "illiberal" lands as violent, in need of (Western) intervention (see Khalid 2017). These logics are also gendered and gendering, insofar as "gendered orientalist discourses of intervention have long been deployed in the service of intervention and other forms of imperialism" (Khalid 2017, 156). At the Tribunal, this takes shape through Balkanist logics, where discourses of gender, sexuality, and violence intersect through the wielding of juridical violence (see Chapter 4). Consider, for example, the following two quotes taken from the ICTY's annual reports:

> The very stability of international order and principle of civilisation is at stake over the question in Bosnia. (Mazowiecki in ICTY Annual Report 1996, 48)

> The Tribunal is the voice of a universalism based on hope ... [and] is the first step in rebuilding a community from the ruins of a society divided by ethnically-based slaughter. (ICTY Annual Report 1998, 66)

The annual reports, produced by the Tribunal's presidents (Antonio Cassese in 1996, Gabrielle Kirk McDonald in 1998), provide insight into the progress of investigations, indictments, arrests, and prosecutions. But as the quotes above demonstrate, they also invoke the ICTY's origin stories, that the Tribunal exists as the "civilized" answer to the "ethnic hatred" of "the Balkans" (Kovačević 2008, 118). As with *Origin Stories I* and *III*, the former Yugoslavia is rendered knowable in relation to Europe, but is also pathologized and constructed through Balkanist logics. Following *Origin Story IV*, it is international law that provides the solution to "a society divided by ethnically-based slaughter." In the ICTY texts, civilization is modeled on Western and Eurocentric visions of the world. This European character of international law, and its manifestation at the ICTY, (re)produces global hierarchies.

The Tribunal must be understood within the broader project of international law, a project implicated in the "production of empire" (Heathcote 2019, 180). Makau Mutua argues that the "savages-victims-saviours" metaphor in human rights and humanitarian discourse typically positions Europe as the savior, insofar as Europe is constructed as "superior and as centre of the universe" (Mutua 2001, 233). The history of colonial and imperial conquest is testament to this (white) saviorism, wherein Christian missionaries and a "humanitarian need" to enlighten or civilize natives justified the larger colonial project (Mutua 2001, 233). In contemporary global politics, the savior subject position is still—at least from a Western and Eurocentric perspective—located in the "enlightened" lands of North America and western Europe. The UN has also taken on this label. As Mutua argues, "the United Nations is, in a sense, the grand 'neutral' saviour, and Western liberal democracies treat it as such" (Mutua 2001, 237–38). While calls for a tribunal were multiple and varied, including from Yugoslavs themselves (see Chapter 6), the UN's creation of the ICTY in some ways continues a longer (colonial) history of saviorism. As I discussed in relation to *Origin Story III*, in the context of failed and lack of humanitarian interventions, the ICTY represented a chance for redemption. International law provided an acceptable mechanism for these Western "saviors" to redeem themselves, to retroactively save Balkan victims. For those State representatives voicing their support and praise of the Tribunal's establishment in the UNSC meeting (UN Doc S/PV/3217 1993), the ICTY offered a chance to allay historical guilt (see *Origin Story I*). The Tribunal was a mechanism through which to channel their outrage at the "uncivilized" violence taking place in the former Yugoslavia. At the ICTY, this civilizational saviorism is anchored in Balkanist logics.

At the ICTY, Balkanist logics constitute the idea of the "Balkan body" as both dangerously hyper-heteromasculine and helplessly feminized and infantilized (see Chapter 4).[5] Balkanism was formed and sedimented over "the course of two centuries and crystallised in a specific discourse around the Balkan wars and World War I" (M. Todorova 1997, 19). While it continued to develop and add new features over the course of the twentieth century, Balkanism refers to the "derivative but distinct project of constructing the Balkans as 'the other within' Europe . . . built on much more diffuse and indirect relationships of domination and subordination vis-à-vis 'the west,'" in contrast to the overt colonial dynamics animating the concept of Orientalism (Helms 2008, 90). Indeed, a key dynamic of Balkanism is the designation of "the Balkans"—the geographical area that is generally accepted to include Albania, Bosnia-Herzegovina, Bulgaria, Croatia, Kosovo, Moldova, Montenegro, North Macedonia, Romania, Serbia, and Slovenia (see also M. Todorova 1997, 31). Through Balkanist logics, "the Balkans" is understood as geographically European (i.e., southeast Europe, see *Origin Story I*) but culturally distinct (Kovačević 2008, 3, 12). As with Orientalism (Said 1978), Balkanism is made meaningful precisely through its distinction from Europe.

Maria Todorova argues that "the Balkans" is racially and religiously like western Europe; that is, white and "predominantly Christian" (1997, 188). Race, ethnicity, and religion in the former Yugoslavia are plural, shifting, and entangled identity and group constructions. As Catherine Baker writes, "race, distinct from yet related to ethnicity and religion, undeniably forms part of identity-making projects in the region" (2018b, 161).[6] While most academic and popular discourse frames the former Yugoslavia as ethnicized rather than racialized (Baker 2018b, 1), such emphasis on the former should not preclude an awareness of the historical and contemporary practices of racialization that position "the Balkans" as a racial and civilizational Other to Europe, and minorities within the region as internal racial Others (Baker 2018b, 4, 10, 17; see also Rexhepi 2023). Through Balkanism, the former Yugoslavia serves as an "internal other within the Western European imagination" (Abazi and Doja 2017, 1016), which allows the "enlightened" Europe to distinguish itself from the strangeness of "the Balkans." Thus, "the Balkans" is designated as white, but "ambiguous or indeterminable, as only conditionally white" (Baker 2018a, 766–67; 2018b, 19; see also Rexhepi 2023; The Yugoslawomen + Collective 2020, np). This attention to the racial rendering of the former Yugoslavia is important. But Todorova's assumption of Balkan whiteness problematically erases the internal racial hierarchies in the region, such as discrimination against the Roma community, migrants, and refugees (M.S. Todorova 2018). Balkanist logics therefore cast Balkan populations as more white than non-Europeans, but nevertheless subject to a devalorized racialization. This often means that a "racialised European colonial perception of Muslims, especially Muslim women, as profoundly non-modern and non-European and, therefore, non-White," persists (M.S. Todorova 2018, 121–22). These civilizational logics find resonance in the broader racial and colonial logics that organize international law.

Moreover, discussions of race in the Yugoslav context need to be considered relationally, positioned differently to others in global assemblages of racism. For example, during the 1990s conflict, "Bosnian refugees could still come closer to western European collective selves than black African refugees in hierarchies of foreignness" (Baker 2018b, 123). Following these colonial logics, the racial ambiguity assigned to "the Balkans" situated the region as something in-between European "civility" and Oriental "savagery." These racialized, Balkanist logics organize the ICTY origin stories I have introduced in this chapter. For example, in *Origin Story I* and *Origin Story II*, the comparisons between World War II, the Holocaust, and the Nazi concentration camps constructed Bosnia as geographically, historically, and racially European. But as I have argued here, Balkanist logics situate the former Yugoslavia as both Europe and not-Europe, and such a distinction manifests in the pejorative racial and cultural infantilization of Bosnians during the conflict.

Balkanist logics therefore attribute the region as Europe and not-Europe (see Swimelar 2019, 776), a kind of *and/or* logic that allows "the Balkans" to occupy a transient, liminal space in geopolitical and international legal imaginaries. For example, when "the Balkans" is characterized as European in the ICTY's origin stories, it justifies and propels the international legal project to establish an ad hoc tribunal. Largely, however, "the Balkans" is scripted as Europe's Other, envisioned as a place and people who "live in another time and a barbaric land" (Abazi and Doja 2017, 1019). In this way, "the Balkans" exists on a different anachronistic plane to western Europe (Abazi and Doja 2017), characterized by features of a civilization that do not constitute a "modern," "peaceful," and "enlightened" Europe. As I previously discussed, in *Origin Story I*, Bosnia is coded as European when compared to World War II and calls for "Never Again." But such qualification is unstable. For a violent war to take place in Bosnia during the 1990s, Balkanism conjures "the Balkans" as anachronistically distinct, as "evil," "barbaric," and characterized by ancient violence markedly different from the contemporary, peaceful (western) Europe. Todorova argues that "the Balkans" is therefore cast as "semideveloped, semicolonial, semicivilised, semioriental" (M. Todorova 1997, 16). In this way, it occupies a state of "in-betweenness"—of being not quite other but an "incomplete self" (M. Todorova 1997, 18). "The Balkans" therefore has the potential to be more like (western) Europe, but only through (legal, political, military, economic) interventions. As Kimberley Coles argues, "the Balkans" are constructed as "a European alter-ego," whereby "Europe" itself, while also an unstable designation, is frequently "associated with EU [European Union] neo-liberal institutions, multiculturalism and civil liberties" (Coles 2007, 258–59, 260; see also Slootmaeckers 2023, 89). Thus, "the Balkans" is scripted "as a part of Europe that used to be under Ottoman, hence oriental, rule and, as such, different from Europe 'proper'" (Bakić-Hayden 1995, 920–21). Balkanist logics place the region in "an imaginary location somewhere between civilization and barbarism as the West's immediate and intermediary other," a "boundary marker" that distinguishes and protects Europe from its ultimate Other—the Orient (Imre 2014, 117–18).

Neda Atanasoski provides some insightful critiques of these subject positions in her analysis of the ICTY documentaries (see also Biddolph 2024a). Her research provides compelling evidence of the ways in which the Tribunal, as a Eurocentric mechanism of international law, (re)produces Balkanist logics. She argues:

> The documentaries of the ICTY visually remake the frontier zone between Europe and the world outside by rendering the physical space of the

Tribunal as the site where justice is seen to be done. In contrast, the Balkan landscape is frozen as a war crime scene, as each documentary circulates footage of camps, dead bodies, human remains, and war criminals as signifiers of Balkanness. (Atanasoski 2018, 75)

The ICTY is thus a cultural response to the "exceptional" violence occurring in the former Yugoslavia. Atanasoski's analysis demonstrates the extent to which the former Yugoslavia is read through Balkanism, made legible by being positioned as different to Europe (Atanasoski 2018, 73). She continues, arguing that "the ICTY films uphold the institutional supremacy of international tribunals as the sole locus of justice and juridical progress ... exemplifying the best of Euro-American values" (Atanasoski 2018, 69). In the justification for the existence and continuation of the ICTY's work, these documents produce an image of internal chaos in the former Yugoslavia, one that is also gendered and sexualized and that calls for international law as a response.

Through Balkanism, then, "the Balkans" and "Balkan people" are characterized by harmful stereotypes. Drawing on Todorova's work, Lene Hansen notes that binaries such as controlled/violent, rational/irrational, developed/underdeveloped, civilized/barbarian, organized/tribal, national/primitive, orderly/savage, and mature/childish distinguish between Europe and "the Balkans" (Hansen 2006, 42), binaries which also apply to racist logics of coloniality. As these predicates indicate, Balkanism produces a Balkan subjectivity that is culturally inferior to western Europe, defined by its nationalist propensities (Hatzopoulos 2003), its emotional instability (Hansen 2000, 350), and its "socioeconomic and civilisational backwardness" (Abazi and Doja 2017, 1014). Of course, all these characterizations are representational practices that do not accurately reflect the region, but instead obscure the polysemy and diversity of southeast Europe (Abazi and Doja 2016, 594). As a logic, then, Balkanism is pejorative and inherently exclusionary. It is intelligible only by erasing the realities of life in the region and cleaving to an ethnocentric account of "the Balkans" that has never really existed except through the white, Western gaze.

The violence of Balkanist logics manifest in a number of ways, including, as I argue in Chapter 4, through the legal denunciation of Balkan perpetrators. The violence of Balkanism also appears in the internalization of these logics. According to Todorova and others, all of the negative characteristics that constitute Balkanism are internalized by Balkan populations (M. Todorova 1997, 39). This manifests in a set of "nesting orientalisms" or

Balkanisms that allow "members of one nation . . . to portray themselves as superior/western/European while casting their southern and eastern neighbours as part of the inferior, oriental 'east'" (Helms 2008, 91; see also Bakić-Hayden and Hayden 1992; Bakić-Hayden 1995). Indeed, a large part of the discursive battle in the lead-up to conflict involved Serbs/Bosnian Muslims/Croats/Albanians portraying each other as variously patriarchal, ultraconservative, rapists, sexual deviants, and homosexuals, all of which cast the Other as inferior and the Self as superior (see Bracewell 2000; Slootmaeckers 2023; Zarkov 2007).

Balkanist logics thus reinforce gendered and ethnicized hierarchies. This is because Balkanism, in its reference to civilization, violence, and culture, depends on gendered presuppositions. Todorova sees this most clearly in the articulation of the Balkan man, although the Bosnian conflict brought renewed focus to Balkan women. Balkanism holds that "the standard Balkan male is uncivilised, primitive, crude, cruel, and, without exception, disheveled" (M. Todorova 1997, 14). This subject position carried through into the 1990s conflict. Indeed, "in both Western scholarship and West Balkan media outlets, [Balkan] masculine identities stand-in for anti-modern forces: backwardness, parochialism, and (neo-)traditionalism" (Dumaničić and Krolo 2017, 155). A significant addition to this was the ways in which the Balkan man was intelligible through his victimization of Balkan women (Zarkov 2014, 9). As I elaborate in Chapter 4, Balkanist logics render (cis-)men perpetrators as sexually perverse, in part through reducing them as threats to "their own" and "other" women. Predicating men as gendered and sexual perversions is vital to the Othering process (see Spivak 1988, on "white men saving brown women from brown men"). Gendered and sexualized discourses are crucial to the construction of this Other, who is seen to be simultaneously hyper-heteromasculine and homophobic as well as feminine, homosexual, and queer in the "dehumanizing sense" (Otto 2022b, 24; see also Manchanda 2015).

Feminist approaches to international law have made it clear that "the Tribunal's analysis, however unwittingly, raises the spectre of orientalist beliefs about the character of 'the Muslim,' particularly, Muslim women" (Buss 2007, 19; see also Nadj 2011, 650–51; Nadj 2018, 113). The subject position of Bosnian woman in the ICTY texts simplify and essentialize the diversity of women's identities and experiences during the Yugoslav conflict. Other subject positions are created, too—sadistic perpetrators and hyper-heteromasculine rapists (to name a few, see Chapter 4)—all replete with multiple and even contradictory discourses of gender, sexuality, and violence. In this way, the ICTY is both constituted by, and (re)produces, multiple subjectivities. For example, the ICTY judges, prosecutors, and presidents are constructed in the texts as adjudicators and arbiters of international law. In contrast, victims and perpetrators are Balkan, ethnicized, and require international intervention to bring peace and justice to the region (see Chapter 4). These subject positions and the discourses of gender, sexuality, and violence that constitute them are explored in the following two chapters.

Balkanist logics not only essentialize Balkan men and women but also position the West and Western interveners (e.g., NATO, UN forces, the ICTY) as paternal protectors and saviors (O'Reilly 2012, 531; see Chapter 4). This tracks with broader civilizational logics that script white Western forces as saviors of other "uncivilized" lands. These subject positions manifest at the ICTY and constitute international law as a governance mechanism that is both constituted by, and (re)produces, discourses of gender, sexuality, and violence. For example, the ICTY annual reports cast the former Yugoslavia as hyper-masculinist and patriarchal in its "viciousness" and "savagery," but also as feminized and infantilized, unable to save itself from the "forces of evil" and cycles of "ethnic hatred" (ICTY Annual Reports 2003, 71; 1996, 50; 1999, 4; 1994, 25). In contrast, the ICTY (embodied by judges, prosecutors, investigators, and other legal actors) is imbued with a virtuous masculinism, a protector and a savior of the former Yugoslavia and of international peace and security more broadly. This logic is driven by the belief that "geography is all that separates the ... dead, mutilated and raped in the former Yugoslavia" (ICTY Annual Report 1998, 62), so responsibility is placed on those actors of international law to denunciate such violence and hold perpetrators to account. I continue to trace the work these gendered Balkanist logics do at the ICTY to uphold the broader civilizational ordering of governance and international law in the following chapter.

Concluding Thoughts on Logics of Governance and International Law

In this chapter, I analyzed some of the logics of governance and international law that constitute the ICTY. Building on the arguments established in Chapter 1 (that international law is a (queer) governance mechanism), and Chapter 2 (that logics organize discourses and make them intelligible), in Chapter 3 I developed the following core arguments. First, the ICTY is coherent and coheres through (at least) four "origin stories": "Never Again" and the war crimes tribunals; the camps in Bosnia; (non)interventions in the post–Cold War period; and the promise of international law. Through these stories, the ICTY's creation was made possible through Balkanist logics about the former Yugoslavia, mass atrocity, and intervention. These origin stories reflect the invocation of international law as a suitable response to governing global violence.

Second, and central to this chapter, the ICTY both engages with and (re)produces civilizational logics that perpetuate pejorative characterizations of the former Yugoslavia. These are Eurocentric logics that position the former Yugoslavia as inherently "violent" and "uncivilized," in contrast to the "peaceful" and "civilized" (western) Europe. Balkanism is gendered and gendering. In the ICTY's foundational texts, these logics work to construct a former Yugoslavia that is populated with hyper-heteromasculine criminals and feminized victims (see Chapter 4). These Balkanist logics reflect, and are an example of, the broader logics of civilization, coloniality, and race that constitute international law. Balkanist logics are evident across the ICTY texts I analyze in this book, and contribute to cis-heteronormative discourses of gender, sexuality, and violence. It is to these logics I now turn, exploring, through the case of the ICTY, how the adjudication of violence through international law (re)produces particular gendered, civilizational legal subjects as the common sense.

4
Governing through Adjudication

Legal Violence at/of the International Criminal Tribunal for the Former Yugoslavia

International law is a (queer) governance mechanism founded on violence. It is a response to violence and a form of sanctioned, legal violence that performs harms as wide-ranging as incarcerating individuals, legitimating military intervention, installing economic sanctions and embargoes, disempowering victims and survivors, and upholding racial hierarchies and the cis-heteronormative common sense. The violence in each of these examples often begins in the process of adjudication: of ordering, classifying, and passing judgment on the legality or criminality of acts under international law. Adjudication is a form of governance that depends on designating bodies, populations, and acts in gendered, sexualized, racial, and civilizational ways. International law is certainly a violent governance mechanism. But it is also a site of queer potential, where resistance to legal violence coexists and offers hope for those seeking justice within the law. To see the queer potential of international law, however, requires first tracing its violences and the possibility of disrupting them.

Chapter 4 offers a queer critique of the adjudicatory practices of international law and problematizes the violent legal-political possibilities they enable and foreclose. Using the case of the ICTY, I identify and deconstruct how international law governs through adjudication, engaging in practices of legal violence that (re)produce civilizational logics and cis-heteronormative discourses of gender, sexuality, and violence. In this chapter, I am concerned with the ways in which international law engages practices of juridical violence, which are entwined with cis-heteronormative assumptions of gender and sexuality. This focus on practices of legal violence rests on the broader argument that international law is violent and "grounded in violence" (Heathcote 2011, 21). Through the case of the ICTY, I show how international law's gendering, agential, and violating capacities enable cis-heteronormative discourses of gender, sexuality, and violence to intersect. These discourses have the effect of governing through adjudication. As an example of international law, the ICTY establishes and reinforces ethnicized, straight, and cisgender legal subjects. It engages in practices of victimization (which construct feminized, homogenized, and silenced victims);[1] denunciation (which construct sadistic perpetrators and Balkan rapists); and paternalism (which position the ICTY's legal actors as lawful adjudicators and international law as "the only civilized alternative" to governing violence). Through the case of the ICTY, I map how international law is a site of knowledge production and an agent of violence. It prescribes certain discursive and juridical possibilities, including the designation of gendered, "uncivilized" bodies as criminals or victims, thereby warranting punishment, incarceration, or protection.

By tracing how the ICTY, as an example of international law, governs through adjudication, this chapter traces the civilizational (read: Balkanist) logics and cis-heteronormative discourses of gender, sexuality, and violence that underpin these practices. As a (queer) governance mechanism, international law is therefore simultaneously gendered and gendering, constitutive and agential, and violent and violating. By identifying and problematizing these governing practices and showing that in their discursive (re)production they can be deconstructed or undone, I suggest that even as a source of violence, international law maintains the potential for subversion, queerness, and possibility for addressing (in)justice.

Victimization

International law is often applied in the name of victims. It invokes victims in seeking justice and accountability; it is a project that seeks to provide justice *for* victims. But international law also produces victims: performatively, in the utterances, classifications, and discursive articulations of victimhood; and in the "administrative violence[s]" of the courtroom (Spade, quoted in Baars 2019, 20), through which witnesses and survivors are subjected to the disempowering and reductive effects of legal process. In this section, I interrogate practices of victimization in international law. I do so by analyzing and deconstructing the assumed stability of feminized, homogenized, and silenced victims within the ICTY texts. While the indictments, court proceedings, and trial judgments all attempt to make sense of violence through invoking Balkanist logics and gendered discourses of victimhood, this subject position is far more complicated than legal discourse depicts.

Moreover, the construction of certain gendered and ethnicized bodies as victims in international law contributes to practices of erasure and exclusion, by highlighting some (gendered, ethnicized) victims more than others and by simplifying victim experiences and realities. As an example of international law, the Tribunal engages in victimization, a legal violence that occurs through judges, prosecutors, and defense attorneys limiting witness testimonies, reducing survivors to victimhood status only, and constructing an overall assumption of passive, feminized, Balkan victimhood.

Feminized Victims

Victimization in international law (re)produces feminized subjects of victimhood. Certain kinds of victimhood are attached to certain gendered bodies, at the same time as violence is rendered governable through feminized logics of victimhood. At the Tribunal, as with international law more broadly, victimhood is frequently feminized, with "children, women and elderly people" constituting an overall category of vulnerability (ICTY Annual Report 1994, 18; UN Doc S/PV/3217 1993, 21). In the ICTY texts, women are frequently cast as victims. This is a discourse of "victim essentialism," whereby "women become defined by their sexual violability and their reproductive capacity, and are treated by courts with emphasis on those traits" (Sjoberg 2017b, 133). To acknowledge this is not to undermine the experiences and frequency of trauma faced by women. Nor is it to discount that "Many survivors of wartime rape who testified or who sought to testify before the . . . ICTY believed giving testimony would help them heal" (Mertus 2004, 111). However, in the trial judgments, court transcripts, and institutional documents, where international legal actors (e.g., judges, prosecutors, Tribunal presidents) cast women as victims, they are almost always designating them as victims of sexual violence. This has the effect of simplifying women's experiences to that of "Woman Victim" and of "effac[ing] differences . . . and undermin[ing] agency" (Mertus 2004, 115; see also Bakšić Muftić in Orentlicher 2018, 170; Engle 2020, 11; Nadj 2011, 654; Nadj 2018, 1). For example, in *Kvočka et al.*, the judges describe Omarska as a site of violence, a place where women are undoubtedly subjected to rape:

> In Omarska camp, approximately 36 women were held in detention, guarded by men with weapons who were often drunk, violent, and physically and mentally abusive and who were allowed to act with virtual

impunity. Indeed, it would be unrealistic and contrary to all rational logic to expect that none of the women held in Omarska, placed in circumstances rendering them especially vulnerable, would be subjected to rape and other forms of sexual violence. (*Kvočka et al.* 2001, Trial Judgment, para 327)

In the excerpt above, the judges presuppose the sexual vulnerability of women in the camps. Indeed, the judges find it "unrealistic" and irrational to think otherwise. Victimization here is made possible through practices of denunciation, which I explore later in this chapter. The ICTY engages in gendering work by casting women as natural victims of sexual violence, and by denouncing "men . . . who were often drunk, violent, and . . . abusive" as the perpetrators of this violence. These predicates and subject positions depend on Balkanist logics that organize discourses of gender, sexuality, and violence. As I argued in Chapter 3, Balkanism pejoratively casts Balkan women as helpless to the victimization of hyper-heteromasculine, violent, Balkan men. Balkanist logics of gender and violence permeate this example from the Trial Judgment, revealing how judges have the capacity to (re)produce essentialized and gendering discourses about "the Balkans." These kinds of gendered, Balkanist logics are evident in the ICTY institutional texts as well, embedded within origin stories that position the Tribunal as a response to the victimization of Bosnian (Muslim) women:

Most recently, on 26 June 1996, Judge Vohrah confirmed an indictment against eight accused, Dragan Gagović and others, who are alleged to have participated in the subjugation of Muslim women in Foča to a brutal regime of gang rape, torture and enslavement by Bosnian Serb soldiers, policemen and members of paramilitary groups. (ICTY Annual Report 1996, para 22)

Here, Antonio Cassese, president of the ICTY, describes the factual details that constitute one of the indictments issued by the Office of the Prosecutor (OtP). As the president details, the indictment finds that Muslim women were subjected to "a brutal regime of gang rape, torture and enslavement by Bosnian Serb" forces. My queer reading of this extract does not seek to diminish the realities of these crimes, nor the trauma faced by those victimized in the former Yugoslav conflicts. Rather, I am interested in how the president discursively frames the violence through the subject position of "Muslim women," and the qualifiers used to describe crimes committed by the accused (as perpetrators of a "brutal regime"). The denunciation of perpetrators achieves coherency through the legal victimization of Muslim women, who are conceived of as the ultimate or iconic victims of the Bosnian war in radical feminist, media, and Western accounts (Nadj 2011, 650–51; Nadj 2018, 113; Zarkov 2017, 28). Balkanist logics, as I argued in Chapter 3, essentialize Muslim women as timeless victims of an "innately" patriarchal, conservative, and violent Balkan masculinity. Thus, the president's active construction of the Muslim woman subject position here, while crucial to the ICTY's governing practices as a site of international law, also draws energy from and continues a genealogy that genders "the Balkans" in simplistic and pejorative ways. Indeed, the attachment of "Muslim women" to terms such as "subjugation" and "brutal regime" reinforces the assumed naturalness of Muslim women's victimization. This is a construction that finds saliency in broader racial and civilizational logics of governance and international law. In this way, ICTY actors engage in practices of legal violence through establishing certain feminized, ethnicized victims as common sense in international law. The designation of Balkan women as victims legitimates and reinforces the authority of international law as a violent (queer) governance mechanism, with the ability to determine innocence from guilt, legality from criminality.

This positioning of women as (rape) victims is evident across the ICTY texts. Often, the indictments and trial judgments make the sexual victimization of women detainees legible by invoking a dichotomy between "nonsexual" violence against men and sexual violence against women:

> Beatings and humiliation were often administered in front of other detainees. *Female detainees were raped and sexually assaulted.* (*Brdanin* 2001, Third Amended Indictment, para 55, my emphases)
>
> Inmates were interrogated, beaten, subjected to inhuman and degrading conditions of life and tortured. *Women were raped* and killings occurred on a regular basis. (*Brdanin* 2004, Trial Judgment, para 115, my emphases)
>
> Male detainees were interrogated and beaten. Detainees were beaten in front of other detainees. *Female detainees were raped.* (*Brdanin* 2001, Third Amended Indictment, para 42, my emphases)

Through international law, the ICTY prosecutor and judges performatively (re)produce women detainees as sexual violence victims. This is achieved through predicates and subject positions such as the "rape victim" or the "sexually vulnerable and violable" subject (see N. Henry 2014; Zarkov 2012). In doing so, ICTY legal actors presuppose that beatings and torture (read: "public" practices of violence) occur to men, while rape and sexual assault (read: "private" practices of violence) occur to women (and occasionally men). The binaries between men/women, nonsexual/sexual, and public/private are problematic, not least because they reify essentialist, cis-heteronormative discourses of gender, sexuality, and violence in international law. By scripting women as sexual victims, the examples above (re)produce dominant ideas in global politics and international law that "normal" or "expected" practices of violence are those that beat, torture, and kill men; and rape and violate women (see Sjoberg 2010a, 30; 2017b, 34).

Furthermore, the *Brdanin* Trial Judgment notes that "for a woman, rape is by far the ultimate offence" (*Brdanin* 2004, Trial Judgment, para 1009). Thus, in addition to situating women as exclusively rape victims, international law also (re)produces harmful logics about honor and gendered bodily integrity, which assume that rape is always the most devastating crime a woman could experience (Engle 2020, 93). This "fate-worse-than-death" qualifier prescribes certain international responses to (certain) violence: "to mobilize troops, judges, and counterterrorism measures, sexual violence has to be portrayed as fully destructive" (Engle 2020, 172). As evidenced in this and the preceding chapter, the raped woman victim subject position constructed by international actors was a key motivation in the turn to international criminal law (i.e., mobilizing the judges) as a response to the conflicts in the former Yugoslavia. In international law more broadly, this feminized victimhood subjectivity, tethered as it is to sexual violence, has similarly been weaponized in neocolonial military campaigns and counterterrorism responses that have followed civilizational and racist logics. As Zarkov notes, this kind of exclusive focus on sexual violence against women in conflict also risks obscuring or downplaying other violences, such as the destruction of homes, access to resources, and expulsion "from her ancestral territory" (Zarkov 2017, 28). The ICTY's emphasis on women as rape victims proscribes attention to these other gendered and gendering harms and obfuscates the ways in which sexual violence forms part of these entangled injuries.

The assumption that women are always the targets of sexual victimization informs court proceedings within international law:

Q. Sir, were there any women in the camp?
A. Yes, there were women in the camp. Let me see. There was Grozda Cecez, Milojka Antic....

Q. Sir, I'm not going to ask you for the names of all the women. Let me just ask you again without saying what you heard, can you please tell us whether or not you received information at the camp suggesting that any of the women at the camp had been sexually assaulted?
A. Yes.
Q. Let me go forward. (*Mucić et al.* 1997, Trial hearing 8 July)

This example reflects the gendered binary between "sexual" and "nonsexual" violence. When women are spoken about in the courtroom, they make sense to the legal actors and are "hypervisible" (Sjoberg 2020, 84) almost exclusively through understanding them as sexually violable. Practices of violence evident in the discursive victimization of women proscribe the narration of plural experiences of violence and embodiment (see O'Reilly 2018, 108; Zarkov 2017, 28). The discursive positioning of women as victims attempts to establish a coherent representation of gendered bodies in conflict. The (cis-)woman figure is intelligible and coheres within international law precisely because she occupies this singular, homogenizing subject position (see Simić 2012, 133). As an example of international law, then, the ICTY governs through the adjudication and classification of women as victims.

As a site of international law, the ICTY's discursive victimization prescribes various legal possibilities, with the effect that certain victims are recognized under international law, while others are erased. For example, the decision and justification for charging crimes of rape and sexual violence is wholly dependent on the testimonies of sexual violence victims. Critically, the (cis-)woman rape victim serves this purpose, insofar as she provides the basis for prosecuting these crimes. Their testimony prescribes the prosecution and judgment of individuals responsible for committing crimes of sexual violence. Arguably, this is an integral component of international law. As Ratna Kapur writes: "To be recognised a victim of sexual violence ... is important. But such recognition is part of an already existing process that only recognises certain gender arrangements and performances as legitimate and addresses complaints that emanate a subject who complies with such arrangements" (2015, 271). This manifests in several ways, including, as I have discussed so far, through the reduction of women to singular subject positions of international law in ways that regulate their testimonies within the courtroom (see also the following section).

Certain legal possibilities are also curtailed in the process of designating women as the ultimate victims of sexual violence. This subject position presupposes a particular kind of woman: cisgender, "heterosexual, of a certain age, monogamous, within the same ethnic group" (Engle 2016, 225; 2020, 48), and thus anything to the contrary—including expressions of sexual agency and of nonconforming sexual and gender identities and practices—is made unthinkable within international law. For example, the experiences of LGBTQIA+ individuals are entirely erased from the ICTY's governing practices. In my queer analysis of the Tribunal's texts, I found little evidence to suggest that queer bodies were subject to violence. This is not to say that no there were no queer victims, or that there weren't any attempts by the ICTY legal teams to prosecute crimes against them, but that the cis-heteronormative status quo of international law made seeking justice for LGBTQIA+ victims and survivors close to impossible. The resounding presumption is that victims (and perpetrators) are either straight cis-men or straight cis-women, erasing the diverse gender and sexual identities and expressions that constitute bodies. Such an exclusion from the Tribunal is deeply concerning, not least because queer bodies are frequently the targets of violence but also because international law accepts that the victim is unquestionably straight and cisgender (Biddolph 2024b). In other words, "the stabilizing of (straight, cisgender) . . . legal subjects by the ICTY erases any possibility of queer lives as subject to violence and as agents or recipients of justice" (2024b, 230). Thus, the subject of the (cis-)woman as rape victim has proscriptive value. It prohibits attention to other victimhood subjectivities, thereby (re)producing a coherent, simplified narrative of sexual violence in international law (see Sjoberg 2020, 84). As a result, these discursive practices predominantly obscure or conceal non-normative experiences of sexual violence.

The ICTY texts, in (re)producing the (cis-)woman victim subject position, establish a referent object through which agents of international law can retroactively save and protect "helpless," feminized Balkan victims from their perpetrator counterparts. The Tribunal thus "creates memories of sexual violence in war and conflict, it institutionalises its idealised victims and makes seeing nontraditional victims (and perpetrators) all the more difficult" (Sjoberg 2017b, 169, emphasis in original).This positioning of women as "legitimate" victims (Andrić-Ružičić 2003, 107–8) justifies the exceptional actions taken by the Tribunal and international law more broadly, such as the prosecution and imprisonment of perpetrators through practices of denunciation. While the subject of women as victims reaffirms cis-heteronormative discourses of gender, sexuality, and violence, women are not exclusively defined by this category in international law. Furthermore, under international law, the ICTY posits not just women, but all of Bosnia and "the Balkans," as a victimized place of burden.

Homogenized Victims

While the ICTY reinforces essentialist discourses of international law that situate women as victims of sexual violence, it also challenges it, by focusing much of its prosecution on crimes committed against men. This is because, as the ICTY texts reveal, it was mainly men who were detained in prison camps across Bosnia (see *Kvočka et al.*, *Tadić*). My analysis reveals that the victim subject position goes beyond a binary of victimized men and victimized women, instead constructing "[a]bstract universal victims" that characterize all bodies subjected to violence (Kumarakulasingam 2014, 69). In this way, ICTY actors invoke a homogenized Balkan victim subject position. While the "Balkanness" of victims is not always explicitly invoked at the ICTY, it is central to the Tribunal's work, because international criminal law depends on the (Balkan, Others') perpetration of crimes and the creation of maimed, debilitated, or dead victims for its functioning (see Heathcote 2018b, 88).

The ability of international law to operate as a (queer) governance mechanism depends on acts of violence. For example, legal actors at the Tribunal make sense of and conjure homogenized victimhood (see Rudling 2019, 422) by situating the camps as a place of evil. In *Kvočka et al.*, the judges describe Omarska camp as "a hellish environment in which men and women were deprived of the most basic needs for their survival and of their humanity" (*Kvočka et al.* 2001, Trial Judgment, para 707). The judgment continues, reiterating that "[n]o one could mistake Omarska for merely a badly run prison; it was a criminal enterprise designed to operate in a way that destroyed the mind, body, and spirit of its prisoners" (*Kvočka et al.* 2001, Trial Judgment, para 707). In the indictments, the prosecutor similarly establishes the camps as "abject and brutal" (*Kvočka et al.* 1998, Amended Indictment, para 11), "brutal and inhumane," and "foul" (*Kvočka et al.* 1998, Amended Indictment, para 8), all predicates used to discursively (re)produce the camp as a space of exception, a site where bodies are victimized and left to die. While these descriptors are accurate labels for the living conditions of the camps in Bosnia, their (re)production in the ICTY texts provides the ideal background or presuppositional knowledge needed to produce the ultimate victim subject position. In other words, it is not only the moment of violence that discursively (and materially) produces victimized bodies. Rather, it is also in the moment (and ongoing processes) of representation and adjudication, in the ways in which international law (re)produces testimonies of violence, that a homogenized, faceless, and injured victim is constructed at the Tribunal. In *Mucić et al.*, for example, the judges employ the same types of predicates to establish the violent context of the camps and the violence of the perpetrator:

> Even should it be conceded that Mr Landžo's request to Dr. Grubač is evidence of some remorse for his actions, rather than a mere expression of his fear of recriminations from Mr. Delić, this can hardly detract from the *gross nature* of his [the accused's] conduct in *mercilessly* beating an elderly person with a heavy implement. It appears that the only reason for his assault on Mr. Samouković was that the latter was a Serb from Bradina and thus somehow deserving of punishment for the acts of other Serbs from Bradina in killing several Bosnian police officers. The *ferocity* of the attack can further be gauged from the fact that the victim did not survive for more than half an hour afterwards. Such a *brutal* beating, inflicted on an old man and resulting in his death, clearly exhibits the kind of *reckless behaviour* illustrative of a complete disregard for the consequences which this Trial Chamber considers to amount to wilful killing and murder. (*Mucić et al.* 1998, Trial Judgment, para 855, my emphases)

In this excerpt, the victim, Boško Samouković, is helpless in the face of the perpetrator's violence. The judges' characterization of the beating and killing of Mr. Samouković reflects the factual details of the crimes but does so by way of tethering the old man to his suffering and subsequent death. While Landžo, the accused, ethnically objectifies and homogenizes Mr. Samouković, the judges (re)produce this reading of the victim as a Serb and therefore subject to the violence of a Bosnian Muslim. The ethnicized discourses utilized by the judges assist in the criminalization of the accused, particularly given the OtP's task of proving crimes of ethnic cleansing. Mr. Samouković is thus doubly victimized: in the camps and under international law. The judges need to position him as an elderly Serb man, maimed, helpless, and interchangeable among the other victims who succumbed to the violence of the camps, to denunciate the accused. Put simply, the victim acts as a conduit or an instrument through which international law condemns perpetrators (see Elander 2013, 101). This is not unexpected; as an example of international law, tribunals are mandated to hold individuals responsible for breaches of international humanitarian law. All the evidence presented at the Tribunal (at least by the prosecution) serves to establish the culpability of the accused. While the ICTY texts emphasize that the testimonies of witnesses and survivors are significant (i.e., in their contribution to facts about the conflict, individual and collective healing, and broader goals of justice), the victim exists only so long as there is a perpetrator who wields such violence. Thus, to govern through adjudication, international law is an agent of legal violence, discursively (re)producing a homogenized victimhood that condemns perpetrators but denies the complex, plural identities of witnesses and survivors.

The (re)production of particular kinds of legal subjects in/through international law, including victims, is legible through cis-heteronormative discourses of gender, sexuality, and violence. For example, victims' subjection to crimes involving sexual humiliation, incest, and necrophilia is seen as so abhorrent before the Tribunal (a site charged with prosecuting the most serious crimes), that their humanity is rendered meaningful only in relation to their debility and trauma. The representation of these crimes places camp detainees as the ultimate victims under international law. It prescribes the ICTY to intervene on their behalf: as lawful adjudicators providing the "only civilized alternative" (i.e., criminal justice) to "the Balkans." Through this logic, it is the perpetrators who are sexual aberrations, not the victims (as deigned by the perpetrators). In this way, victims are instrumentally positioned in international law to attribute criminal status to those individuals (and populations) who engage in crimes against humanity.

As a site of international law, the ICTY also participates in practices of discursive victimization in more tacitly gendered and gendering ways. In *Mucić et al.*, predicates of passivity are used to describe victims as "defenceless" and "obliged to helplessly observe the horrific injuries and suffering caused by this mistreatment" (*Mucić et al.* 1998, Trial Judgment, para 1086). The judges are correct to acknowledge the dehumanizing violence of the Čelebići camp. However, the predicates deployed in this example speak to the broader discursive positioning of bodies as interchangeable and faceless symbols of (feminized) passivity and vulnerability (see Schwöbel-Patel 2021, 133–37). That the victimized body is one that is weak and powerless speaks to the need for international law to govern controllable, docile bodies, to protect them and punish dangerous, hyper-heteromasculine perpetrators. In this way, the victim under international law is constructed as simultaneously worthy and unworthy; worthy enough for legal actors to establish a sympathetic juridical subject, but not worthy enough to be identified beyond their victimization. As I detail in Chapter 5, though, it is possible to subvert this subject position, to expose the tensions and inconsistencies that produce bodies as constituted by queer complexities of meaning.

This dynamic must be situated within the wider project of international law, about the need to provide justice to victimized, helpless populations. Debilitated, maimed, and injured bodies (Heathcote 2018b) are valuable victims for international law, their suffering offered as evidence of criminal wrongdoing and justifying legal intervention. Those in need of saving are ideally those who are reduced to bare life, are feminized, and offer no resistance in their actual or symbolic rescue by international legal actors. When bodies are conceived in this way, it produces a victim subject that needs the protection of "civilized" or "superior" actors who object to and punish "illegitimate" violence wielded by "unruly" Others. At the ICTY, the Balkan victim is the ultimate victim because they are docile and powerless in their subjection to violence, thereby allowing paternalistic interventions into their fates. Whether well-intentioned or not, this serves to (re)produce the very discourses that justified the violence in the first instance. It invokes infantilizing language that constructs the victim as some*thing* (not someone) to be acted upon. Thus, just as the (re)production of the victim figure in/through international law is possible because of the need to denunciate perpetrators, so too is this victim required to reaffirm the authority of international law.

Silenced Victims

International law (re)produces the homogenized, feminized victim subject by discursively tethering violated bodies to their victimhood. But it also does so by silencing or curtailing testimony in the courtroom (see Dembour and Haslam 2004). Witnesses who are silenced or have their testimony restricted by judges, prosecutors, and defence attorneys are "juridified" (Elander 2018a, 26), cast into a limited victimhood subject position that allows legal actors to adjudicate crimes. Silencing occurs through the interruption, diversion, and in some cases admonishment of witness testimonies. Judges, prosecutors, and defense attorneys interfere and disrupt witness attempts to share their stories, in ways that uphold the primacy given to the procedural functioning of the courtroom and devalue the embodied and affective realities of the witnesses (see O'Reilly 2016, 425). International law is an agent of violence because it violates the human justice of witnesses, survivors, and those who were killed in acts of atrocity. Legal victimization reinforces simplistic discourses of gender, sexuality, and violence, rendering bodies valuable only so long as they contribute to the functioning and governance of the courtroom. The silencing or restriction of witness testimony in the ICTY texts say as much about the legal actors as the victims. The following objection from two defense attorneys in *Mucić et al.* is illustrative of this point and is worth quoting at length:

MR. ACKERMAN: Your Honour, I have an objection— . . . By the way the testimony is proceeding, it appears the witness has a well-prepared statement that he wants to give to the court, which is relatively unrelated to the questions that are being asked. The last question that was asked of him could have been answered "yes" or "no." He went into about a five-minute dissertation that had relatively little to do with the question that was asked. I hope we could proceed in this court in a way that the witness will at least listen to the question that he is asked and attempt to answer that question rather than proceed off with these long-winded statements that go off to nowhere. I would hope the witness could be instructed by the court to listen to the question and make every attempt to answer that question only and as precisely as possible. . . . *I suggest very strongly that the court admonish this witness that he will be removed as a witness if he cannot listen to the questions and answer the questions; otherwise he has no business being here. This is a court of law, not a place to make speeches.* [. . .]

MR. GREAVES: Your Honour, with great respect, *the witness cannot be allowed to defy the control of the court in the way he has just done so. That is intolerable and it is not the way it should be done.* In my submission to your Honour, he must be told in the clearest terms that *he cannot do as he wishes.* It must be in answer to the questions which he is asked and under the control of learned counsel for the prosecution.

JUDGE KARIBI WHYTE: Thank you very much. Occasionally you will meet witnesses of this nature, but I think we will make him to answer questions directed at him in the way the counsel wants him to answer. I do not think he will behave differently. He will try and answer. (*Mucić et al.* 1997, Trial hearing 5 May, my emphases)

The defense attorneys very clearly admonish the witness, who, as I explore in Chapter 5, attempts to share more of his story to the court. Mr. Ackerman's and Mr. Greaves's objections violently curtail the possibility of this witness being more than a victim, prohibiting him from sharing, in his own way, his experiences in and beyond the camps. The witness is made both a victim of atrocity and a victim under international law (see Elander 2018a, 24–25). The defense attorneys violate this witness through an admonishment that is disempowering and patronizing. Mr. Ackerman reaffirms that the Tribunal "is a court of law," a mechanism through which victimized bodies can only ever be victims, victims who can speak only in response to limited lines of questioning. To ensure a time-sensitive and fair trial, preserving the rights of the accused, and attempting to shorten the mandate of the Tribunal, the ICTY has justified curtailing the length of witness testimony. Consider the following disclaimer by the presiding judge, Carmel Agius, to another witness before his testimony:

> The important thing is that you try to answer the question, the whole question, and nothing but the question. We don't want long stories. We want the truth. But please stick—you are a professional man. Stick to the question that is put to you either from the Prosecution or the Defence. Don't try to go off at a tangent or give us explanations that we don't need or you haven't been asked to give. (*Brdanin* 2002, Trial hearing 3 June)

Even before testimony begins, the judge limits the extent to which the witness can share his experience of violence. The juridical functioning of the law is centered, rather than the witness's own subjectivities, including but not limited to being a survivor. The judge presupposes that the witness will understand the necessity of remaining on topic and responding only to the questions asked. The statement also assumes that there is only one (correct) answer to the questions being posed by the prosecution and defense.

My queer analysis of the ICTY texts entails tracing how international law and ways of juridical governing are violating and thus enactments of violence. Part of this queer approach means being attuned to the regulatory violences of juridical practices, and the ways in which as a (queer) governance mechanism, international law both depends on and erases the plural discourses and logics that give it meaning. Thus, while the ICTY judge expects witnesses to conform to particular answers, this expectation eclipses other truths and realities about violence, including the various ways in which bodies experience violence through bodily senses, memories, and affects (see Sjoberg 2016). As I have argued elsewhere, the "language of the Tribunal is depoliticizing and dehumanizing, and it seeks a retributive justice that cannot make sense" of queerness and complexity (Biddolph 2024b, 232).

Similarly, the judge presupposes that legal actors at the Tribunal can access a singular, tangible truth through which to make sense of and adjudicate crimes. In this way, the judge, as an agent of international law, engages in practices of legal violence that reduce witnesses to objects of instrumental value, as victims, as embodied forms of evidence through which to govern violence and criminalize perpetrators. This reflects what Dubravka Zarkov calls the "staccato exchange" through which the witness "is reduced to a dismembered and passive victim" (2007, 177; see also Mertus 2004, 113). The example also reveals the essentialist discourses of gender that infuse the courtroom. Judge Agius refers to the witness as a "professional man." The predicate of professional coupled with the gendered subject position (of man) renders the witness a rational but compliant subject of international law. Judge Agius appeals to the witness's identity as a "professional man" in an attempt to regulate the testimony given as evidence. This disclaimer announced before witness testimony prescribes and proscribes actions and possibilities during the court session. It entitles the prosecutor, defense, and judges to interrupt witnesses whom they deem to be going off track. It also enables the provision of witness evidence that is tailored to the crimes under discussion. As Julie Mertus writes, "the legal process does not permit witnesses to tell their own coherent narrative; it chops their stories into digestible parts, selects a handful of parts and sorts and refines them to create a new narrative" (2004, 113). This prohibits the witness from embodying his own survivor subject position, instead rendering him of utilitarian value for the Tribunal and international law more broadly.

In contrast, while certainly not the case for all rape testimonies, the testimony of one rape survivor (Witness A) was dismissed because "her testimony was so confused as to details of the rape that it cannot be relied upon to establish guilt" (*Kvočka et al.* 2001, Trial Judgment, para 557). This is not to downplay the Tribunal's commitment to admitting testimonies of sexual violence based solely on the testimony of the survivor. The ICTY's Rules of Procedure and Evidence stipulate that in cases of sexual assault, "no corroboration of the victim's testimony shall be required," among other rules that protect the rights of sexual assault survivors (ICTY Rules and Procedure of Evidence 1994, Rule 96). The judges' discounting of Witness A's testimony, however, violently reduces her experience and trauma. In a legal setting, evidence must be coherent and clearly established to attribute innocence or guilt to the defendant (see Anderson 2020, 30). Within this context, it is therefore understandable that confusing or inconsistent testimony may be dismissed. But this overlooks the context in which her testimony was provided. Witness A was recounting her rape which occurred several years prior to giving evidence. Furthermore, in her willingness to stand before the Tribunal, she revealed harrowing experiences of trauma. Each of these details, while recognized under international law, should contextualize the survivor's "confusing" evidence. Instead, the messiness of her testimony is an excess in the courtroom, something that does not fit within juridical frames of justice (see K. Campbell et al. 2019, 261). International tribunals, "which demand that truth be told in a complete and linear fashion, mistrust the natural voice of survivors" (Mertus 2004, 120). Thus, judges deem the rape survivor's testimony unreliable, and therefore invalidated before the court. It is not the response the judges are looking for. In other words, the "court cannot hold the complexity of victimisation" (Elander 2013, 114). The traumatized rape victim, while given the space to bear witness in the courtroom, is devalued, her testimony only authorized under international law so long as it conforms to established norms of evidence and truth.

Seen through the case of the ICTY, international law engages in gendering and violating practices that categorize and govern bodies according to civilizational logics and cis-heteronormative discourses of gender, sexuality, and violence. Victimization is one example of how international law governs through adjudication and is an agent of juridical violence. International law therefore "requires a 'perfect' or 'legitimate' victim who is allowed to gain access to justice but required to adjust their testimony to fit the script provided by the dominant narrative" (Mibenge 2013, 7, quoted in Sjoberg 2017b, 134–35). Victimization freezes witnesses and survivors as feminized, homogenized, and silenced victims, thereby crafting compliant bodies who can provide (the "right" kinds of) evidence to govern, prosecute, and punish perpetrators.

Denunciation

International law, as a (queer) governance mechanism, engages in gendering, discursive, and violating practices. One of the most prominent ways it does this is through denunciation: the denouncement and condemnation of certain actors and actions as violent, criminal, and deserving of punishment. In this way, international law regulates violence, determining who and what is illegal, dangerous, and perverse. To govern violence is also to wield violence, whether that be through the imprisonment of individuals charged with crimes, or the demonization and excoriation of perpetrators. Denunciation forms another practice of legal violence in international law, in ways that (re)produce pejorative civilizational logics and essentialist, cis-heteronormative discourses of gender, sexuality, and violence. At the ICTY, the accused and perpetrators are the targets of this denunciation, crafted by the judges, prosecution, and presidents as sadistic perpetrators and rapists with a distinctly Balkan propensity for hyper-heteromasculine, ethnicized violence (see O'Reilly 2012, 538). Denunciation reinforces and prescribes the authority of international law to govern through adjudication, to make sense of, regulate, and punish certain bodies because they are seen as directly in opposition to "accepted," "civilized," and "European" values. Such a legal violence both depends on and (re)produces these perpetrator subjectivities, for there must be "bad" bodies to criminalize and imprison, just as these processes performatively constitute "bad" bodies to be criminalized and imprisoned (see Engle 2020, 82). Civilizational logics and gendered discourses thus construct perpetrators as perverse and queer (in the derogatory sense), who require *straightening* and correction through retributive means.

Sadistic Perpetrators

The Tribunal's legal actors both tacitly and explicitly invoke Balkanist logics (see Chapter 3) in their denunciation of perpetrators. Balkanism organizes cis-heteronormative discourses of gender, sexuality, and violence, constituting perpetrator subject positions through predicates of sadism, cruelty, and brutality. Denunciating practices that frame perpetrators as dangerous, hyper-heteromasculine sadists prescribe the arrest, indictment, prosecution, judgment, and punishment of individuals. Sadistic perpetrators are legible through their Otherness in international law. At the ICTY, while the perpetrator is frequently conjured along ethnic lines (i.e., by attributing more criminality to certain ethnic or religious groups), gendered, Balkanist logics of governance enable legal actors at the Tribunal to criminalize perpetrators, whether Serb, Croat, or Muslim. The perpetrator is a discursive construction, performatively (re)produced and legible through plural and contradictory signifiers and practices (see Chapter 2). My queer analysis underscores the instability and contested nature of this perpetrator category (see Chapter 5), as well as the overt and implicit ways that discourses of gender, sexuality, and violence imbue the perpetrator with meaning.

The ICTY characterizes perpetrators through predicates such as "brutal," "merciless," "cruel," "vicious," "sadistic," and "savage" (*Mucić et al.* 1998, Trial Judgment). These adjectives are often invoked in the indictments and judgments. They are textual practices that literally judge and make judgments about the subjects in question: rendering individuals criminally liable, classifying violence according to legally established categories, and grading both the severity of the crimes committed and the extent of criminal responsibility to pass sentence. In other words, denunciation is what these judgments are about. Woven into these practices are judging or moralizing predicates that make adjudication possible in international law. The descriptions of "savage" and "sadistic" perpetrators help the Tribunal (i.e., the judges, prosecutors) conclude criminal liability by framing the accused through these value-laden adjectives. By employing these discursive practices, the trial judgments permit the pronouncement of judgment and the subsequent punishment to be meted out (see Garbett 2016, 44). As an example of international law, the ICTY, through its gendering, agential, and violating capacities, attributes predicates such as sadism and viciousness to perpetrators to distinguish them as dangerous, criminal, and perverse, thereby warranting the curtailing of their freedoms (e.g., through incarceration).

The predicates used to describe perpetrators at the ICTY continue a history of Balkanist logics (see Chapter 3). Balkanism is echoed in the ICTY judgments I analyzed, and serves to construct a homogeneous, threatening Balkan perpetrator. For example, in *Mucić et al.*, the judges found that Mr. Delić (one of the accused) "is a man who derived sadistic pleasure from the suffering and humiliation he caused," laughing as he inflicted an electric device normally used for cattle on detainees (*Mucić et al.* 1998, Trial Judgment, paras 1053, 1057–58). Another statement from the same judgment establishes the inhumanity of the perpetrator:

> The Trial Chamber has further made factual findings that Esad Landžo tied a burning fuse-cord around Vukašin Mrkajić, forced two brothers to commit fellatio with each other and ordered a father and son to beat one another. While Mr. Landžo was not charged directly with these offences and thus is not sentenced in relation to them, the Trial Chamber again notes the heinous nature of the acts involved and the depravity of mind necessary to conceive of and inflict such forms of suffering. (*Mucić et al.* 1998, Trial Judgment, para 1275)

In this excerpt, the judges establish Esad Landžo, the accused, as depraved for the "heinous" acts he committed against detainees. The judges construct Landžo's perversion through reference to sexual violence, specifically, the forcing of two brothers to commit fellatio. The perpetrator gains meaning in international law as cruel and sadistic through explicitly gendered and sexualizing meanings. As I continue later in this section, the denunciation of perpetrators in international law frequently depends on legal actors conjuring individuals as hyper-heteromasculine, sexually deviant rapists who are simultaneously homosexual and homophobic. In doing so, the denouncement of perpetrators in judgments such as the one above distinguishes between "acceptable" (sexual) behavior and the criminal actions of Balkan perpetrators.

Furthermore, perpetrators are constructed through binaries of good and evil. The statement that "Omarska was a place where beatings occurred daily and with devilish instruments" (*Kvočka et al.* 2001, Trial Judgment, para 707) functions according to Othering and pathologizing discourses. This establishes the undeniably "bad" actions of perpetrators, and therefore the "good" work of the Tribunal in bringing them to justice. Sadism, depravity, and evil constitute the perpetrator in these examples. While the perpetrator subject position at the ICTY does not explicitly stand in for a homogeneous Balkan subject, the characterization of multiple perpetrators across different ethnicities as "sadistic" and "merciless" works to distinguish them as violent, nonhuman, or monstrous entities in contrast to the law-abiding and law-enforcing actors who adjudicate violence in international law (see Engle 2020, 13, 82). This language that frames perpetrators as sadistic, monstrous, and categorically different from civilized humanity is so normalized within international law that it attains the status of common sense. My concern with this discursive practice of demonization and denunciation should not be taken as underplaying the severity and trauma of violence inflicted by perpetrators. Rather, my queer analysis alerts me to the power relations that make these designations possible across intersecting discourses of gender, sexuality, ethnicity, and violence. As a site of international law embodied by legal actors prosecuting Balkan individuals, the ICTY's denouncing of perpetrators as sadistic needs to be understood within a broader racist, (neo)colonial, and Eurocentric history of designating "Other," "Oriental," African, and Balkan populations as uncivilized, premodern, and victims to their own violent natures. Consider, for example, the following extracts from *Mucić et al.*:

Hazim Delić has criminally caused the death of two detainees in the Čelebići prison-camp. He was a party to the brutal and merciless beatings of Sčepo Gotovac. He beat this elderly man to death on the basis of an accusation that he had been responsible for the deaths of Muslims in the Second World War. (*Mucić et al.* 1998, Trial Judgment, para 1261)

The evidence indicates that, as well as having a general sadistic motivation, Hazim Delić was driven by feelings of revenge against people of Serb ethnicity. Before raping Ms. Antić, he stated that "the Chetniks were guilty for every thing that was going on. He [Delić] started to curse my [Ms. Antić's] Chetnik mother." (*Mucić et al.* 1998, Trial Judgment, para 1269)

In these excerpts, Balkanist logics about the former Yugoslavia as a place and people of ancient, ethnic hatreds constitute the presuppositional or background knowledge of these denunciations (see Chapter 3; Nadj 2011, 656–57). It is therefore accepted that Delić would engage in retaliatory violence against Serbs because of Balkanist assumptions about interethnic conflict in the former Yugoslavia. Predicates such as "brutal" and "merciless" conjure Delić as a sadistic perpetrator, while the raping of Ms. Antić is understood by the judges as a reflection of Delić's vengeful feelings and propensity to inflict sexual violence and gendered, ethnic slurs (with *chetnik* an ethnic slur against Serbs). Thus, while the judges render this violence horrific (and rightly so), such denunciation perpetuates gendered, Balkanist logics that pejoratively cast the Balkans as a place and people of timeless ethnic and heteropatriarchal violence. This becomes common sense at the Tribunal and allows legal actors to govern through adjudication. It therefore makes sense that Bosnia is a place where crosses are carved into flesh (*Brdanin* 2003, Trial hearing 3 March), and where old men and the intellectually disabled are beaten (*Mucić et al.* 1998, Trial Judgment; *Tadić* 1997, Trial Judgment; *Brdanin* 2003, Trial hearing 4 June). The prosecution and conviction of Balkan perpetrators before the ICTY is justified on the basis that truly sadistic perpetrators must be punished, castigated, and denounced on an international stage.

Practices of denunciation are not limited to the demonization of men perpetrators. Where women are represented as agents of violence in international law, their presence stands in contrast to heterosexist, gendered presuppositions that reinforce essentialist notions of peaceful womanhood and exceptionalize women's violence as irrational, unnatural, and profoundly unfeminine (see Sjoberg and Gentry 2007). For example, the ICTY texts tell of acts of violence where two women threatened to cut a detainee's penis off (*Mucić et al.* 1997, Trial hearing 17 March), and of an elderly Serb woman who wielded "a sabre or a long knife," threatening the detainee and said: "Are there any balijas[2] around, remaining? Fuck their mothers" (*Brđanin* 2003, Trial hearing 26 February). The presence and representation of these moments in the broader corpus of ICTY texts is significant, because seen as exceptional instances of women's violence, they (re)produce problematic gendered assumptions of normal, peaceful femininity and the ability for violent women to pervert them. As with men perpetrators, the violence of these women legitimates the authority and governing practices of international law, to denunciate perpetrators and contribute to their disciplining, enlightenment, and redemption.

The judges echo this logic in *Delić*. The Trial Judgment details an incident at Kamenica camp, where a "Mujahedin" decapitated a detainee, placed the head on a butcher's hook, threw the head at other detainees and ordered them to "kiss your brother," and then hung the head up in the room for all the detainees to see (*Delić* 2008, Trial Judgment, para 261).[3] In contrast to previous examples, this violence is not qualified with predicates such as "savage" and "sadistic." Instead, the indictment, the witness testimony, and the trial judgment let the violence speak for itself. Similar effects are evident in the inclusion of testimonies that detailed detainees who were forced to kiss a dead boar (*Mucić et al.* 1997, Trial hearing 16 June 16), and to drink each other's urine (*Mucić et al.* 1997, Trial hearing 2 April). In undertaking this analysis, I do not mean to diminish the ways that witness and survivor testimonies contribute to human justice, nor of the role of testimonies as evidence within the procedural justice functions of the courtroom. What my analysis of these instances instead shows is that even in their direct narration, the ICTY's creation of a detailed record of violence committed by perpetrators also creates a perpetrator subject position that can be easily denounced and subjected to judgment and sentence.

As with Omarska, Kamenica camp is constructed as a place where violence occurs. This presupposition renders the crime legible within the scope of the case. In contrast to the prior examples, the perpetrator is not identified by name, nor by his broader role as a guard. Instead, the judges characterize the perpetrator as a Mujahedin, what the ICTY texts frequently refer to as the sometimes organized, although more often "rogue," "foreign," or "Arab" Muslim fighters supporting the Bosnian Muslim forces against the Serbs (see also Baker 2018b, 137). In this case, the sadistic perpetrator is not the expected Serb perpetrator that comes to characterize much of the Tribunal caseload. Instead, he is "dangerously" Muslim (in contrast to "good" Bosnian Muslims), unequivocally different from the (predominantly) Christian Balkans, and from the Judeo-Christian, Eurocentric project of international law (see Atanasoski 2018, 76). Indeed, throughout the Trial Judgment, Orientalist descriptions of the Mujahedin abound. For example, the judges preface the denunciation of the crime by describing who they refer to when they invoke the term "Mujahedin":

> The term "Mujahedin," meaning "fighter of Allah," has been widely used to refer to the foreigners—mainly from the Arab world—who came to Bosnia and Herzegovina during the war in support of Bosnian Muslims. Those foreign Mujahedin were of a darker complexion, wore long beards and did not speak the local language. (*Delić* 2008, Trial Judgment, para 165)

In another excerpt, the judges include an extract from a Bosnian military report describing the Mujahedin as "characterised by fanatical courage that comes from religious fanaticism" and that "[b]asically, members of the [Mujahedin] Detachment consider as enemies all those who are not of the Islamic faith" (*Delić* 2008, Trial Judgment, para 502). While this is not the language of the judges, the inclusion of this extract is revealing, contributing to an overall emphasis on, and distinction of, the Mujahedin within the ICTY texts. The judges later go on to say that these military reports indicate that "members of the EMD [the Mujahedin] had a propensity for violence and to commit crimes" (*Delić* 2008, Trial Judgment, para 513). The judges' denunciation of Mujahedin violence in *Delić* must be situated within the time frame of the trial, held between 2005 and 2008, during the post-9/11 context. The Mujahedin subject is already cast as the dangerous Other or threat to the United States (and the West), conjured as both hypermasculine, patriarchal, homophobic oppressors *and* "monster-terrorist-fags" (Puar and Rai 2002), within distant, Arab lands such as Iraq and Afghanistan (see also Khalid 2017; Manchanda 2015). This post-9/11 imaginary and War on Terror discourse contributes to the ICTY's (and international law's) framing and construction of Muslim and Arab men as dangerous, sadistic, violent, and queer in the derogatory sense. Thus, when the perpetrator is made meaningful at/by the ICTY through this threatening subject position, acts of decapitation and taunting are not unsurprising; they are *expected* of these perpetrators.

A queer reading of this example is also attuned to the moment of violence itself, of how the perpetrator invokes sexualized discourses and taboos to make the violence meaningful. Seen through the Eurocentric gaze of the ICTY, the perpetrator is especially violent because he is (sexually) perverse, forcing detainees to kiss a decapitated head. As this example illuminates, the perpetrator is positioned as the barbaric criminal not only through the judgments made about what constitutes acceptable violence (i.e., civilized vs. barbaric), but because it depends on discourses of acceptable versus dangerous masculinity and normal versus perverse sexuality. These discursive effects are similarly evident in witness testimony detailing how a boy was forced to rape his dead mother in front of other detainees (*Tadić* 1996, 21 June). To be sure, this is a horrific crime, but its horrifying quality is presupposed through the assumed sadism of a perpetrator who would subject victims to both incest and necrophilia, violations that are seen as the ultimate taboo and perversion of human dignity (Drumond 2019, 159). These gendered and sexualized discourses that constitute the barbaric criminal subject position are explicitly deployed to produce and therefore denounce the Balkan perpetrator as a (sexual) predator in international law. As such, the legal actors embodying and acting for the Tribunal establish this subject position through practices of denunciation. This allows them to not only make sense of but also adjudicate violence. Pathologizing predicates of sadism and viciousness that distinguish perpetrators under international law have prescriptive value, allowing judges to condemn and punish individuals and to discursively categorize them according to pejorative civilizational logics (such as Balkanism).

Vicious Rapists

The perpetrator subject position is entangled with gendered and sexualized meaning. In addition to broader constructions of perpetrators as "cruel," "sadistic," and "merciless," legal discourses also establish them as sexually dangerous, homosexual, *and/or* homophobic.[4] This finding reveals how the Tribunal, as an example of international law, is a discursively powerful and agential actor that continues Balkanist logics of governance to adjudicate violence. By deconstructing the cis-heteronormative discourses that construct perpetrators as sadistic and vicious rapists, knowable through their "Balkanness," I disrupt and expose the violent ways international law distinguishes between "good" and "bad" bodies.

The denunciation of perpetrators as hyper-heteromasculine and sexually perverse rapists is, as expected, especially noticeable in the adjudication of rape and sexual assault cases. For example, in *Brdanin*, the judges include reference to "a Bosnian Croat woman who was forced to undress herself in front of cheering Bosnian Serb policemen and soldiers" (*Brdanin* 2004, Trial Judgment, para 1013).[5] They also referred to a perpetrator who "made no secret that he wanted a Bosnian Muslim women to 'give birth to a little Serb'" (*Brdanin* 2004, Trial Judgment, para 1011). In another court proceeding, it was told that "Hazim Delić and others... bragged that 60 Delić girls and boys will be born because that is how many women he raped" (*Mucić et al.* 1997, Trial hearing 18 March). The judges emphasize the perpetrators' pleasure and arrogance to demonstrate and denounce their sadism and hyper-heteromasculine sexuality. Other examples highlighted in the *Brdanin* Trial Judgment follow a similar discursive pattern:

> Outside interrogation, Bosnian Muslim and Bosnian Croat male and female detainees were forced by a Bosnian Serb policeman to perform sexual acts with each other, in front of a crowd of cheering men.... Two other male detainees, at least one of whom was a Bosnian Muslim, were forced to perform *fellatio* on each other by the "Specialists" whilst being subjected to ethnic slurs. (*Brdanin* 2004, Trial Judgment, para 824, emphasis in original)

In this excerpt, there are no predicates to distinguish the perpetrators as especially bad, such as "sadistic" or "cruel." Instead, the emphasis on fellatio and the acknowledgment that these acts were committed in front of cheering men continue an overarching tendency to depict crimes in ways that enunciate the distinct wrongness of these acts, committed by ethnically motivated perpetrators. The *Brdanin* Trial Judgment also attests to evidence that men detainees were threatened with their mothers and sisters being raped in front of them. Each of these examples invoked by the judges builds toward the designation of perpetrators as sexual predators; dangerously hyper-heteromasculine men with the capacity and drive to violate helpless victims. Other ICTY cases reinforce the vicious rapist subject position. For example, the following extract from *Mucić et al.* describes instances of rape in ways that reinforce the perpetrator's (hypermasculine) threat and the victim's (feminine) vulnerability:

> Hazim Delić is guilty of torture by way of the deplorable rapes of two women detainees in the Celebici prison-camp. He subjected Grozdana

Ćećez not only to the inherent suffering involved in rape, but exacerbated her humiliation and degradation by raping her in the presence of his colleagues. (*Mucić et al.* 1998, Trial Judgment, para 1262)

Grozdana must be a humiliated and degraded subject, the ultimate rapable/raped victim for Hazim Delić to be/become the vicious Balkan rapist in ICTY discourse (see Mertus 2004, 115). This trope of dangerous hyper-heteromasculinity depends on the construction of a docile, victimized subject, just as much as it depends on a discursive rendering of violence that is distinctly "backward" in contrast to "legitimate" forms of maiming and killing. These Balkanist assumptions simplify and obscure the lived realities of what it means to be "Balkan," instead representing the region through frames of gendered backwardness. Legal actors at the ICTY invoke Balkanist logics that position ethnic and religious identity as inherent to Balkan culture, a sign of tradition, patriarchy, and premodernism that distinguishes "the Balkans" from an enlightened, secular Europe (see Chapter 3). Consider the following examples from *Mucić et al.*:

> The Prosecution contends, *inter alia*, that Hazim Delić personally participated in monstrous crimes. He murdered a number of detainees, he brutally raped a number of the women in the prison-camp and then boasted about it, and he frequently beat detainees, often with a baseball bat, causing his victims to suffer broken ribs. (*Mucić et al.* 1998, Trial Judgment, para 1254)
>
> The rapes were committed inside the Čelebići prison-camp and on each occasion Hazim Delić was in uniform, and viciously threatening towards Ms. Antić. (*Mucić et al.* 1998, Trial Judgment, para 963)

"Monstrous" and "viciously threatening," the judges categorize Hazim Delić as a perpetrator beyond the limits of acceptable behavior. These predicates and subject positions are especially meaningful because they performatively (re)produce the perpetrator as a sexual predator and rapist. This discursive practice is necessary for the Tribunal to prosecute and charge the accused with crimes of rape and sexual assault. As an example of governance and international law, the ICTY must denunciate perpetrators in its ability to make sense of and regulate violence. But in doing so, the judges cast the perpetrator out, criminalizing him through the invocation of Balkanist logics of difference, sexual predation, and monstrosity. The characterization of the dangerous masculinity and hypersexuality of Balkan perpetrators allows the Tribunal to govern through adjudication: to make legal decisions and pronouncements that have legal-political effects. A criminal tribunal established in the name of international peace and security requires a demonized and denunciated Other in order to function and bring justice to victimized populations. The ICTY was created to prosecute individuals responsible for war crimes and crimes against humanity in the former Yugoslavia. It contributes to the attribution of "good" and "bad" bodies in international law, and these representational practices depend on Balkanist logics and cis-heteronormative discourses of gender, sexuality, and violence.

International legal mechanisms are required to investigate and govern practices of violence, such as the acts of rape referred to above. At the same time, however, international law is not just about violence, but maintains its own violating capacities, such as the (re)production of exclusionary logics that justified crimes in the first place (see Zarkov 2007, 7). For example, while the ICTY condemns forced fellatio as an act of sexual violence and torture, it nevertheless (re)produces the cis-heteronormative discourses driving the violence. It does so by reinforcing the shame associated with "homosexual" practices such as fellatio (Lambevski 1999). In *Mucić et al.*, the prosecutor frames the testimony through logics of embarrassment and shame:

Q. Mr. Dordic, could you describe better how did Mr. Landzo wrap the fuse around you? Was that while you were dressed or not?
A. He ordered me to take off my trousers and my pants and then he wrapped the fuse round my body.
Q. Exactly how did he wrap it round your body? Describe better without being embarrassed.
A. May I stand up and show you?
Q. Yes, please.
A. Thank you. (Indicating). A part of the fuse was right here, under here (indicating) and then back. Then he put an end into my anus, and then the other end was showing up here. Then later he forced me to put on my knickers and trousers.

Q. All right. Thank you. So you were saying a while ago something about oral sex. Could you please now describe this other incident about oral sex in detail, please, without being embarrassed. (*Mucić et al.* 1997, Trial hearing 7 July)

The crimes deliberated in *Mucić et al.* contribute to jurisprudence on sexual violence against men and are therefore significant for their recognition of crimes. But the prosecutor's embarrassment around asking about these crimes (re)produce rigid sexual norms and gender categories. Such a reassurance by the prosecutor to the witness could reflect the sense of shame all victim-survivors (including women) might feel in recounting sexual violence, including heterosexual rape. However, this explicit invocation of embarrassment by the prosecutor is not one I have found in other court proceedings across the selected cases. This could be an isolated example where the prosecutor has shown consideration to the witness's dignity in narrating these crimes. But traces of shame related to forced homosexual practices, and between brothers no less, haunt the line of questioning. Indeed, in a different ICTY case outside of my selected cases, a witness tells of a "well-known ... homosexual" and how "the military policemen would often—to get their kicks, they would make him do all sorts of things with this man Trebinjac" (*Prlić* 2007, Trial hearing 1 May). In response, the defense counsel asks that "This might be something that could be handled in private session given the gentleman's—I mean—given the content of what—I just think out of respect for the individual" (*Prlić* 2007, Trial hearing 1 May). The counsels and judges read these instances of violence as evidence of the perpetrators' criminality and guilt. But by invoking logics of shame and embarrassment over "homosexual(izing)" violence, they nevertheless reinforce the same cis-heteronormative discourses of violence they seek to denounce.

Within cis-heteronormative discourses, fellatio is considered particularly abhorrent because it goes against cis-heterosexual normality, but its perversion is compounded by the act being forcibly practiced and occurring between brothers. The ICTY's adjudication of these crimes is a vital part of establishing criminal responsibility demanded under international law. But the repetition and reiteration of these cis-heteronormative discourses demonstrates how international law perpetuates harmful assumptions about the "proper" expression of gendered and sexual embodiment, including those that "are derived from the same gendered, sexualized, and ethnicized practices from which the violent acts receive inspiration, justification, and/or sanction" (Zarkov 2007, 7). In this sense, international law configures violence through multiple (and often competing) discourses of gender, sexuality, and violence. The judges and prosecutors use this evidence to denunciate the (homo)sexual *and/or* homophobic "deviancy" of the guards and establish the brothers as sexually violated victims (see Zarkov 2007, 169). At the same time, the judges also classify such violence through cis-heteronormative systems of meaning, whereby violence that serves to "homosexualize" or "feminize" (cis-)men is considered much more abhorrent than "nonsexual" forms of torture. As gendered and gendering, constitutive and agential, and violent and violating, international law (re)produces and institutionalizes cis-heterosexuality and denigrates homosexuality. At the ICTY, legal actors castigate Balkan perpetrators for their "vicious" and "monstrous" sexual acts against detainees. In doing so, they invoke Balkanist logics that pejoratively characterize "the Balkans" as a place of homophobia, intolerance, and the international judges and lawyers who embody the Tribunal as lawful adjudicators of justice. Practices of denunciation in sites of international law, therefore, are practices of violence, ways of organizing, regulating, and punishing "uncivilized" perpetrators, to the exclusion and excision of other criminally responsible actors.

Paternalism

International law governs and adjudicates through violent practices of paternalism. Legal actors at/of the Tribunal—including prosecutors, defense attorneys, judges, presidents, and the State Representatives at the UN who helped establish this mechanism—engage in a paternalism that is gendered, condescending, and predicated on civilizational (i.e., Balkanist) logics that position international law as the most appropriate, lawful, and civilized response to the war in Bosnia (see Biddolph 2024a, 10). Paternalism is violent and violating because it depends on exclusionary and pejorative discourses. These discourses infantilize racialized and civilizational Others as either helpless victims or perennial perpetrators who require the adjudicatory powers and authority of international law to correct their violent ways. Discourses of gender, sexuality, and violence intersect through practices of paternalism that underpin victimization and denunciation. International legal actors are positioned in the legal texts as lawful adjudicators and concerned representatives of the law committed to avenging feminized victims and condemning hyper-heteromasculine perpetrators (see Heathcote 2011, 146). This is a kind of masculine paternalism that counters the "dangerous," "violent" masculinity of the Other. In this way, "violence and protection are not opposites, but complementary concepts that necessitate each other: protection requires violence; violence requires protection" (Sjoberg 2010b, 67). At the ICTY, paternalistic practices are not only violent and violating because they position Balkan bodies in gendered and pejorative ways. They also legitimate or prescribe the juridical authority of the Tribunal: to organize, punish, and regulate through the criminalization and incarceration of individuals. Here, I explore two ways in which paternalism materializes in the ICTY texts: through the subject position of legal actors as lawful adjudicators, and the positioning of the Tribunal and international law as "the only civilized alternative" to conflict.

Lawful Adjudicators

My queer analysis of the ICTY texts found that legal actors such as the judges, prosecutors, and presidents are positioned as moral, lawful adjudicators authorized to govern violence. The decision to establish the ICTY is frequently heralded in the Tribunal's texts as a moral necessity. The institutional texts invoke origin stories and genealogies of international law to develop an image of the Tribunal (and international law more broadly) as the moral and lawful adjudicator of feminized, Balkan victims (see Chapter 3). For example, one annual report refers to the postwar tribunals of Nuremberg and Tokyo, situating the ICTY as a continuation of these courts' goals and as having been "entrusted with the *noble* but difficult task" of holding Balkan perpetrators criminally responsible for atrocities against innocent victims (ICTY Annual Report 1994, 49, my emphasis). As I show in the next subsection, this comparison to the postwar tribunals was similarly invoked in the verbatim record of the UN's establishment of the Tribunal, but with a more explicit focus on the condemnation and denunciation of Balkan perpetrators. Here, however, the predicate of "noble" represents a vital discursive move in situating the ICTY as an authorized juridical intervener. The ICTY judges are encased by a particularly heroic aura, as servants of the law and carriers of justice. In the same annual report, the judges are said to have "solemnly under[taken] to fulfil their mission ... as a result of the obligations undertaken by them towards the international community and the United Nations body which elected them" (ICTY Annual Report 1994, 50). The judges "owe a compelling *moral obligation* to the population of the former Yugoslavia," and by extension the Tribunal they represent "fervently hopes to contribute, by its own means, to restoring humane and peaceful conditions in *that torn region* and to alleviating the anguish and grief of those who have suffered and still suffer from armed violence and brutality" (ICTY Annual Report 1994, 50, my emphases).

This moral obligation depends on the construction of a worthy victim in need of saving. In other annual reports, the UN and the ICTY are depicted as "concerned" onlookers of, or sympathetic "listeners" to, "the special problems faced by people who have witnessed or suffered the traumatic events ... in the former Yugoslavia" (ICTY Annual Report 1995, 27, see also ICTY Annual Report 1998). The distinction between the lawfulness of the Tribunal and the helplessness of feminized, Balkan victims hinges on civilizational logics of governance and international law. Legal actors who embody the ICTY attain legibility as lawful adjudicators through the existence of, and emphasis on, the victimhood subject position, prescribing international law to help contribute to "the rule of law" and "lasting peace" in the former Yugoslavia (ICTY Annual Report 1999, 51). It is also, though, a chance for redemption, for the UN to demonstrate their ability to act in the face of violence, even if those actions were delayed (or themselves violent). Or, as one annual report says, to show that "the United Nations was not sitting back idly while thousands were being brutally abused or massacred" (ICTY Annual Report 1994, 10; see also Chapter 3).

These discursive practices (re)produce an image of the ICTY and the legal actors who embody it, as noble, moral, and heroic actors. These predicates and the subject position they constitute do not exist through "universal" values of ethical responsibility. Rather, they depend on civilizational logics and gendered discourses of international law, whereby the ICTY represents the paternal, juridical intervener, while victims are feminized, infantilized populations who lack the capacity to protect themselves (from themselves). As Heathcote reminds us, the "dichotomy between the protectors and the protected[] seem[s] natural rather than constructed through law and gendered" (2011, 164). A queer approach involves deconstructing this assumed naturalness and exposing the overt and tacit ways in which gender, sexuality, and violence make this dichotomy possible. This gendered dynamic is not exclusive to discourses (re)produced in the ICTY texts but reflects broader civilizational logics of governance and international law. The examples from the ICTY's annual reports cohere within this broader understanding of Othered populations as helpless, feminine, infantilized, and in need of protection and external intervention from "benevolent," "masculine" protectors (see Peet and Sjoberg 2019, 46). Practices of sexual violence, torture, beatings, neglect, and death are portrayed at the ICTY, and all work to position victimized bodies as helpless and feminized. Unable to save them from these violent acts, the Tribunal condemns the violence on their behalf. Thus, practices of paternalism establish legal actors as moral, noble, and lawful adjudicators who protect and avenge victims through the denunciation of Balkan perpetrators.

"The Only Civilized Alternative"

The ability of the ICTY to govern violence, and to be an agent of violence, depends on and (re)produces the assumption that international law is the superior mechanism through which the violence in Bosnia can be addressed. Moreover, it is deemed common sense that any approach must be retributive, juridical, and carceral. This is a paternalistic practice that engages Balkanist logics and essentialist discourses of gender, sexuality, and violence to construct the ICTY as authorized to govern, regulate, and punish. The following extract from the 1994 Annual Report is worth quoting at length, and is emblematic of this Balkanist, paternalistic posturing:

> How could one hope to restore the rule of law and the development of stable, constructive and healthy relations among ethnic groups, within or between independent States, if the culprits are allowed to go unpunished? Those who have suffered, directly or indirectly, from their crimes are unlikely to forgive or set aside their deep resentment. How could a woman who had been raped by servicemen from a different ethnic group or a civilian whose parents or children had been killed in cold blood quell their desire for vengeance if they knew that the authors of these crimes were left unpunished and allowed to move around freely, possibly in the same town where their appalling actions had been perpetrated? *The only civilised alternative* to this desire for revenge is to render justice: to conduct a fair trial by a truly independent and impartial tribunal and to punish those found guilty. If no fair trial is held, feelings of hatred and resentment seething

below the surface will, sooner rather than later, erupt and lead to renewed violence. (ICTY Annual Report 1994, para 15, my emphases)

This excerpt reveals much about the paternalism of international law. It is telling that the president, the author of the annual report, conjures the role of the ICTY and the violence in Bosnia through discourses of therapeutic governance (see Chapter 3). Predicates such as "stable," "constructive," and "healthy" are used to establish the ICTY as a site of international law able to "fix" the "ethnic hatred" and violence "endemic" to the region. Furthermore, the president constructs gendered subject positions in his justification for the Tribunal's existence. The raped woman serves as the ideal referent through which to designate the former Yugoslavia as a place not only beset by (gendered, sexualized, and ethnicized) violence but also teeming with "feelings of hatred and resentment." Balkanist logics and essentialist discourses of gender, sexuality, and violence intersect to (re)produce the ICTY and international law as the "only civilised alternative," rather than risk descent into "vengeance" and "renewed violence." This excerpt not only reflects the violent and violating practices of paternalism (which enable condescending and gendering acts of governance) but legitimates legal practices of victimization and denunciation. By positioning international law as "the only civilised alternative," judges and prosecutors are empowered to criminalize certain acts of violence as well as certain violators. The president justifies punishment as a moral necessity. According to this logic, rather than let former Yugoslav countries seek justice themselves (lest they pursue vengeful justice), the ICTY steps in as the lawful, "civilised" way to hold perpetrators responsible, and thereby punish them, for crimes committed during the conflicts.

As an example of governance and international law, the ICTY espouses a protective, masculine paternalism through its adjudicatory powers. In the case of the Tribunal's early legal texts, this designation of international law as "the only civilised alternative" does crucial justificatory work. In the 1994 Annual Report, the UN is seen to uphold "an impressive corpus of international standards," with the establishment of the Tribunal proof that international justice will be served on "all the individuals found guilty of rape, torture and massacre [who] will be severely punished for their unacceptable disregard of the dignity of other human beings" (ICTY Annual Report 1994, 49). In other instances, "the Balkans" is legible as a place of "madness" and a symbol of the "depths" of "evil" humanity can sink to

(ICTY Annual Report 1998, 66). In these examples, "the Balkans" is presupposed as queer (in the dehumanizing sense): a place of violence, a people characterized by their propensity for committing horrific crimes. The selective listing of atrocities committed during the conflict ("rape, torture and massacre") reaffirm the gendered, Balkanist logics of perpetrators at the ICTY, at the same time as it excises "the Balkans" from "civilized" (western) Europe (see Chapter 3). Elsewhere in the 1998 Annual Report, the ICTY directly addresses perpetrators, reinforcing the assumption of "rational," "moral," and lawful adjudicators in contrast to "irrational," "sadistic" perpetrators:

> To those who made them victims, its proceedings demonstrate why justice is better than revenge. Responding within a framework of law to an attack on the human being, and not within a framework of violence and destruction, is the first step in rebuilding a community from the ruins of a society divided by ethnically-based slaughter. (ICTY Annual Report 1998, 66)

In this excerpt, the ICTY seeks justice, while perpetrators seek revenge. It tacitly (re)produces Balkanist logics and gendered discourses of protective (read: accepted) and dangerous (read: perverted) masculinism. The "rational," paternal need to deliver justice on behalf of victimized populations stands in opposition to the "irrational," "unruly" masculinism that threatens to continue "cycles" of "ethnic hatred." The predicates and subject positions evident in the excerpt above demonstrate how legal discourses establish realities for "the Balkans" and international law. In this way, the designation of an uncontrollable perpetrator justifies, legitimates, and prescribes the exceptional actions of international law. It also contributes to an assumption that "uncivilized" perpetrators are exclusively responsible for violence, absolving practices of violence committed by Western actors (e.g., NATO) and therefore distinguishing between legitimate and illegitimate forms of maiming and killing in international law.

The paternalist practices of international law rely on the condemnation and denunciation of "uncivilized" perpetrators. This is evident in the ICTY's early documents, which (re)produce origin stories about the ICTY and its connection to the postwar tribunals (see Chapter 3). In the 2000 Annual Report, the UNSC is constructed as paving the way for a return to postwar justice. The report notes that "[b]y establishing the Tribunal in 1993, the Security Council made a historic decision and took up one of the greatest challenges since Nürnberg: to say that crimes against humanity and genocide would not go unpunished" (ICTY Annual Report 2000, 47). Similarly, in the UNSC verbatim record of the meeting that marked the Tribunal's establishment, Venezuela's Permanent Representative to the UN explicitly invoked Nuremberg and Tokyo in his address to the UNSC:

> The evolution of international society reveals the need to create a corrective and punitive forum, particularly in the case of crimes affecting the very essence of the civilized conscience, as in the case of crimes against humanity. In Nuremberg and Tokyo we saw the emergence of international courts to try those guilty of the crimes committed during the course of the Second World War. Now the Security Council has decided to act on behalf of the global community of States by establishing an International Tribunal which, as a forum representing all of humanity, will bring to trial and punish those guilty of abominable crimes. (UN Doc S/PV/3217 1993, 6)

By invoking the memory of the postwar tribunals, both the annual report and the statement from the Venezuelan representative (re)produce Balkanist logics of the duty of a "civilized" UN to act and condemn those pre-emptively designated as "guilty of abominable crimes." Here, even before the Tribunal begins its operations, the Balkan perpetrator is denunciated. This presupposition prescribes the actions taken by legal actors at/of the ICTY, so that atrocities committed by Balkan bodies "cannot pass without political condemnation and penal sanctions. Such a situation would be intolerable in modern society" (UN Doc S/PV/3217 1993, 7). Importantly, what the Venezuelan representative makes clear in this statement is the pre/proscriptions enabled by practices of paternalism. At the very least, individuals found guilty under international law face some sort of sanctioned punishment (e.g., imprisonment, criminal charges). But even if found not guilty before the Tribunal, or acquitted of charges, the designation of "war criminal," of perpetrator, remains (see Dauphinée 2007).

Paternalism also manifests in the ICTY's later legal texts, in the guise of condemning whole governments for failing to cooperate with the Tribunal's mandate. For example, in the ICTY Statute, it "[c]alls on all States, *especially* Serbia and Montenegro, Croatia, and Bosnia and Herzegovina, and . . . the Republika Srpska within Bosnia and Herzegovina" to apprehend fugitives of the Tribunal (ICTY Statute 2009, 58, my emphasis). The singling out of former Yugoslav countries is not unexpected. But the subject positioning of these countries and their governments follows a paternalistic logic that infantilizes the region. Statements such as "[t]he Prosecutor . . . has been *especially disappointed* with the failure by Serbia and the Republika Srpska" (ICTY Annual Report 2006, 3, my emphases) and "[t]he Prosecutor has *expressed concern* over the comments made by the new President of Serbia . . . [with] [s]uch rhetoric *a step backwards*" (ICTY Annual Report 2012, 17, my emphases), employ condemnatory language that reinforces the distinction between the "civilized" Tribunal and the "uncivilized" Balkans. In the 2017 Annual Report, Serbia's "non-cooperation with the Tribunal" in arresting remaining fugitives is considered particularly disappointing in light of Serbia having "cooperated in the past," and for the ICTY, this warrants doubt about "the country's commitment to justice for war crimes and its adherence to the rule of law" (ICTY Annual Report 2017, 13; see also ICTY 2007, Completion Strategy, 16 May).

The ICTY (re)produces binary logics that equate international law as representative of order and justice, and "the Balkans" as perpetually prone to "disobedience" and illegality. This subject positioning is not surprising given the assumption built into the foundational ICTY texts that international law offers a superior form of justice than the former Yugoslav countries (ICTY 2004, Completion Strategy, 24 May, para 29). Its legal systems "inadequate," its "sub-standard" adherence to "accepted" norms of accountability and justice, and its recovering political institutions in their "infancy," "the Balkans" is fashioned by the ICTY texts as "incapable," susceptible to "illiberal" values and deeds, and in need of the Tribunal's juridical governance. As one completion strategy report states, "[e]xperience shows that, unfortunately, it is only under international pressure that the States of the former Yugoslavia cooperate with the ICTY" (ICTY 2004, Completion Strategy, November 23, para 26).

The paternalistic language adopted in the ICTY texts sustains broader civilizational logics and gendered discourses in international law. Paternalistic practices legitimate and infuse the legal violences of victimization and denunciation. The ICTY manifests in the Tribunal's foundational documents as the acceptably paternal, masculine figure of international law. But as my analysis has shown, this subject position is far from static, and the (re)production of the ICTY (and international law more broadly) as lawful adjudicator and "the only civilized alternative" is constituted by unstable and impermanent discourses. Indeed, these discourses have the potential to be challenged, deconstructed, and subverted. As I demonstrate in Chapter 5, queering legal violence can also mean unearthing alternative representations of embodiment in international law.

Concluding Thoughts on Governing through Adjudication

Using the case of the ICTY, I have traced how international law and its various legal actors are agents of violence that engage in practices of victimization, denunciation, and paternalism. In this chapter, I argued that the ICTY is an agent of violence, engaging in gendering, agential, and violating practices that (re)produce Balkanist logics and cis-heteronormative discourses of gender, sexuality, and violence. Practices of victimization, denunciation, and paternalism legitimate and prescribe legal actions and categorizations of gendered, sexualized, and ethnicized bodies in international law. International law discursively (re)produces victimization, which attempts to freeze bodies into feminized, homogenized, and silenced victim positions. It engages in denunciatory practices that allow prosecutors and judges to classify, essentialize, and criminalize "uncivilized" perpetrators as sadists and rapists. Moreover, international law engages in paternalistic practices through which violent and violated bodies are juridically known and governed. In the case of the ICTY, the gendered, sexualized, and ethnicized legal subjects constructed through these practices of violence legitimate a carceral response to the Bosnian conflict, and the pejorative classification of "Balkan" bodies as "bad," "perverse," and in need of paternal intervention.

International law is a (queer) governance mechanism that has gendered and gendering, constitutive and agential, and violent and violating capacities. These are enabled by and (re)produce civilizational logics and cis-heteronormative discourses of gender, sexuality, and violence. By engaging in a queer reading and critique of governance and international law, I have paved the way for alternative accounts of bodies at the ICTY. To this end, Chapter 5 challenges these civilizational logics and cis-heteronormative discourses, reflecting on the queer, subversive potential of governance and international law.

5
Subverting International Law and Violence at/of the International Criminal Tribunal for the Former Yugoslavia

The queer reading of governance and international law I have offered thus far is in many ways a bleak one. The various legal actors who embody the Tribunal, including its judges, prosecutors, and defense teams, rely on and perpetuate cis-heteronormative discourses and engage in paternalist, Balkanist logics of governance. Queering governance and international law exposes these violences, but it also reveals moments of resistance, of subverting expectations of how violent and violated bodies encounter the violence of international law. This plurality, of being simultaneously violent and subversive, constitutes international law as a (queer) governance mechanism. This chapter identifies and deconstructs subversive discourses and practices of gender, sexuality, and violence in international law through the case of the ICTY. Practices of subverting violence include challenging practices of victimization, denunciation, and paternalism (see Chapter 4).

Subverting international law and violence is both gendered and gendering, albeit in more tacit ways. For example, in the ICTY texts I analyzed, subversive practices did not extend to the challenging of cis-heteronormative and exclusionary discourses of gender and sexuality. Rather, both the wielding and subverting of violence depended on these gendered discourses. In this chapter I problematize the (re)production of cis-heteronormative and essentialist discourses in and through practices of subversion. Representations of the agency and complexity of survivors and perpetrators disrupt the adjudicatory simplification and violence of international law. But exclusionary discourses of gender and sexuality are still upheld. In other words, cis-heteronormative discourses of gender, sexuality, and violence are crucial to the governing practices of international law, including examples where people subvert violence. As a (queer) governance mechanism, then, international law invokes and (re)installs the straight, cisgender subject of law and violence as common sense, even while it maintains space for subversion. Bodies who resist or do not conform to this gendered expectation are excluded and erased from the stories told about violence. Thus, international law is gendered and gendering, constitutive and agential, and violent and violating through the governance *and* subversion of law's violence.

Subverting violence entails those practices by various actors (e.g., detainees, perpetrators, witnesses, survivors, prosecutors, etc.) who challenge or disrupt the juridical violence of international law. Subversive practices are relational, shifting, and contingent (Touquet and Schulz 2020, 217). For example, the ability of a witness to subvert the legal victimization of the courtroom is restricted by the space afforded for the witness to speak outside the directed lines of questioning, or the power of judges, prosecutors, and the defense to restrict testimony. Chapter 5 develops a queer reading of bodies who resist and subvert dominant discourses of violence in international law. My approach to international law as a (queer) governance mechanism reveals how embodied actors in sites of international law are agential, plural, complicated, and messy. These are actors who are empowered to subvert representations and practices of violence in international law. This chapter traces the pluralities and contradictions that constitute international law as a (queer) governance mechanism and reveals the queer logics that enable its gendered and gendering, constitutive and agential, violent and violating, *and* subversive capacities. This is about exposing the multiple and subversive experiences of violence in international law, and how discourses of gender, sexuality, and violence make these encounters legible. It also means being attentive to how plural, messy, and "noisy" legal subjectivities are seen and heard within international law, even if such recognition is partial and contested.

This chapter proceeds by identifying "noisy" witnesses and survivors, those who challenge the expectations of the court by speaking their trauma beyond what is demanded by international law. Witnesses and survivors subvert their victimization by legal actors, which includes practices that silence, homogenize, and feminize victims (see Chapter 4). These subversive practices reveal the tensions between procedural justice (the justice of the court) and human justice (the justice of the survivors). "Noisy" survivors are also those who challenge the violence of atrocities. Practices of refusal, bodily autonomy, and resistance, or even simply existing, subvert the expectations of how victimized, dehumanized populations should behave, and how they are understood by legal actors. I then introduce the concept of "complex" perpetrators. This is not to say that some perpetrators are complicated, and others are not, or that only perpetrators are complex and other bodies are not (such as survivors). Rather, I use the term "complex" to signal the ways in which perpetrators—both during conflict and in international law—are multidimensional and messy, just as all humans are. Dominant portrayals of perpetrators by ICTY legal actors cast them as vicious rapists (see Chapter 4). But there are examples that reveal the ambiguous position the perpetrator occupies. Moments of compassion toward detainees, or of kindness to neighbors before the war, for example, complicate representations of perpetrators as innately bad. A queer analysis reveals the contingent, plural, and contradictory nature of these representations, of the queer logics that constitute bodies in sites of international law (Heathcote 2019; Weber 2016). In other words, while international law is violent and violating (see Chapter 4), it is also queer, because it is made meaningful through plurality, ambivalence, and resistance to law's violence.

"Noisy" Survivors

Practices of subversion challenge the violence of international law. Within this context, certain people are given the authority to speak (i.e., judges, prosecution team, defense counsel, witnesses) within certain parameters. As I explored in Chapter 4, the authority granted to some actors to speak depends on and reinforces the silencing of others. It might then be useful to describe the Tribunal as an "audio" space, the courtroom functioning to amplify some voices (i.e., court officials) and silence others (i.e., "unruly" witnesses). "Noisy" survivors challenge and subvert the legal violence of silencing in international law, revealing more complicated, multidimensional experiences and accounts of real lives and bodies in sites of conflict. In the previous chapter, I explored examples where during court proceedings, a trial judge may clarify procedural questions, speak to witnesses directly, or adjudicate between the prosecution and the defense regarding lines of questioning. A judge's authority to speak, therefore, is informed by the goals of the trial and of international law: to establish whether individuals are culpable for violations of international humanitarian law (Anderson 2020, 29). This same dynamic is present for all individuals participating at the ICTY, although the level of importance and space allotted to speak vary according to the actor. For witnesses and survivors, their testimonies are significant to the Tribunal to the extent that they prove or disprove a crime or the responsibility of the accused. Similarly, the space given to survivors to bear witness and represent their experiences is limited to the extent that their trauma can be used by the prosecution and defense teams to establish a minimum basis of criminal responsibility (Dembour and Haslam 2004, 154). Procedural justice—the justice of the Tribunal to hold individuals culpable for crimes or to exonerate them and reaffirm their innocence—is the primary goal of witness testimony. Human justice—the justice of the survivors, of those both present in the courtroom and those whose experiences were never investigated by the Tribunal—is seen as a secondary, albeit desirable, function. I address the inequalities between these forms of justice in the discussions that follow.

While survivors are predominantly forced to adhere to the legal performances of the courtroom (see "Victimization" in Chapter 4), there are examples of subversive, "noisy" survivors who challenge the hierarchy between procedural and human justice. These "noisy" witnesses refuse to be silenced, subverting juridical expectations of how legal subjects are supposed to behave. This is not to valorize voice over silence: indeed, as I explore in this chapter, "resistance ..." doesn't "need to be speech-based and vocal to effect a liberating praxis" (Santos de Carvalho 2022, 6). It can also manifest in the ways in which bodies resist the totalizing encounters of violence and push back against their dehumanization. Similarly, as Juliana Santos de Carvalho remarks, "remaining silent can mean a defiant refusal to speak... when a disciplining authority orders an individual ... to give an account of their story, to justify their actions, or to prove their innocence" (2022, 9). In this way, silence can be "noisy" or subversive. Both forms of resistance are gendered and gendering, made meaningful through discourses about what it means to be feminized, homogenized, and silenced victims of violence, and what it means to resist these discourses. "Noisy" survivors challenge the assumption of powerlessness that so often envelops victims of conflict and push back against the strictures of procedural justice. Subversive practices reveal the messiness, complexity, and queer dynamics of international law.

In this chapter, and particularly in this section, I use the concept of resistance to analytically frame moments of subverting violence in international law. As Foucault argues, "[w]here there is power, there is resistance" (1976, 95), so that "discourse can be both an instrument and an effect of power, but also a hindrance, a stumbling-block, a point of resistance and a starting point for an opposing strategy" (1976, 101). Through the case of the ICTY, I see resistance as an analytical tool to conceptualize acts of subversion and refusal to obey the expectations of the courtroom. At the same time, I use resistance to describe the practical resisting moves by witnesses, survivors, and legal actors in international law.[1]

Subverting the Violence of Atrocity

As I argued in Chapter 3, the dominant portrayal of the camps in Bosnia (seen in *Origin Story II*, Chapter 3) consists of emaciated, men enclosed behind the bars of the camp. The camp victim is typically assumed to be a (cis-)man, while images of suffering women show them as victims in mourning seen at sites of mass atrocity (e.g., Srebrenica, see Jacobs 2017; Simić 2014). While each of these portrayals universalize and simplify the gendered experiences of war, they also silence the stories of the very people constituting these images. According to this discourse, victims conform to submission, passivity, and silence (see also Chapter 4). Moments of agency and resistance represented in the ICTY texts and in other forms of bearing witness subvert this figure of the defeated war victim. In this way, international law can be empowering, with agential actors such as witnesses, prosecutors, and perpetrators able to (re)produce and/or subvert victimization. This reflects much of the hope that oppressed groups place in the justice possibilities of international law (see Chapter 6).

While representations and acts that subvert violence at the Tribunal are minimal, they still offer opportunities for deconstructing the assumed mutability of the passive victim in international law. Their acts of subversion take many forms. For some detainees, resistance is an explicit refusal or denial of the violence inflicted on them. Omer Filipović, one of these detainees, powerfully represents how violence was something that could be subverted, even in a context of relentless violation. I speak to Omer's life, survival, and death in Manjača throughout this chapter to trace a life beyond the suffering of the camps. According to one witness, Omer was "a born leader" and was outspoken about the inhumane conditions of the camp (*Brdanin* 2002, Trial hearing 25 February). Before the war, Omer was a history and geography teacher, and vice-president of the municipality in Kljuc. His presence in the camp was a significant source of morale for fellow detainees, as his brother and survivor, Muhamed, reveals to the courtroom:

Q. Was your brother in the same barn as yourself?
A. Yes, until he got in their way, because they realised that my brother was helping the morale of the prisoners. People had become resigned to their fate. They were eating grass. In the daytime people would eat grass they were so hungry. And then my brother would come by and say, "Don't do that. Don't give them pleasure seeing us Muslims eating grass." (*Brdanin* 2002, Trial hearing 5 September)

In this statement, Muhamed presupposes the camp's dehumanizing conditions. Poorly fed by the camp authorities, detainees across the camps in Bosnia were forced to eat grass out of pure hunger. But Omer challenges the dehumanizing effects of the camps. In the various accounts of Omer in *Brdanin*, friends, family, and fellow detainees revere Omer as a hopeful and selfless figure. This subject position becomes even more powerful considering how Omer was treated and violated in Manjača. Muhamed explains:

They were so base that in the morning this damn Bulatovic would bring him breakfast and hot tea. Instead of giving it to him—I apologise to the ladies—instead of giving him the tea to drink, he would take off his pants and poor the hot tea over him. He humiliated him in such a way, but Omer would not give in. (*Brdanin* 2002, Trial hearing 5 September)

The gendered and gendering violence of this moment is expected to humiliate Omer, but as Muhamed makes clear, the violence of the camps could not break him. Omer subverts the perpetrator's expectations of what would happen in this moment of violence, that is, the physical suffering and (sexual) humiliation of hot tea being poured over his naked body. While I am not able to speak to how Omer felt in this moment, Muhamed's retelling of this incident reveals a strength to resist and survive despite the overwhelming violence of the camps. Furthermore, Omer subverted the gendered and sexualized meanings imbued in this moment of violence, by refusing to "give in," to be humiliated by it. At the same time, Muhamed's prefacing of the testimony with "I apologise to the ladies" (re)produces the gendered notions of honor and shame that make this violence meaningful in the courtroom (see Chapter 4). Here, cis-heteronormative discourses of gender, sexuality, and violence are both (re)produced and subverted. In another example, Omer told one guard that if he survived the camp, he would write a book with the guard as one of the main characters (*Brdanin* 2002, Trial hearing 5 September). Thus, at every mention of Omer in the courtroom, his suffering is always countered with his stoicism, subversiveness, and wit. So much so, that at least within the camp, Omer affectively moved the camp detainees. Omer did not survive Manjača, but when his body was placed in a van and taken away, "All the inmates in the camp stood at attention so that the Serbs are [sic] ... afraid of a rebellion" (*Brdanin* 2002, Trial hearing 5 September).

Each of these examples describing Omer challenge what it means to be a victim under international law. Omer embodies the "noisy" survivor, one who resists the legal violence of victimization that constructs homogenized, passive victims. His actions subvert the assumption of a universal experience of victimhood (see Chapter 4), instead revealing the multilayered realities of those subjected to violence. Omer's story—told by his brother and other witnesses as agential and empowered actors in international law—is an example of how the violence of atrocity can be subverted. It also reveals how international law is a mechanism that can amplify these subversive practices. International law offers a space for witnesses and survivors to provide evidence of crimes. This fulfills the juridical mandate of the Tribunal: to prove or disprove the criminal responsibility of indicted individuals. But importantly, my queer analysis of the ICTY texts, and of Omer's experiences represented within them, reveals the pluralities, contingencies, and contradictions that make the Tribunal, and international law, knowable. By being attuned to the *and/or* of international law, of its gendered and gendering, constitutive and agential, violent and violating, *and* subversive practices, it is possible, at the very least, to capture some of the moments (both difficult and hopeful) that constitute the complicated lives of victim-survivors.

At the ICTY, subverting violent acts takes many forms, and as the case of Omer demonstrates, these practices frequently engage multiple people in the hope of uplifting others. In *Kvočka et al.*, one survivor tells of their friends who managed to organize a "ransom" to pay the guard so if they had to die, it would be out of the camps, surrounded by friends and family (*Kvočka et al.* 2000, Trial hearing September 1). Solidarity extended in other ways too. In *Mucić et al.*, a survivor tells of her fellow detainee, Grozdana Cecez, who offered her contraceptive pills to take while being subjected to rape in Čelebići camp (*Mucić et al.* 1997, Trial hearing April 3). While Ms. Antić (the survivor testifying) reveals that she did not need them due to her having had a hysterectomy prior to the war, Grozdana's actions challenge the expectation of a passive, feminized victim in international law (see Chapter 4). It was not always possible to resist violence, but Grozdana's taking of contraceptive pills during her imprisonment is a powerful refusal of the violent and violating practices of atrocity.

Consider, for example, how one survivor told the Tribunal of being raped in the camp: "I defended myself, and I asked him why he was doing that. But I had to, under pressure from him, to take my clothes off and lie down on the foam mattress" (*Kvočka et al.* 2001, Trial Judgment, para 554). Here again, violence is met with resistance, even if such violence cannot be curtailed. In this example, the survivor positions herself as a resisting woman, someone who would defend herself against sexual violence. Gendered and sexualized presuppositions inform this decision. To what extent did questions of bodily honor and integrity inform how the survivor sees herself, and feels the need to prove to the Tribunal, and under international law, that she resisted being raped? It is also possible that this emphasis on defending herself could be a way to reclaim herself, to prove to herself and the courtroom that she is more than a victimized body. While there are no clear answers to this without speaking to the witness herself, my queer reading of her subverting violence and emphasizing it in the courtroom urges me to consider both and all ways of making sense of her resistance. It is possible that gendered discourses of "expected" sexual relationships and "unacceptable" ones constituted her testimony *as well as* a desire to move beyond the victimized, raped woman subject position so frequently invoked in international law (see Chapter 4). This speaks to both the "split subject" (Heathcote 2019) and queer *and/or* logics (Weber 2016). The witness is not one or the other, but a plurally embodied, gendered actor.

The examples from the ICTY I have so far discussed engage with detainees and survivors who have vocalized their resistance. But the agential, resisting detainee is not universally "noisy," and can indeed embody subversion through acts of silence and a determination to live (Touquet and Schulz 2020, 220). The ability to exist, and to survive atrocities, is perhaps the ultimate form of resistance against those who seek to annihilate the detainees. In one testimony recounting his subjection to beating, one survivor was asked if the beating hurt him very much, to which he replied: "Yes, there was pain but I was fighting, I wanted to live. I wanted to live" (*Tadić* 1996, Trial hearing 19 June). In another testimony, one survivor simply said: "Well dammit, we survived" (*Brdanin* 2002, Trial hearing 8 July). For one rape survivor who contemplated committing suicide (itself an act of bodily resistance to which I return below), fellow detainees urged her: "No, please do not; we shall survive, we shall live, to tell the truth" (*Tadić* 1996, Trial hearing 19 July). And even in less explicit ways, decisions such as pretending to be dead to avoid being killed represent moments of resistance (*Delić* 2008, Trial Judgment, para 216).

In each of these examples, the determination to live subverts the dominant discourses in international law of silenced, passive victims (see Chapter 4). Their ability to challenge this simplified image of victimhood is not to deny the reality of dehumanization and violation experienced by victims and survivors. I do not identify these acts of subversion as signs of superiority, of the strength and determination of some detainees against the "weakness" and "hopelessness" of others. Understandably, many victims are hollowed by the violence they endured, and the capacity to survive or resist against their destruction is not always possible within the totalizing confines of the camp. Seeking to remain invisible, to "go along" with some forms of violence to survive, "can in turn be seen as a resistance ritual" (Bacic 2017, 86; see also Scott 1989, 50). I identify acts of resistance within the ICTY's representation of atrocity because they signal the multiplicity of the human condition and illustrate the necessity of sites of international law to pay attention to plural experiences of trauma and survival. The resolute statements and intention to survive in the ICTY texts open possibilities for international law to embrace plural realities of war and to consider how these discourses might contribute to human justice.

Similarly, acts of reclaiming autonomy through suicide and bodily materiality disrupt juridical scripts of victimhood in international law (see Chapter 4). Acts and attempts of suicide challenge the power of perpetrators over detainees, through detainees reclaiming autonomy over their ability to live and die. In the ICTY texts, moments where detainees consider committing suicide or attempt to do so are accompanied by testimonies of severe trauma.[2] As the earlier examples demonstrate, survivors who reveal their thoughts and attempts at suicide to the Tribunal recall the intervention of other detainees. In one example, two women planned to commit suicide, but according to the testimony of one of them, the other "took me by the shoulders and pulled me out," the reason for deciding to live not explained but pivotal to them making it out of the camp alive (*Mucić et al.* 1997, Trial hearing 18 March). In other examples from the ICTY texts, the decision to commit or not commit suicide is driven by thoughts of family and the future:

> [T]hinking about the future, the history, and I thought well, my children will say it wasn't the Serbs who killed my—our father but he killed himself. And then I decided not to kill myself, to let them do it. And somehow I felt better after that. (*Brdanin* 2002, Trial hearing 3 June)

Both the decision to die and then to live are acts that subvert the simplified victim subject in international law. The detainees' desire to die (on their own terms) becomes apparent in the context of the violence of the camps. While suicide is frequently depicted as an act of (feminine) weakness, of an inability or unwillingness to stoically suffer through pain, I read these moments as forms of resistance that subvert the power relations of the camp and complicate victimhood in international law. Lauren Wilcox's analysis of Palestinian suicide bombers offers insights into the agential capacity of suicide in places of violence. Wilcox argues that suicide "upsets the assumption of the subject driven by self-preservation" (2015, 81). Her focus on suicide bombing draws attention to the unique ways in which this violence destroys the boundaries of bodily materiality. Wilcox's insights are valuable to analyses of suicide as resistance because they challenge the notion of disembodied subjection. Detainees in the camps across Bosnia are not powerless in death, as their reclamation of bodily autonomy, of "suicidal resistance[,] is a message inscribed on the body when no other means will get through" (Spivak 2004, 95, quoted in Wilcox 2015, 89).

Spivak's point here is also illustrative of the inhumane conditions of living and subjection to violence that forces people to consider suicide to regain their humanity. While within the context of the camps in Bosnia, suicide is a form of agency that allows detainees to exert control over their fate (see *Mucić et al.* 1997, Trial hearing 25 March), the conditions of violence which constitute the decision to live or die restrict detainees' options for expressing agency. While I read testimonies of attempted suicide as an indication of bodies who subvert traditional understandings of victimization in conflict, I also recognize that in the absence of sustained violence and trauma, suicide likely would not have been the only option for expressing resistance. Suicide as a form of resistance—as an example of "noisy" survivors—disturbs how survival and dignity is typically understood in international law. It also reveals the conditions under which certain forms of resistance are enabled or curtailed.

While suicide as an act of subverting violence points to the severity and trauma of atrocity, I close this subsection of the chapter with an example of bodily refusal and play. This example offers glimpses into even the smallest moments of humor, joy, and hope within the context of, and subjection to, violence and dehumanization. The example in *Kvočka et al.* reveals how detainees were ordered by guards to signal the three-finger Serb salute. One detainee recounted:

> We all obeyed, but it's a little funny, because one man didn't have a finger. He was lacking a finger, so he couldn't press these three fingers together. And they liked that, and they beat him and they said, "Well, he's fucking around with us. He doesn't want to make this three-fingered sign but only does it with two of his fingers." (*Kvočka et al.* 2000, Trial hearing 1 September)

The detainee, by virtue of missing a finger, subverts the guard's orders and undermines the three-finger salute simply by not having the bodily features to do it. His missing finger cannot be made to conform to the violence, a fact of bodily refusal that offers a moment of humor in the presence of trauma. This resistance affects the guards, seen in the frustrated expressions that the detainee is "fucking around with us," despite the fact, of course, that he physically does not have the finger to form the salute. This example is a moment of queerness. It shows how "the fleshy materiality of the body" is "affected by, and saturated with, power, and how protean yet banal many of its tactics remain" (Solomon 2015, 66). It is also strange, nonconforming, and playful, a moment juxtaposed with the ubiquitous violence of the camp. In the context of the grave testimonies represented in the ICTY texts, this is an example that embodies the multidimensional subjectivities who inhabit spaces of violence and international law. While it was the only example in the cases I analyzed that reflected even the briefest experience of humor and play, it nevertheless challenges the construction of homogenized, silenced, and "uncivilized" victims in international law (see Chapter 4).

Subverting Violence in the Courtroom

As a (queer) governance mechanism, international law is embodied by, and makes space for, agential actors to make sense of violence. Survivors who testify in the courtroom exert their power to bear witness and give testimony, something that subverts the hierarchy between victim and perpetrator, insofar as the victim/survivor/witness now holds power over the perpetrator/defendant (K. Campbell et al. 2019, 259). "Noisy" witnesses also challenge the juridical violence of international law by pushing back against judges', prosecutors', and defense attorneys' attempts to silence and homogenize them (Elander 2013, 115, 2018a, 7; see Chapter 4). At the Tribunal, the primary purpose of testifying is to provide evidence to prove or disprove a crime and the culpability of the defendant (Dembour and Haslam 2004, 154). While the ICTY recognizes that providing testimony has cathartic value, offering survivors the opportunity to bear witness and reclaim their experiences of violence, the goal of procedural justice often eclipses that of human justice. For example, it is telling that in the ICTY's completion strategies submitted to the UNSC, the president and the prosecutor note that the "evidence of the commission of crimes . . . is presented . . . wherever possible in writing in lieu of live testimony of witnesses" (ICTY 2007, Completion Strategy, 16 May, para 11). Moreover, the prosecutor is encouraged to "restrict the examination of witnesses to key points" and that all trials are to have "strict time limits," meaning that prosecutors should "reassess the numbers of witnesses they need to call" (ICTY 2007, Completion Strategy, 16 May, para 11). In Chapter 4, I showed how practices of silencing and curtailing witness testimonies constitute legal violences integral to international law's ability to govern through adjudication. It is within this constraining environment where procedural justice is prioritized over processes of trauma and memory, that some witnesses subvert the conventional subject position of the obedient legal subject.

The "noisy" witness in the courtroom is a subversive force in international law. For example, some witnesses refuse to embody certain ethnic categories (re)produced by the Tribunal. In *Mucić et al.*, one witness responds to a question that their ethnicity is "Yugoslav," before being pressed by the prosecutor to respond with "Serbian" (*Mucić et al.* 1997, Trial hearing 3 April; see also *Kvočka et al.* 2000, Trial hearing 3 July). In *Brđanin*, Judge Carmel Agius plays a forceful, intervening role in attempting to construct witnesses as members of particular ethnoreligious communities:

Q. What is your religion?
A. Bosnian.
Q. Do you practice a religion?
A. No.
Q. You were married in 1964 and have two sons aged 33 and 25 years?

JUDGE AGIUS: One moment. Because I'm sure there must have been a mix-up in the interpretation here, because when he was asked for his ethnicity he answered a Muslim when he was asked for his religion, he answered a Bosnian. And when he was asked whether he practices a religion—practices a religion, he said no. Are you a Bosniak?
THE WITNESS: [Interpretation] Well, yes, for me it's all the same thing, and that's why I said what I said. A Bosniak, yes. Okay.
JUDGE AGIUS: Of Islamic faith—of Muslim faith.
THE WITNESS: [Interpretation] Yes. (*Brdanin* 2002, Trial hearing July 8)

In this example, the judge attempts to and eventually succeeds at constructing the witness as Bosnian Muslim in international law, a subject position Judge Agius and the prosecutor deem important in the context of trying to prove ethnically motivated crimes (see also *Brdanin* 2002, Trial hearing 16 October). The judge is dissatisfied with the witness's answer, not least because it challenges the ethnic and religious essentialism of the Tribunal. Judge Agius seeks a straightforward answer that separates religion from ethnicity, one that validates his idea of how cultural identities are seen and practiced in Bosnia, in contrast to how Bosnians actually live and identify. The judge's presuppositional knowledge is legible through logics of Balkanism, ones that misrepresent the region and elevate (western) European knowledge of "the Balkans" as *the* truth, rather than follow how the witness understands his own ethnic identity.

Beyond challenging ethnic categories, witnesses subvert legal violence by speaking freely about the atrocities they have experienced (*Brdanin* 2002, Trial hearing 25 April). To subvert violence in international law is to challenge the hierarchy between procedural and human justice (re)produced in the courtroom. In the example below, the survivor centers his embodiment by refusing to perform the legal script of the Tribunal:

> I apologise. I cannot just say simply "yes" and "no." I am not in Celebici. I am not in the silo. I am not in Musala. I am not in Trnovo. Please allow me to respond completely in details. If necessary, we can stay here for one year so that in details we can spell everything out from A to Z. I recognise this court and I want to tell what I have lived through. (*Mucić et al.* 1997, Trial hearing 5 May)

The survivor's statement reveals the persistence of trauma beyond the confines of the prison camps. Taking this survivor's testimony seriously means recognizing that "people experience war not only materially, but also emotionally" (Sjoberg 2015, 450). The survivor points to his imprisonment and dehumanization in the camps as justification for why he cannot reduce his testimony to "yes" and "no" responses. These places are presupposed as sites of violence, spaces where physical and psychological harm reduced possibilities for resistance and agency. The survivor's desire and need to share his trauma speaks directly to the dehumanization he faced in the camps. His subject position in international law, then, is not one of the silent, submissive detainee, but a powerful survivor and witness with the ability to expose the crimes of the accused and the broader structures that allowed violence to occur. This survivor's statement is a clear example of how "witnesses do continually resist the legal counter-narrative" of the international criminal trial (Mertus 2004, 114). He states, "I am not in the silo," a declaration laced with meaning about both the literal and symbolic siloes detainees were forced into at the camps. It also challenges the silo effects of international law, of the disempowering implications of testifying at the ICTY not on one's own terms, but according to the terms of the courtroom.

While reinforcing his respect for the Tribunal ("I recognise this court"), seeing it as a vehicle for justice and a space for him to bear witness (see also Chapter 6), the survivor also challenges the underlying norms of international law, of what a witness is expected to do and say before the Tribunal. As I revealed in Chapter 4, his statement is met with admonishment from the defense counsel, who undermines the intentions of the witness to provide evidence and threatens to have him removed if he continues to exhibit this behavior in a court of law. The possibility of being removed from the courtroom and having his testimony deemed unreliable is prescribed by his challenge to the ICTY's procedural processes. But this example reflects the possibility of international law to adapt and center survivor's needs, so that "the courtroom ... [could be] a site for social mobilisation: a platform that gives people a voice and makes them visible" (Haddeland and Franko 2021, 3). Tribunals are arguably sites of formality and adherence to legality, and so other mechanisms of justice (e.g., truth commissions, people's tribunals) are frequently offered as more "suitable" spaces for survivors to provide unfettered accounts of their trauma. But the ICTY, as this example illustrates, is a site constituted by complicated and subversive bodies, a site of international law that cannot avoid the human and embodied experience of violence. The survivor in this instance is (paternalistically) scolded for his response, revealing the unyielding power of the Tribunal over its legal subjects. His presence, however, is a promising indication of the possibility for tribunals to better center survivors, whether that be through survivor impact statements prepared prior to the trial and delivered in the courtroom, or the opportunity to fully reflect on their experiences during the trial.

This kind of sensitivity to human justice is exhibited in *Brdanin*, an exception to the dominant posturing by the judges, defense team, and prosecution evident across the texts I analyzed. Prosecution attorney Ms. Korner made the following statement in response to a witness testimony being curtailed by the elevation of procedural justice: "Your Honour, I'm—I'm slightly distressed that the witness's account of what is clearly a harrowing event is being interrupted by an argument of law" (*Brdanin* 2002, Trial hearing 5 September). Ms. Korner's statement demonstrates the subversive potential of these kinds of actors in international law. It reveals a dissatisfaction with the legal processes of the courtroom and its implications for human justice.

"Noisy" survivors (as well as the exceptional statement by Ms. Korner) are strange, queer subjects in the context of the courtroom, because they challenge the assumed obedience of witnesses to a court of law. Beyond this legal space, their experiences reflect trauma and survival, and the human complexity that characterizes all embodied subjectivities. "Noisy" survivors are queer because they occupy the *and/or* (Weber 2016) and inhabit plural subjectivities (Heathcote 2019). They resist singular narratives of violence and embody multiple and contradictory subject positions, simultaneously (see Chapter 2). It is the messy and multilayered human experience that challenges the coherency of international law. This is a coherency that depends on denunciating "uncivilized" perpetrators, silencing feminized and homogenized victims, and paternalistically positioning international law and its representatives as "the only civilized alternative" (see Chapter 4). Despite this, my analysis of "noisy" survivors reveals that practices of subverting violence do not necessarily entail subverting cis-heteronormative and essentialist discourses of gender and sexuality. While I discussed some instances of resistance to violence intended to sexually humiliate detainees evident in the ICTY texts, subversive practices are mainly intelligible through an overarching adherence to cis-heteronormativity as the common sense. Similarly, international legal actors construct perpetrators in ways that maintain the cis-heteronormative juridical subject, even when perpetrators subvert what is expected of them as agents of violence. This reaffirms the seemingly contradictory ways that international law is both violent and subversive, a (queer) governance mechanism that maintains cis-heteronormative discourses and civilizational logics, while always already containing queer potential for addressing (in)justice.

"Complex" Perpetrators

All actors who are the subject of or are engaged in the governing practices of international law maintain multiple and complicated subjectivities. As with victim-survivors, perpetrators also have the capacity to subvert violence, and my queer reading of the ICTY illuminates the simultaneous construction of perpetrators as sadistic criminals *and* as kind, sympathetic people by witnesses, prosecutors, and judges. This speaks directly to Heathcote's concept of the "split subject," one that is "split, splitting, or able to be fractured in multiple ways" (2019, 120). "Complex" perpetrators are simultaneously sympathetic and violent, plurally embodied and legible in international law. So far, I have demonstrated that international law mainly (re)produces civilizational logics and cis-heteronormative discourses of gender, sexuality, and violence (see Chapter 4). Deconstructing the perpetrator subject position allows me to disturb the dominant governing logics and gendered discourses of international law, of the perpetrator as the hyper-heteromasculine homophobic *and/or* (homo)sexually aberrant villain. Here, I argue that examples of perpetrators subverting violence challenge these scripts by tempering the gendered Othering predicates used to describe the perpetrator. When perpetrators resist violence in the ICTY texts, legal actors do not frame them as hyper-heteromasculine and dangerous Balkan criminals, but neither do they move beyond the cis-heteronormative and heteropatriarchal discourses that are held as common sense in international law.

My analytical framing of perpetrators in this section complicates a one-dimensional perpetrator subject position. I tease out some of the ways in which people and bodies are messy and complex, and that representations of violence both highlight and obscure such complexity. This is because practices of denunciation such as those explored in Chapter 4 "tend to obscure the intensely personal and varied processes through which ordinary, otherwise law-abiding civilians can become active participants in genocidal violence" (Anderson and Jessee 2020, 4). My queer analysis deconstructs the dominant framings of perpetrators in international law and how they both make legible, and are made legible through, the governance of violence. As with earlier discussions in this chapter, discourses of gender and sexuality tacitly signify the examples and excerpts discussed in this section. Here, I complicate the perpetrator subject position by exposing the plural identities and experiences that constitute them, at the same time as these moments are laced with heteropatriarchal discourses. I analyze examples of perpetrators showing moments of compassion, mercy, and friendliness within the ICTY texts. These examples must not undermine the severity of crimes committed by prison guards and authorities, nor excuse responsibility for the trauma of victims and survivors. Instead, they illuminate the humanity of perpetrators as messy and complicated participants of violence. Unearthing the broader human actions of perpetrators challenges the simplistic, civilizational logics and gendered discourses of the conventional perpetrator subject position constructed in/by international law (see Chapter 4). This is a possibility for international law to become more attuned to the plural and complicated subjectivities that constitute humanness, as well as to acknowledge the potential for rehabilitation, forgiveness, and societal healing. These discussions, then, are about embracing the queerness of *and/or* logics, of the ways in which practices of violence are refracted through plural and contradictory systems of meaning.

The unsettling and uncomfortable coexistence of human morality with deadly violence appears strange in the context of simplistic, civilizational predicates of perpetrators evident in Chapter 4. But my queer reading is about engaging with the plural ways that bodies are lived, imagined, and understood. It is not a matter of *either/or*; that is, of individuals as innocent victims *or* guilty perpetrators. Instead, queerness is present in the split, in the *and/or* of this binary (Heathcote 2019; Weber 2016), for the perpetrator simultaneously inhabits merciful *and* violent subjectivities. While my analysis of perpetrators subverting violence through the case of the ICTY challenges dominant gendered scripts of criminality invoked by the trial judgments (see Chapter 4), I deploy queer theorizing here as a way of grappling with the messiness, multiplicity, and contradictory ways in which perpetrators can be both humane and violent. I begin by briefly reflecting on how Miroslav Kvočka (the first defendant in the multi-accused *Kvočka et al.*) exhibited kindness to the Muslim community before the war. I then identify examples where camp authorities and guards protected detainees from the violence of others. Each of these examples reveals the complicated subjecthood of those positioned as perpetrators of violence. They also resist and subvert the conventional discourses of criminality in international law by illustrating the complicated presence of kindness that can also constitute the perpetrator subject position.

Friendly Neighbors and Familial Ties

While the ICTY predominantly casts perpetrators as vengeful and violent (see Chapter 4), there are some examples where perpetrator subjecthood is complicated by prior expressions of friendliness to the enemy Other (see Anderson and Jessee 2020, 4). In the court proceedings, Miroslav Kvočka describes his behavior as kind and benevolent to his Muslim neighbors. It is significant that as an individual accused before an international tribunal for crimes against Bosnian Muslims, Kvočka details his history of friendship with the Muslim community. His marriage to a Muslim woman (with whom he had two children), and his close relationship to Muslim friends and acquaintances suggests an individual far removed from the ultra-nationalist figure responsible for crimes against Bosnian Muslims (*Kvočka et al.* 2001, Trial Judgment, para 331). By his family's and his own account, Kvočka was an upstanding citizen, an ally to the Muslim community, even sheltering them in his home as tensions increased in Bosnia (*Kvočka et al.* 2001, Trial Judgment, para 331). The Trial Judgment outlines how "during the conflict, when Muslim funerals became difficult to hold, he provided security to such ceremonies at the request of the local Muslim clergy" (*Kvočka et al.* 2001, Trial Judgment, para 332). While much of his testimony recounts examples of his relationship to Muslim friends, extended family, and acquaintances, from the outset, he emphasizes his marriage to a Muslim woman. Kvočka's own predication of himself as a kind and caring friend of the Muslim community is upheld through heteropatriarchal familial discourses. He provides examples of serving as best man (*kum*) to a Muslim man and a Serb woman in their marriage ceremony, explaining that to be someone's *kum* is "very intimate, very close, [a form] of friendship, and the kum is almost equivalent, and in fact is equivalent to a brother" (*Kvočka et al.* 2000, Trial hearing 29 February). Gendered discourses of matrimony, brotherhood, and familial life anchor Kvočka's testimony and shape his own understanding of himself as an upstanding citizen and part of the Muslim community. Kvočka demonstrates to the court that there is no better test of his amity to Muslims than through familial and matrimonial ties. His ability to subvert discourses of violence is one that therefore relies on, and upholds, cis-heteronormative discourses and practices.

Kvočka positions himself as the benevolent neighbor. By narrating these moments of kindness, he is predicated as innocent and peaceful, a person detached from the crimes against humanity that he would later commit in the Omarska prison camp (see Anderson 2020, 36). If the Tribunal is to put faith in these accounts—which were supported by witness testimony—then Kvočka's perpetrator subjectivity becomes complicated by the dual presence of kindness and violence. It reaffirms Hannah Arendt's (1963) thesis of the "banality of evil," the ability of "normal" or ordinary people to commit atrocities by following orders and performing their duties. Kvočka is not predicated as psychopathic or monstrous in the descriptions of his deeds prior to his position at Omarska. On the contrary, his behavior to the Muslim community before the conflict could be deemed kind and thoughtful. The Tribunal took this evidence into consideration in its sentencing, noting that the "Trial Chamber is ... persuaded that Kvočka is normally of good character" (*Kvočka et al.* 2001, Trial Judgment, para 716). But in the same paragraph, the judges also acknowledged that "holding a position of respect and trust in the community" likely allowed for his criminal conduct in the camp (*Kvočka et al.* 2001, Trial Judgment, para 716). While Kvočka and other defense witnesses attest to his kindness to Muslims, the Trial Chamber concludes that such kindness only extended to his friends and relatives in the camp (*Kvočka et al.* 2001, Trial Judgment, para 715).

This example illuminates the complicated and contradictory actions and identities that constitute the perpetrator subject position. It stands in contrast to the sadistic perpetrator discourse that dominates representations of war criminals in international law (see Chapter 4). Kvočka's crimes and personhood appear even more peculiar and queer, precisely because he embodies the paradox of the banality of evil. He is both "normal," evidenced in his kindness and humanity; and violent, exemplified in his responsibility and complicity in the crimes committed at Omarska. His actions and personhood, therefore, are far from simplistic. His kindness subverts the figure of the sadistic war criminal and disturbs the conventional discourses of who and what constitutes criminality in international law. Rather than uphold a dichotomy between kindness and violence, or to cast violence out as an abnormality, this case reveals that perpetrators embody the messiness of the human condition. Violence *and* kindness constitute humanity. The act of committing violence, of being violent, is not unhuman or monstrous; it characterizes human life. While this statement should be obvious, it demands further consideration, because the predominant framing of perpetrators as brutal sadists proscribes their humanity. As my queer analysis of perpetrators indicates, these figures are complicated human beings, precisely because they occupy multiple subjectivities, even those that ought to contradict each other. While the perpetrator is characterized through the act of perpetration, it is important to remember that "the perpetrator, as a person, existed before the moment of perpetration and continues to exist afterward" (Anderson 2020, 33–34). Being attentive to the multiple lives and identities of perpetrators thus offers opportunities to move beyond discursive practices that denunciate and incarcerate "evil" perpetrators in international law.

Mercy and Violence

Across several of the ICTY cases I analyzed, evidence suggests that some perpetrators engaged in acts of mercy, if not moments of kindness, in the face of pervading violence. While these examples are minimal in contrast to the overwhelming evidence of violence against detainees, they provide an alternative discourse of perpetrators in international law. For example, a guard prevented another guard from killing three women with a knife (*Delić* 2008, Trial Judgment, para 317), other guards defended detainees and ordered guards "not to touch" them (*Brdanin* 2002, Trial hearing 4 September; *Kvočka et al.* 2000, Trial hearing 31 August), while another refused to rape a woman after being ordered to by his superior (*Mucić et al.* 1997, Trial hearing 3 April). I am interested in the gendered and gendering discourses and practices that organize these examples of resisting and subverting violence. That is, I am curious about the essentialist discourses of gender that constitute these moments, of the gendering norms through which the guards refuse to violate women detainees. Do these same guards intervene or resist violence against men detainees? Are some forms of violence deemed acceptable, and others—because of whom they target and what forms they take—deemed perverse? Without speaking to the guards, these questions remain unanswered. But they are ones that arise from my queer analysis of the ICTY texts and what insights it provides for international law more broadly.

Perpetrators can subvert individual acts of violence through these examples, but they can never escape their complicity in the broader structures of violence that enabled atrocities to occur. While my queer reading of perpetrators reveals that they have the capacity to resist and challenge violence, this must be contextualized against the many more examples where they willingly participated in or enabled the systematic violation of detainees. The judges came to this conclusion in the *Kvočka et al.* Trial Judgment, where they argued:

> Kvočka was more than merely a passive or reluctant participant in the criminal enterprise. He actively contributed to the everyday functioning and maintenance of the camp and he remained culpably indifferent to the crimes committed therein. His participation enabled the camp to continue unabated in its insidious policies and practices. (*Kvočka et al.* 2001, Trial Judgment, para 407)

Similarly, the judges addressed Kvočka directly, emphasizing that "not only did you know of the system of persecution which Omarska camp represented but you also agreed with it and made it possible for the system to function" (ICTY 2003). Thus, examples of perpetrators subverting violence need to be understood alongside their complicity in and responsibility for the severe and traumatic conditions enabled within sites of atrocity. The following example from *Delić* reveals how practices of subverting violence frequently occurred within and enabled broader forms of suffering:

> I was brought to that place, when they then raised my legs to the back. Our faces were facing the ground. It was very difficult to breathe. At one point, the Mujahedin that I knew called "Habib," who was in that group that had captured me, ran up to help me. He brought a piece of cardboard and placed it under my face so that I could breathe. He brought me a cup of coffee so that I could drink. And at one point, he untied my hands as if to help me. (*Delić* 2007, Trial hearing 4 October)

Habib's actions in this example offer a moment of reprieve for the witness, who was in the middle of being tortured. Being given a moment to breathe, a drink to quench his thirst, and a break from having his wrists bound are undoubtedly significant for the detainee. But Habib did not stop the torture. On the contrary, these "kindnesses" allowed the violence to continue. This is a clear example of how perpetrators can both subvert and maintain violence, a seeming paradox but one that is crucial to the functioning of the camp. My queer reading of governance and international law through the ICTY texts exposes these *and/or* logics, of the ways that various actors (e.g., witnesses, victim-survivors, perpetrators, defendants, prosecutors, judges, etc.) are agential participants in the governance of violence, just as much as they are constituted by them.

My analysis of these individuals is difficult, insofar as I cannot comfortably characterize these guards as merciful or kind, because they remain complicit in the persecution and dehumanization of detainees. It is this discomfort, this unsettling presence of both cruelty and kindness that constitutes the perpetrator subject position in international law. Acts of kindness are peculiar or queer in contrast to the pervading violence of the camp. The following extract from *Brdanin* exemplifies the complicated coexistence of violence and mercy. Omer, the "noisy" survivor I discussed earlier in this chapter, was killed in the camp. Two guards removed the wedding ring from

Omer's body, and the loss of the ring was a severe source of trauma for his relatives. I quote Omer's brother, Muhamed, at length:

Q. The day he died, did you see him?
A. I did see him on the 29th. Omer passed away in the evening of the 28th, and I was allowed on the 29th to see him. So I did see him on the 29th, about 4.00. And when I saw him, I saw him dead. He was absolutely naked. He had been stripped. And on his hand he didn't even have his wedding ring. As my cousin Nihad Filipovic was with me, I said to Nihad, "Examine him closely whether there is a wedding ring." And then according to the Islamic custom, I read a prayer. But Nihad went down again and said, "There's no wedding ring." I bent down and kissed my brother. And if [sic] person who was in charge of those two Chetniks—he was an officer, a captain—he came up to me and expressed his condolences and said literally, "Please accept my sincere condolences, and be assured that I am not in favour of these things." And then I said, "Thank you, dear God, that in this fucking Bosnia there is someone who doesn't agree with this. Did they really have to take his wedding ring off?" ... And when Omer was exhumed, when I transferred Omer's body from Banja Luka to Kljuc, I found the wedding ring on Omer's skeleton and I assume that the captain that expressed his condolences forced these other two Chetniks to return the wedding ring, because he knew that they were the people who stripped him and they could—they were the only ones who could have stolen it. So the wedding ring was found and when he was exhumed, we buried him with the wedding ring. (*Brdanin* 2002, Trial hearing 5 September)

This testimony is a powerful example of how small moments of compassion complicate *and* enable cruelty. The captain in this example cannot be absolved of his complicity in Omer's death. As a captain and authority over other guards, a more merciful action would be to prevent the violence and killing of detainees, or to use his position of power to help detainees escape the camp. Of course, it can be difficult to ascertain the whole context of this captain's situation, of the modes of power that might have prevented him from resisting or refusing violence. But to valorize this captain based on this one moment of kindness is to risk exonerating the other times when he (willingly or otherwise) participated in violence. I identify this example not to dishonor the victims and survivors, but to contrast this seemingly "kind" act against the predominant representations of perpetrator cruelty (see Chapter 4).

The captain's retrieval of the wedding ring illustrates his humanness, his capacity to do and be beyond the sadistic Balkan perpetrator subject position identified in Chapter 4. As Muhamed recounts this moment to the courtroom, he also recognizes the compassion of the captain. By proclaiming: "Thank you, dear God, that in this fucking Bosnia there is someone who doesn't agree with this," the witness positions the captain as an exception to the norm of violence that constitutes not only the camp, but Bosnia itself. The strange yet welcoming kindness of the captain is juxtaposed by "those two Chetniks," ostensibly seen as cruel, compassionless guards. The witness's use of *chetnik* to describe the perpetrators in this instance, and the lack of this signifier when describing the captain, is also significant. *Chetnik* is an ethnic insult used against Bosnian Serbs in this context. By invoking this subject position for the perpetrators and not for the captain, the witness is distinguishing "those two Chetniks" as the enemy, those who seek the suffering of Bosnian Muslims in service of Serbhood. Describing them as *chetniks*, it is therefore not surprising to Muhamed that the guards would take Omer's ring, another form of violence expected in the Bosnian conflict. But the actions of the captain subvert this expectation. The apparent exasperation evident in Muhamed's thanking of the captain is present because he could not possibly believe that kindness could exist alongside systematic violence. As with the Kvočka example, this excerpt reflects the complex constitution of the perpetrator subject position in international law. By deconstructing the assumption of perpetrators as absolute monsters, it is possible to reveal the complicated layers of humanity that enable both kindness and violence to coexist.

This example of how the perpetrator can embody both violence and mercy is a paradox that disrupts dominant binaries and instead occupies the split and *and/or* logics. My queer reading of this excerpt also reveals that this moment of subverting violence is gendered and gendering, evident through the presuppositional knowledge that constitutes the significance and removal of the wedding ring, as well as its subsequent retrieval. As I argued in Chapter 2, my QPDA toolbox consists of predication, which entails tracing how subjects *and* objects are endowed with qualities and meaning. Thus, while the discussions in this book mostly center human bodies, I also acknowledge the gendered power of objects and artifacts. Meaning is stored and invested in objects, in the materiality of these artifacts, "but also in them being inherently bound to a special person, a place or an event, or a combination of these" (Rydén 2018, 515). The wedding ring embodies the potential for further violence; to remove the object from the dead, and from the family of the dead, presents the opportunity for a sustained infliction of harm. As a symbol of love, intimacy, and human connection, the predication of the wedding ring is (re)deployed in ways that pre/proscribe the subject positions of guards and victim-survivors.

The violence involved in this example—of removing the wedding ring from a deceased man's body—is predicated on heteropatriarchal discourses of gender and sexuality. The wedding ring is meaningful because it is presupposed by norms and values of marriage, family, and the role of the father/husband in this familial arrangement. The captain understands the significance of the wedding ring to Omer's surviving relatives, and to the dignity of Omer's dead body (see Simić 2014, 166). A close reading of this interaction—of the guards removing the wedding ring, and the captain eventually returning it to Omer's remains—reveals the emotional investment in personal artifacts, of (dis)respecting the dead by removing/replacing the wedding ring. Indeed, one of the first things Muhamed and his cousin Nihad do is check to see whether Omer still had his wedding ring. The wedding ring is meaningful, personal, and significant for how Omer's family remember and memorialize him. It symbolizes Omer's subject position as a husband, a role that fulfills the cis-heteromasculine expectations of manhood in Bosnia (Pavlović 1999, 132). For the two guards to remove his wedding ring, this is an added violence, an insult to his family members, a way of stripping Omer of this gendered role, and of disconnecting him from his family. In contrast, the captain's decision to retrieve the ring and place it back with Omer can be read as a kindness that reinforces the heteropatriarchal significance of the wedding ring and of Omer's lasting identity as a husband and an important member of his (extended) family.

While this moment (re)produces gendered assumptions of cis-heteromasculinity, it also subverts the expectation of violence that characterizes sites of atrocity. The captain's display of kindness contrasts with the apparent cruelty of the two guards. It is in this context—where a moment of kindness takes place against normalized violence—that Omer's brother is so moved by the captain's actions. I read this moment as an example of the multifaceted nature of perpetrators and victim-survivors in international law. The captain exemplifies the complex ways in which violence and kindness are entangled. While the captain and other perpetrators in the camps are willing and/or reluctant participants in violence, moments of mercy provide opportunities for deconstructing the assumption of perpetrators as sadists and rapists (see Chapter 4). The coexistence of violence and care also demonstrates how discourses of compassion can reinforce systems of violence. The captain's covert retrieval of the ring appeases Omer's relatives, but it does not disturb the overarching structures of violence and dehumanization that allow the maiming and killing of detainees. Therefore, complicating the perpetrator subject position offers opportunities for challenging one-dimensional accounts of criminality in war and international law. It also reveals how violence manifests through overt acts of harm as well as in seemingly kind acts of mercy.

In the context of international law, the existence of these figures—of guards who resist violence or display moments of kindness—challenge the overarching discourse of helpless victims violated by villainous perpetrators (see Chapter 4). It complicates an unwavering predication of perpetrators as cruel and vicious, and therefore innately perverse and criminal. In international law, representations of remorseful and unwilling perpetrators muddy the clear denunciation of individuals as evil criminals. These moments of reluctance in the face of violence, and kindness in the face of atrocity, make it possible to imagine individuals as more than victims or perpetrators: as embodied subjects with plural and complicated values and identities. The monstrous perpetrator subject proscribes the recognition of their humanity. In contrast, the presence of these subversive bodies at the ICTY, of individuals who even minimally resist violence, prescribes the recognition of multiplicity, messiness, and contradiction that constitutes all bodies in international law.

Concluding Thoughts on Subverting Violence

For Muhamed, the ability of friends to turn violent, and the trauma of losing his brother, is something that cannot be easily understood within the juridical context of the Tribunal, which seeks criminal justice but cannot restore loss. Muhamed's words are a powerful reminder of what is really at stake when international law governs, adjudicates, and subverts violence. As Sjoberg (2018, 245) writes in the context of "war families," we must remember the "yet unwritten" stories of their lives, of how Omer's family continues to live beyond what can be said and spoken at the Tribunal. As Muhamed says:

The last day they came for Omer everyone knew he was going to die. Omer waved to me and said goodbye. When I close my eyes at night, I see him waving again and again. When they carried me off the plane in London, I didn't feel relieved, just helpless. I wondered if I'd ever see my family again. Of course I knew I wouldn't see Omer. He was buried the same day I left Bosnia. I often think back to the old days when Omer, Vinko, and I would eat together. I ask myself, what was really going through Vinko's mind as we sat around the table laughing together. My Red Cross certificate says I'm 38. It is not true. I'm really only one year old, because it's only in the last year I've learned what people are really like. (*Brdanin* 2002, Trial hearing 5 September)

The examples of subverting violence at/of the ICTY challenge the ways in which violence is made legible within juridical settings. International law is both an agent and site of violence. But the various actors who embody international law not only (re)produce violence; they also subvert it. In this chapter, I focused on how these actors subvert dominant discourses of violence that engage civilizational logics to adjudicate and denunciate in international law (see Chapter 4). The discussions in this chapter interrupt these discourses by tracing how violence is subverted in international law, and the legal-political effects of these practices. I explored how subversive discourses of violence—evident through examples of "noisy" survivors and "complex" perpetrators—are legible through cis-heteronormative discourses of gender and sexuality. While these subversive practices reinforce the assumption that violent and violated bodies in war and law are straight and cisgender, they also offer moments of resistance by complicating expectations of the passive victim and the monstrous perpetrator in international law. Detainees in the camps engaged in practices of refusal, bodily autonomy, and resistance, and witnesses disrupted the procedural mandate of the courtroom. While "noisy" survivors and witnesses are plurally embodied and challenge violent and violating practices in powerful ways, these subversive practices largely depend on, and (re)produce, cis-heteronormative discourses of gender and sexuality. Chapter 5 thus highlighted the plural subjectivities that constitute international law, pushing back against assumptions of the "static legal subject" (Heathcote 2019, 7).

I also explored how perpetrators, as similarly plural and complicated subjectivities, subvert violence in representations of atrocity in international law. Instances of perpetrators showing moments of kindness or mercy to detainees challenge the violent legal practices of denunciation I deconstructed in Chapter 4. By showing that perpetrators are not solely "bad" and are instead more complicated than juridical discourses depict, I found that perpetrators who engaged in acts that subverted violence also reinforce (rather than disrupt) cis-heteronormative discourses of gender and sexuality. This is a significant finding, revealing that discourses of gender, sexuality, and violence intersect in ways that (re)produce cis-heteronormativity and heteropatriarchy as common sense at the ICTY, and international law more broadly. As a (queer) governance mechanism that is gendered and gendering, constitutive and agential, violent and violating, and subversive too, international law perpetuates exclusionary governing practices. By amplifying subversive discourses of violence, this chapter offers some hope to the story I develop in this book about how the dynamic, messy, and real lives of (gendered, sexualized, and ethnicized) bodies are legible through, and governed by, international law. As a (queer) governance mechanism, international law consists of queer logics that enable the coexistence of both violence and subversion, justice and injustice. This is a complicated vision of international law, one that I consider more deeply in the following, final chapter.

6

Queer Reckonings with International Law

Hope, Violence, and Critique

I hate the Tribunal but I need the Tribunal.
(Madacki, quoted in Orentlicher 2018, 127)

[Q]ueer legal analysis is driven by the need to reveal and understand how law works to sustain structures of domination. But queer is also a political movement that seeks to address lived realities in the present, which requires working with and through the received framework of international law at the same time as contesting it.
(Otto 2022b, 26)

International law is a mechanism of contradictions: it calls for (legal, authorized) violence (such as the incarceration of perpetrators) to address (illegal, unsanctioned) violence (such as the incarceration of victims) (Grady 2021, 367). Victims and survivors invest hope in it, only to be homogenized and silenced. And amid all of this, it seeks and imposes singularity and adheres to procedural clarity while also being a site of multiplicity and mess. Queering governance and international law reveals these contradictions. It recognizes the civilizational logics and cis-heteronormative discourses that make international law a violent and exclusionary mechanism. At the same time, queering also finds ways of reading international law as potentially subversive, evident in glimpses and moments of refusal within the law. In this book, I have argued that international law is a (queer) governance mechanism, one that is both violent and subversive. It is characterized by legal violences of victimization, denunciation, and paternalism, which are underpinned by cis-heteronormative discourses and civilizational logics that prescribe interventionist responses, including incarceration. But international law is also suggestive of queer possibilities, of oppressed groups, victims, and survivors resisting these civilizational logics and paternalist legal practices and using international law as a mechanism for human justice, however limited

Queering Governance and International Law. Caitlin Biddolph, Oxford University Press. © Oxford University Press (2025). DOI: 10.1093/9780197803172.003.0006

it might be. I have called international law a (queer) governance mechanism. This is perhaps a controversial and contested label, given the cis-heteronormative common-sense sites like the ICTY (re)produce. But I have done so with the goal of showing that queerness—plurality, ambivalence, transgression—is always possible, occurring within and outside international law. In this sense, the book has developed a hopeful critique of law's violence, one that complicates singular visions of what justice is and what it can be.

This concluding chapter offers queer reckonings with international law. It draws out the arguments and implications of the book to ask what it means to read international law as a (queer) governance mechanism for both its study and practice, and for those communities seeking justice within and beyond its walls. I return to some of the questions I proposed in the introductory chapter, that is: What might it mean to read international law as queer, even as it (re)installs exclusionary gendered, sexualized, and racialized configurations of (il)legality? And how might queer work complicate international law's exclusionary *and* subversive discourses of gender, sexuality, and violence? Such questions reflect Grietje Baars's provocation: "What possibilities exist for queer emancipation through law, and at what cost?" (2019, 20). I trace these tensions, these queer logics of plurality and ambivalence, through queer reckonings with international law as hope, as violence, and through queer critique. I return to hope in the last move, offering a generative critique that responds to the violences and possibilities I mapped in this book, and the implications of these for those who turn to, reject, and live beyond international law. Such an approach echoes Michelle Burgis-Kasthala and Barrie Sander's "(re-)engaging with the field of [international criminal law]" through "critical engagement," "tactical and strategic engagement," and "decolonial and abolitionist (dis-)engagement," and that international law "may be productively (re-)engaged in the pursuit of emancipatory ends" (2024, 130).

On Hope

When the ICTY closed its doors in 2017, it formally ended over two decades of justice-seeking, a call to law that was often the loudest from victims and survivors. The ICTY's creation and operation was not without criticism from victims and survivors; the quote that opens this chapter from

Saša Madacki reflects the complicated relationship many have with a governance mechanism that was simultaneously welcomed and a source of disempowerment. But it does reflect the hope many groups place in international law to address inequality, ongoing violence, and oppression. The stories and testimonies of those who live and breathe the violences documented in and by international law deserve to be heard and listened to. While much of this book has critiqued the cis-heteronormative discourses and civilizational logics that constitute international law, such critique must be grounded in the hope of international law as a source of justice and queer possibility, even as it (re)produces violence and global hierarchies. Indeed, the discussions in Chapter 5 explored the subversive potential of legal justice, where victims and survivors pushed back against the homogenizing, silencing, and paternalistic violences of the courtroom. But it is a complicated picture, a tapestry of hope, frayed by despair, longing, and the passage of time.

The story of hope I begin with starts with Bosnian victims and survivors, who found in the ICTY the possibility for international law to address injustice. Of course, Bosnian victims and survivors are not a homogeneous group, and it is not my intention here to preclude Bosnian dissent and criticism of the Tribunal, as well as the role of international actors in their country more broadly (see later discussions in this chapter). Rather, I start with this story to chart a hopeful beginning, honoring the faith victims and survivors placed in international law, even if such faith would be later misplaced. Indeed, as Diane Orentlicher remarks, "For many, the Tribunal has rendered a measure of justice that, however flawed, is infinitely preferable to no justice at all. In their eyes, the Tribunal's creation was amply justified because it rendered 'a little piece of justice'" (2018, 128; see also Deronjić, quoted in Orentlicher 2018, 127). Similarly, Maria O'Reilly notes that all the people she interviewed from survivors' associations valued legal justice and the ICTY:

> For Enisa Salčinović, retributive justice was important for "punishing the perpetrator" and for "verify[ing] the truth." Alisa Muratčauš also argued that "all war criminals should be arrested, [. . . and] justice is very important for all sides [of the conflict]" . . . Amela Meduseljac . . . argued that trials were important because they ensured that perpetrators were officially recognised ("registered") as "war criminal[s]" and "held responsible" for their crimes. (2018, 141–42)

Members of the Mothers of Srebrenica association echoed this belief in the power of retributive justice by the ICTY to bring some measure of justice. Redzija, the daughter of the recently passed Kada Ramic, reflects: "She would always say that her only wish was to find her children, to bury them and to see the people who killed the children of Srebrenica sentenced. She always talked about that" (Redzija, interviewed by Omerovic 2021). Fazila Efendic, the head of the association, says: "I am looking forward to nothing but seeing him sentenced to life imprisonment, seeing the first-instance verdict confirmed. Nothing else could be anticipated, nothing less than that" (Efendic, interviewed by Omerovic 2021).

The emphasis Bosnian victims and survivors place on the ICTY as a source of justice, and of retributive justice, cannot be discounted. Their powerful statements reflect a faith in international law that is at odds with my own sustained critique of its violence that I have charted in the chapters of this book. But as a (queer) governance mechanism, international law can and is both: a source of hope and a source of violence. The queer logics of this simultaneity do not erase one for the other. Instead, they complicate singular accounts of international law and allow the recognition of plural encounters with law as (in)justice.

Beyond the ICTY and Bosnian victims and survivors, other oppressed groups see international law as a vehicle for change. As John Reynolds and Sujith Xavier note, in an article that largely critiques international law: "the fact that Tamils and Palestinians and a diversity of Third World peoples, social movements and human rights activists continue to place hope in international criminal law beseeches us to consider its counter-hegemonic potential" (2016, 976; see also Rajagopal 2003, 146). Consider, for example, that in response to the austerity measures imposed on Greece, the Greek people turned to international criminal law as a mechanism through which to "cast their grievances" (Nouwen and Werner 2015, 161). Or that African states were actually early investors of hope in the ICC, as the Court represented the possibility for Western states to be prosecuted for colonialism and genocide, a story often obscured by the dominant narrative of African criticism of the Court's selectivity and neocolonialism (Ba et al. 2023, 1–2).

Such hopeful investments in international law by oppressed groups have a longer history. Indeed, the nineteenth-century Mixed Commissions for the Suppression of the Transatlantic Slave Trade reveals how the antislavery and abolition movement found credence in law and criminal justice (notwithstanding critiques of the Mixed Commissions, to which I return in the following section of the chapter, see Nesiah 2019; Ba et al. 2023). The following century, William L. Patterson, Paul Robeson, and other members of the Civil Rights Congress produced a powerful indictment against the US government, the document titled *We Charge Genocide: The Crime of Government against the Negro People* (Civil Rights Congress 1951). The authors appealed to international law, namely, the Genocide Convention, and "applied [it] . . . to many practices of racist violence in the United States including lynching, mental harm, reproductive control and segregation" (Meiches 2019, 23). The last quarter of the twentieth century also saw a similar appeal of international law to expose and address injustice, "the 13-year period during which, under the leadership of Doudou Thiam, the International Law Commission of the United Nations debated and almost ended up including crimes like apartheid, colonialism, ecocide, mercenarism in international law, only to be thwarted by Western states" (Ba et al. 2023, 4). Within the current moment, "Ukraine has embraced international law as an emancipatory tool in its struggle against Russia" (Labuda 2024), while the struggle for a free Palestine is pursued through multiple channels, some of which include legal mechanisms like the ICC and the International Court of Justice (ICJ) (Sirleaf 2024).

The turn to international law in these examples offers an important counter to a sustained critique (my own included) of law as violent and oppressive. But, as I explore in more detail in the next section, it is possible to recognize international law's possibilities *and* its violences. The two are not incompatible, but part of what it means to be a (queer) governance mechanism that offers hope for oppressed groups while simultaneously (re)producing cis-heteronormative, civilizational, and racial hierarchies. Indeed, in the book, I revealed that international law not only is violent and violating but also subverts practices of violence. In Chapter 5, I deployed my queer analysis to moments where bodies subvert violence. At the ICTY, witnesses and survivors challenged the victimizing and silencing practices of the courtroom by engaging in acts of resistance. Similarly, testimonies revealed that both survivors and perpetrators are more complicated than dominant discourses of violence depict, with messy, multilayered, and dynamic lives that traverse conflict temporalities (Biddolph 2020). This finding has important implications for how bodies are understood and acted on by legal actors within international law, complicating simplified discourses of victimhood, criminality, and the governance of these subjectivities. Crucially, though, I found that subversive discourses of violence depend on and (re)produce cis-heteronormative, essentialist discourses of gender and sexuality. Even in subversive moments, then, my queer reading exposed international law's reliance on, and perpetuation of, the straight, cisgender legal subject, one that excises non-normative gendered and sexualized bodies from its governing practices.

Thus, even where there is hope and possibility, there is violence, and while critical of the cis-heteronormative status quo that international law maintains, I also recognize that international law can be transformative. Returning to some of the earlier examples I outlined, Noura Erakat and John Reynolds speak of the "scope for principled anti-apartheid legal tactics to trigger transformational possibilities" in the Palestinian case (2021, 5). This is particularly important given Israel's intensified genocide against Palestinians since October 2023. Thus, international law might be one part of a broader "anti-colonial strategy" (2021, 11). Indeed, South Africa's case against Israel at the ICJ represents what Matiangai V.S. Sirleaf calls "an example of the periphery, attempting to hold a powerful actor in the purported center to its own rules" (2024, 180). South Africa and other Global South, postcolonial states standing up and in solidarity with Palestinians through international law is a powerful reminder of the expressive value of legal justice. Similarly, in their appeal to the Genocide Convention, the authors of *We Charge Genocide* used "the UN's own terminology" to expose the US government's crimes against African Americans and elicit a response from the international community (Meiches 2019, 23). While the Palestinian appeals to international law continue to be met with resistance (notwithstanding some expressions of solidarity),[1] and the crimes detailed in *We Charge Genocide* never received the legal recognition and condemnation it called for, there is persistent hope in international law's transformative possibilities, even if such hope is dogged by frustration and despair.

Moreover, even as international law justifies retributive and carceral justice in the form of international criminal law, it also enshrines transformative possibilities for anticarceral approaches. This is evident in "numerous international conventions, resolutions, and recommendations [that] encourage states to utilize alternatives to incarceration" (Goodman 2021, 1223). International law is permeated by violence, including the legitimation of imprisonment along civilizational and racial logics. But it also contains the seeds for transformation. It is therefore important to consider then, that "while [international law] has only limited potential to help advance a world that is free of gendered hierarchy and violence, it remains an important site of feminist struggle, and all the more if this struggle can be linked with grass roots justice projects and promote systemic change" (Otto 2022a, 414; see also Jones 2023, 89). This speaks to the tension Kapur identifies in queer desires for legitimacy and recognition under law, something that must be "continually pursued" (2015, 275), a form of justice that, drawing on Gayatri Spivak, "is something 'we cannot not want'" (2015, 289). As I have written elsewhere, quoting Katherine Fobear (2014, 54), "[e]ven in the face of [international law's] violence, many scholars and activists argue that queer inclusion is essential and provides the conditions for 'living a safe and secure life in the present'" (Biddolph 2024b, 220–21). International law is thus an imperfect mechanism, a site of (in)justice.

But recognizing the transformative possibilities of international law for oppressed groups—including Bosnian victims and survivors, and queer communities—does not preclude attention to law's violences. Kapur writes: "My argument is that . . . what is important is to pursue justice *along with* an awareness of the work that justice does and is capable of doing . . . to gain some level of tolerance . . . [which] is welcome, [but] it is also simultaneously an intervention that incorporates the subject into a specific vision of the world and of how to be in that world" (2015, 293, emphases in original). At the ICTY, as with international law more broadly, the cost of legal recognition is the perpetuation of the cis-heteronormative and civilizational common sense, where victim and perpetrator subjectivities are constructed as variously feminized, passive, hyper-heteromasculinized, sadistic, queer (in the derogatory sense), and perverse. To acknowledge this violence is not to give up on law, but to situate its transformative and hopeful possibilities against the harms it always already enables.

On Violence

This book has exposed the violence of international law: its various disempowering, civilizational, and gendered discourses and practices that configure certain populations as subjects of international legal intervention, while others maintain a privileged position as moral adjudicators who do the intervening. Throughout the chapters, I have developed and embraced a queer methodology to expose the discursive (re)production of gender, sexuality, and violence in governance and international law, and to show how these discourses intersect in plural and contested ways. The governing practices of international law are pre/proscriptive, that is, they have legal-political effects. These discursive practices authorize and legitimate the existence, mandate, and operation of international law, as well as sanction certain legal-political possibilities (e.g., criminalization, imprisonment, protection, intervention). The civilizational logics and discourses of gender, sexuality, and violence in/of international law maintain discursive violence, (re)producing pejorative civilizational and gendered characterizations of Othered populations. International law also adjudicates and (re)produces violence through installing cis-heteronormativity as the common sense. In this way, legal subjects are unquestionably cisgender and straight and follow essentialist scripts of masculinities and femininities, a discourse which violently erases the existence of queer, trans-, and nonbinary persons in international law (an erasure that was particularly evident at the ICTY, see Biddolph 2024b).

I have developed a critique of these violences through the case of the ICTY, revealing how these discursive practices affect legal actions and enforcement. The book explored how cis-heteronormative discourses and civilizational logics invoked by legal actors legitimate extraordinary juridical measures. For example, Chapter 4 investigated how, through gendered practices of denunciation, prosecutors indict perpetrators, while judges criminalize and punish them. Furthermore, discourses of gender, sexuality, and violence intersect in international law in ways that prescribe or authorize the discursive classification of bodies as "good" and "bad" along gendered, sexualized, and ethnicized lines (see also Mibenge 2013, 5). The ICTY (re)produces cis-heteronormative discourses that construct perpetrators and detainees as particular kinds of gendered, sexualized, and Balkanist victims or aberrations. In this way, the Tribunal continues and reflects the broader civilizational logics of international law that cast Othered populations and geographies like the former Yugoslavia as places of violence, where hyper-heteromasculine sadists violate helpless, feminized victims (see Chapters 3 and 4). These gendered and sexualized subject positions legitimate the juridical authority of international law as the "only civilized alternative" (ICTY Annual Report 1994, para 15). They also contribute to broader governing logics in international law, conflict, and global politics, including those of military intervention. These representations reinforce civilizational binaries of international law, where violence committed by "uncivilized" actors (e.g., "Balkan" perpetrators) is rendered criminal, while violence committed by "civilized" actors (e.g., Western interveners) is authorized and deemed legitimate. By queering governance and international law, I problematized its violent and violating capacities, and its reliance on gendered, sexualized discourses and civilizational, racial logics to sustain global hierarchies.

Such findings of violence echo survivors' disappointment in the broken promise of justice that international law represents. As Julie Mertus argues in the case of Bosnian victims and survivors and their relationship with the ICTY, "Despite their initial faith that they could use international war crimes tribunals to their own purposes, survivors have quickly become disillusioned with the adversarial process . . . The witnesses almost universally experience the trials as dehumanizing and re-traumatizing experiences" (Mertus 2004, 112; see also Biddolph 2024b, 231; O'Reilly 2018, 143; Rigney 2024, 218; Simm 2018, 76). Indeed, Mertus's argument supports my own conclusions in Chapter 4, where I found that legal practices feminize, homogenize, and silence victims and survivors in ways that constitute an additional form of victimization. This is not to displace the hope that survivors place with(in) international law, including the potentially empowering effects of testifying (if given the scope and dignity to do so). But it does indicate the risks of working with(in) a governance mechanism that is both (potentially) transformative and violent.

As I touched on in Chapter 1, postcolonial and TWAIL perspectives have reckoned with the ongoing violences of international law, manifesting in a colonial and racist system. While some scholars are attentive to law's transformative potential (see previous section), others remain cautious, and "ask[] whether, given certain embedded colonial features, the premise and promise of international criminal justice can—for self-determination struggles or anti-imperial movements in the global South—be anything more than illusory" (Reynolds and Xavier 2016, 961). For example, while the Mixed Commissions for the Suppression of the Transatlantic Slave Trade enforced abolition; Vasuki Nesiah incisively argues that it actually upheld the white common sense of international law, where "race is rendered invisible even in legal principles (such as abolition) that purport to hold racism to account" (2019, 180). Furthermore, "the abolition of the international slave trade was intertwined with the sustaining of slavery" and prefigured a (white) humanity that dehumanized Blackness (2019, 183). While these were legal mechanisms operating two centuries ago, the violence sustained and enabled through them linger in contemporary practices of international law. In the case of the Mixed Commissions, "white men had been presorted ... be they as judges who were going to decide on freedom, or as accused seeking to secure their 'cargo.' In contrast, black men and women hovered in an interregnum between a regime of property law and a regime of colonial law; they were objects of property and subject to colonial rule" (2019, 175). In other words, the law (re)produced "moral economies of rescue" that constructed the white savior/rescuer and Black victims to be saved (2019, 185), an economy that is reflected at the ICC, a justice done "in the name of African victims" to protect against African perpetrators (2019, 188). The analysis of the ICTY explored in this book similarly attests to the construction of legal subjects along civilizational and gendered lines (see Chapters 3 and 4), and the legal violences they further enable.

These insights reveal that international law is inherently violent, even when (and precisely because) it seeks justice. When justice depends on cis-heteronormative discourses and civilizational logics of victimization, denunciation, and paternalism, it is always already a violent (in)justice. Even when victims and survivors place hope in international law as a source of recognition (and perhaps even transformation), violence persists in the "regulative justice that is the form that justice takes within the legal apparatus ... one that is incapable of securing unconditional justice" (Kapur 2015, 283). These conclusions are sobering ones, echoed in the arguments of this book and in the mixed feelings queer scholars have with the law. Even while remaining hopeful, Otto nevertheless asks: "Could it be that the established framework of criminal law is even more committed to maintaining the imperial, masculinist, heteronormative *status quo* than other areas of law?" (2022a, 388, emphases in original). The arguments developed in this book would suggest an answer in the affirmative; that overwhelmingly, international law sustains violent cis-heteronormative discourses and civilizational logics, justifying paternalistic practices of protection and carceral forms of punishment.

But Otto's and my own critique of international law as violent does not foreclose the possibility of a queerer approach to justice, within and beyond law. While we may question, as with Kapur, whether legal justice could ever be "a radically transformative project" (2015, 268), the glimpses of subverting law's violence at the ICTY, and the hope victims and survivors place with(in) it, suggest a more complicated reading of international law as a (queer) governance mechanism. A generative critique offers possibilities for alternative visions of justice, recognizing that international law "cannot give us what we want," insofar as it "operates to uphold a specific normative order, which continues to regulate, discipline and monitor the sexual subject" (Kapur 2015, 277).

On Critique

How might queer approaches reconcile the hope and violence of international law? Can international law be simultaneously queer and violent? Do we live with law, *and/or* do we seek justice elsewhere and otherwise? As Baars asks, "is now the time to say 'fuck law'?" (2019, 60). The queer perspective adopted in this book embraces the irreconciled and the paradoxical, of the queer logics (Weber 2016) and split or fracturing ways law does both (Heathcote 2019). I have argued that as a (queer) governance mechanism, international law is gendered and gendering, constitutive and agential, violent and violating, and subversive—it is all of these things. The analyses developed across the book have illuminated the violent workings of international law, where at the ICTY, cis-heteronormative discourses and civilizational logics cast victims and perpetrators in pejorative and limiting ways. But they have also hinted at subversion (see Chapter 5), and that violence is not stable, but subject to ongoing resistance and change. The discussions in this concluding chapter have also reflected on the plural possibilities of law as a source of hope and as an agent of violence, two arguments that might appear irreconcilable but instead suggest queerness, ambivalence, and visions of justice that exceed singularity. The queer analysis or critique of international law I have waged in the book is not a singular endeavor limited to a "paranoid" reading or a "tracing-and-exposure-project" (Sedgwick 2003, 124). It does this, of course, recognizing the power of "exposing the complicity of international law in contributing to instances and patterns of injustice" and the necessity that "critique be repeated, rubbed in, as it were" (Venzke, quoted in Burgis-Kasthala and Sander 2024, 133–134). But it also holds out hope for deconstructing law's violence and imagining alternative modes of addressing (in)justice. In this third move of the chapter, I think on and with the hopes and violences of international law through a hopeful queer critique (see Mazel 2022, 2023), one that offers "generative friction[s]" (Chadwick 2023, 9) and reckonings with law, "that things can be different, that new understandings are possible, that the unexpected can be enriching and transformative" (2023, 10; see also Burgis-Kasthala and Sander 2024, 137).

A queer reckoning with international law asks that we question the possibility of law ever being queer when it "ratif[ies] and normalise[s], rather than unsettle[s] the normative categories of gender and sexuality" (Kapur 2015, 281; see also Baars 2019, 60). Through the case of the ICTY, I have argued that international law does indeed (re)produce cis-heteronormative discourses which construct legal subjects as cisgender, straight, and binary. Combined with civilizational logics, it casts victims and perpetrators as variously feminized, hyper-heteromasculinized, queer (in the derogatory sense), and perverse. A queer critique exposes these violences, but it also acknowledges the fractured, plural, and complicated encounters people have with the law, including those characterized by hope and transformation. To be sure, my argument in this book does not refute law's violence, indeed, it emphatically pronounces the law as violent. But I also argue that this violence must be placed alongside moments of queerness and subversion. So, if a generative critique is one that embodies discomfort, ambivalence, and a reckoning with not knowing, then the critique I embrace here is one that rejects singular answers to international law. I sit with the queer and the messy, that international law is a (queer) governance mechanism consisting of and inflicting violence, hope, disappointment, and possibility. Whether international law is a project that should be sustained, or whether we should "speak in favour of abandoning or dismantling the institutions ... altogether" (Reynolds and Xavier 2016, 977), perhaps, it is both. Queer critique helps to illuminate the (im)possibility of pursuing both reformist and abolitionist agendas.

To get to these questions, a queer critique of international law must first reckon with the failures of legal justice. In the case of the ICTY, these failures abound, but they also materialize in the violation of victims and survivors in the courtroom and beyond (see Chapter 4). When victims are silenced and dehumanized, legible through gendered, civilizational logics and paternalistic legal practices, there will never be human justice. Of course, even if and as the Tribunal provided some semblance of justice for the survivors (as evident in the first section of this chapter), international law and other justice mechanisms can never reverse the loss of victims and survivors. Razija Husejinovic recounts the words of her recently passed mother, Hanifa Djogaz: "She said no punishment was big enough for what they had done, just that they should bring her children back, but they couldn't do that because they had taken them to their deaths" (Husejinovic, interviewed by Omerovic 2021). Nura Alispahic, who passed in 2020, said: "I feel like a cut tree. I am neither alive nor dead.... There is no justice and there will never be" (Alispahic, interviewed by Muslimovic 2017). The hopes and violences of international law fade against the unending, transgenerational grief and injustice of genocide. If justice is the return of the dead to the living, then there is no justice in international law, or elsewhere.

Other survivors attest to their repeated victimization by an international system that ignores their loss and misplaces the responsibility for committing crimes. The ICTY excluded Western actors' crimes from juridical scrutiny, a move that must be understood within the broader governing logics and origin stories of the ICTY that distinguish between the "justified, normalised, and legalised" violence of Western interveners, against the "illegitimate" and "rogue" violence of Others (Heathcote 2005, 132; see also Engle 2015, 1122, see Chapter 3). While the ICTY's mandate did not preclude the OtP from criminally investigating the role of Western actors in Bosnia, such as the inaction and failure of the United Nations Protection Force (UNPROFOR), this was never pursued to the same extent that Balkan crimes were investigated (M. Veličković 2024, 17–18; Wagner 2019, 42). The legal texts I analyzed in this book condemned and denunciated Balkan perpetrators while acquitting international actors of participating in or having any responsibility for acts of violence committed in the former Yugoslavia, including the UN peacekeepers who failed to stop the Srebrenica genocide (Dembour and Haslam 2004, 169–70). This excision of UN responsibility concealed their complicity in crimes, thereby reorienting criminal responsibility to the "sole" perpetrators: dangerous, hyper-heteromasculine, Balkan criminals (see Zarkov 2014). Survivors feel this injustice; one Mothers of Srebrenica member says: "We have been sold out by the UN" (Sehomerović, interviewed by Gaillard and Pineau 2015). This is an ongoing injustice. When the Mothers of Srebrenica pursued legal justice in the Netherlands, "demand[ing] compensation from the UN and the Kingdom of the Netherlands" for their role in the genocide, "the Supreme Court maintained the previous decisions, confirming that the UN enjoys immunity from prosecution; a decision upheld in June 2013 by the European Court of Human Rights" (Gaillard and Pineau 2015).

The possibilities afforded by a queer critique expose the deficiencies and violences of international law for victims and survivors. But they also grant insight into alternative justices beyond the law, of the fact that socioeconomic justice and security often meant and means more for Bosnians than "establishing individual accountability for war crimes" (Lai 2020, 2–3). Elsewhere, alternative forms of justice have been proposed and materialized in ways that counter the limits of international law. Here, I trace some of these alternatives, rejecting a prescriptive approach and instead presenting examples of the "options ... available to those ... who turn away" from the law (Kapur 2015, 287). This is about asking "whether there is another way imaginable, possible, and liveable" (2015, 281), or "how we can imagine justice in other registers" (2015, 294).

People's tribunals are a good example of more transformative, subversive, and queer alternatives to international law (O'Hara 2023; Otto 2016, 2017; Simm 2018). Dianne Otto offers insight into the power of these mechanisms:

> While victim testimonies are given centre stage, the goal is to step outside the law to ask structural questions about the exclusionary effects of the law and whose interests this serves. The injustices recounted in the testimonies are understood not just in terms of individual or state responsibility, but in a broader frame of colonial histories, systemic racism, divisive nationalisms, institutionalised misogyny and homophobia, militarism and inequitable economic and social structures. Rather than "speaking law to power," the idea is to assume a jurisdiction that enables the voices of the people to speak about the effects of power, including law, in their lives. The idea is to promote solidarity between all those participating in the tribunal and have it flow outward with the participants generating new awareness and inspiring action in their communities. (Otto 2017, 240)

This is an alternative justice—couched in the discourse of international law but also critical of it—attentive to affected communities' visions of (in)justice that hint at what could be possible, but what is often thwarted, in and by international criminal tribunals. People's tribunals represent a queer "reimagining [of] international law" (O'Hara 2023, 3), where the (limited) space for subverting legal violence in formal international legal processes is expanded and given center stage. Returning to Otto's remarks on people's tribunals as sites for listening, solidarity, and justice, she writes:

> [P]eople's tribunals also remind us of the infinity of possible claims for justice and the need for expansive ideas of responsibility for injustice, both within and beyond the confines of the law.... People's tribunals point to the need for transformative change, to a much larger justice than legal mechanisms can deliver, and to the responsibility of us all to play our part in bringing this justice into being. (2016, 317)

In the Bosnian case, the Women's Court provided a much-needed alternative to ICTY justice (Women's Court 2012; Simm 2018), a people's tribunal that could also be characterized as a (queer) governance mechanism. It was similarly gendered and gendering, discursive and agential, violent (in that violence was the subject of the Court's discussions), and importantly, subversive, transgressive, hopeful, and queer. This is just one example of how we might think and do "international law otherwise" (Jones 2023, 160).

Transformative justice has also been proposed as an alternative to legal justice, one that seeks "the radical and sustainable transformation of structures and relationships" (Nagy 2022, 195), driven by victims, survivors, and affected communities, and often manifesting in restorative rather than retributive justice (Boesten and Wilding 2015; Ghazal 2022). For Indigenous communities and postcolonial subjects, international law might be a space for transformation, but it is the calls for land repatriation, redistribution, and decolonization (beyond and including formal legal processes) that offer the most promising paths to justice (Moyo 2015; Murdock 2018; Sesay 2022).

There is also abolition: a call to abolish domestic carceral and penal logics of governance (Davis 2003), as well as international ones (Grady 2021; Burgis-Kasthala and Sander 2024; Rigney 2024). As Reynolds and Xavier write, "Not enough space has been opened up in mainstream and even critical legal discourse to challenge the presupposition that there must be an international criminal law" (2016, 977). Such a prompt stems from prison abolitionists' ongoing challenge to imprisonment as the status quo response to violence and social (in)justice. As Angela Davis asks, "How can we imagine a society in which race and class are not primary determinants of punishment? Or one in which punishment itself is no longer the central concern in the making of justice?" (2003, 107).

These justice alternatives deserve far greater attention than I have given them in this chapter, and indeed the book. But by identifying how justice might be pursued elsewhere, beyond the violent workings of international law, I have offered a queer critique of governance and international law that is grounded in both suspicion (of its violence) and hope (in its possibilities within and beyond). Such a critique embodies the queer logics of plurality, paradox, and ambivalence that animate the pages of this book, and the ICTY as an example of international law as a (queer) governance mechanism. It is an uncomfortable and confronting task to trace the ways in which international law can simultaneously be a mechanism of cis-heteronormative, civilizational violence *and* a mechanism vested in hope, possibility, and even queerness. But it is a necessary part of reckoning with international law and its limits, alternatives, and visions for justice.

**

There are no simple answers such a queer reckoning with international law can offer. Indeed, this book has in many respects asked more questions than it has answered, "queerying" (Detamore 2010) and unsettling the cis-heteronormative and civilizational assumptions that constitute international law and its governing arrangements. But there are implications to these questions and for my core argument that international law is a (queer) governance mechanism that is both violent and subversive. I discuss each in turn, drawn from the findings of the book and the discussions that animate this chapter.

First, the discourses observed at the ICTY and within the transcripts interface and interact with wider international legal practices beyond them. They reflect broader gendered discourses and civilizational logics in global politics: of peace and conflict; of international law; of transitional justice—of any forms of intervention that denounce violence perpetrated by gendered, civilizational Others and that prop up Eurocentric/Western exceptionalism (see Vernon 2024). They also speak to the preference or dominance of legal or carceral justice in international law, the limitations of which reflect a need to move beyond these approaches and consider alternatives.

Second, international law inherently relies on violence and the (re)production of cis-heteronormative discourses and civilizational logics, and this matters both for the practice of international law and its study. A pessimistic reading might argue that international law is doomed, because it can never escape the violence it perpetuates and installs through the governance of bodies and populations in these gendered, racialized, and carceral ways. In this sense, such an outlook warrants calls for the dismantling of international law and justice mechanisms as the common-sense response to injustice, and to a more critical scholarly engagement with its violences. For those who study and do international law, it is vital that they recognize that international law is always already violent and predicated on civilizational logics and cis-heteronormative discourses that further prescribe the legal recourse to carceral governance and paternalistic intervention. International legal scholars (even, and perhaps foremostly, the critical ones), must reckon with these violences, their role in the perpetuation of them, and acknowledge that other forms of justice can and ought to be centered. A more hopeful reading, then, is that international law might be transformed so that it can meaningfully respond to oppressed groups' call for justice. The subversive moments in Chapter 5, for example, suggest ways this might happen within a courtroom setting. Both pessimistic and hopeful readings constitute my queer critique and point to plural possibilities for working with(in) or turning away from the project of international law.

Third, there are implications for those who are interested in pursuing justice in the realm of international law. My research has complicated romanticized visions of international law as an arbiter of justice. Of course, there is a need to recognize that oppressed groups and victims/survivors call for international law and see it as a vehicle for addressing injustice (Burgis-Kasthala and Sander 2024, 144–145). This is particularly the case when formal articulations of justice continue to carry such weight and when formal justice in national settings remains limited. However, my findings about the violence and cis-heteronormativity of international law caution over the possibilities of achieving human justice within international law, and about the limited ways cis-heteronormativity is challenged, but nevertheless upheld. As I have discussed in this chapter, even when survivors want international law, it often fails their expectations and can be a source of renewed violation. Thus, those seeking to pursue justice through international law must do so with caution and in recognition of these violences. At the same time, my findings revealed (even if albeit marginally) that there is space for resistance, subversion, and queerness in international law. This brings hope that even within violent systems, change can come from within. But again, it is with caution that I suggest this, knowing, as with Kapur and Spivak, that it is a justice we "cannot not want" but it is one that nevertheless imposes its own violent modes of governance.

Finally, there are implications for those who remain skeptical of international law as a vehicle for liberatory practice and largely think it should be abandoned in favor of alternative measures of justice. Here, I speak to lessons in humility I have learned in the process of this project. Having adopted in this book a queer perspective that is critical of the international legal project, the testimonies and voices of victims, survivors, and oppressed groups serve as a reminder that international law can be a space for resistance and hope, and indeed, even of queerness. As Kseniya Kirichenko argues, "being there is also queer; claiming a voice is queer; choosing our own language is queer; building alliances and coalitions to dismantle—is radically queer" (2023, 15). But my critique of international law as violent and violating speaks to another possibility, one that moves away from international law in its current form. It is one that questions whether international law can ever be a truly radical, liberatory, and queer mechanism when it remains tethered to and creates civilizational hierarchies and cis-heteronormative discourses and should therefore be abandoned in favor of other forms of justice. These two points are not mutually exclusive. International law will work for some, and some will find change/hope within it. But for others it will remain violent, oppressive, and wedded to procedural over human justice. This reflects my overarching argument that international law can and is both things: violent and containing queer potential.

Through the case of the ICTY, my queer analysis allowed me to see how representations of violent acts and the legal violence of international law invoke and (re)install cis-heteronormative and civilizational logics of governance. International law attempts to arrest violence: to organize, regulate, and make sense of it in ways that reduce lived experiences to legal categories and factual evidence. But international law is inhabited by messy, plural, and contradictory meanings. These signifiers are also always gendered and gendering, constitutive and agential, violent and violating, subversive, and infused with civilizational hierarchies of international law. Whether through sites of international law, or through the pages of this book, making sense of violence is a complicated, queer, and violent practice. But it is one that embodies our desire to resist the violent assemblages that constitute our world/s.

By queering governance and international law, I have offered a reading of gender, sexuality, and violence, their legal-political effects, and how various legal actors are constituted by, (re)produce, and subvert them. My queer approach has revealed that international law is a (queer) governance mechanism and maintains its authority to represent, adjudicate, and sustain violence, through its gendered and gendering, constitutive and agential, and violent and violating practices. These practices are plural, contingent, and maintain the possibility of being subverted. I remain hopeful that where there is resistance to violence, there always already exists the capacity to deconstruct the pejorative, cis-heteronormative (re)production of violence. Within this hope, there always already inhabits possibilities, both within international law and beyond, for rewriting future lives and stories of those affected by conflict. Queering governance and international law exposes and disrupts violence, but it also "involves dreaming" (Otto 2022b, 22). The frames of violence, justice, and international law that animate our lives can and must be reimagined, reconfigured, and queered. This is a commitment to subverting governance and international law, to dreaming of and making more peaceful, inclusive, and nourishing worlds.

APPENDIX 1
ICTY Case Information

CASE	ACCUSED, DETENTION CAMPS, INDICTMENTS, AND CHARGES
Tadić (IT-94-1)	Duško Tadić; Omarska, Keraterm, and Trnopolje camps (Prijedor, BiH); Individual criminal responsibility for: (i) persecutions on political, racial, or religious grounds; rape; murder; inhumane acts (crimes against humanity); (ii) willful killing; torture or inhuman treatment; willfully causing great suffering or serious injury to body or health (grave breaches of the Geneva Conventions); (iii) cruel treatment; murder (violations of the laws or customs of war). Sentenced to 20 years' imprisonment.
Mucić et al. (IT-96-1)	Zdravko Mucić, Hazim Delić, Esad Landžo, Zejnil Delalić; Čelebići camp (Konjic, BiH); Superior and individual criminal responsibility for: (i) willfully causing great suffering or serious injury; unlawful confinement of civilians; willful killings; torture; inhuman treatment (grave breaches of the Geneva Conventions); (ii) cruel treatment; plunder; murders; torture (violations of the laws or customs of war). Found not guilty or sentenced to 15–20 years' imprisonment.
Kvočka et al. (IT-98-30/1)	Miroslav Kvočka, Dragoljub Prcać, Milojic Kos, Mlado Radić, Zoran Žigić; Omarska, Keraterm, and Trnopolje camps (Prijedor, BiH); Individual criminal responsibility for: (i) outrages on personal dignity; murder; torture; cruel treatment (violations of the laws or customs of war); (ii) persecutions on political, racial or religious grounds; inhumane acts; murder; rape; torture (crimes against humanity). Sentenced to 5–25 years' imprisonment.
Brdanin (IT-99-36)	Radoslav Brdanin; Omarska, Keraterm, and Trnopolje camps (Prijedor, BiH); Individual criminal responsibility for: (i) genocide; complicity in genocide (genocide); (ii) persecutions; extermination; torture; deportation; inhumane acts (forcible transfer) (crimes against humanity); (iii) wanton destruction of cities, towns, or villages or devastation not justified by military necessity; destruction or willful damage done to institutions dedicated to religion (violations of the laws or customs of war); (iv) willful killing; torture; unlawful and wanton extensive destruction and appropriation of property not justified by military necessity (grave breaches of the Geneva Conventions). Sentenced to 30 years' imprisonment.

APPENDIX 2
List of ICTY Documents

ICTY Annual Reports (n = 24)

International Criminal Tribunal for the former Yugoslavia (1994) Annual Report, A/49/342–S/1994/1007. 29 August 1994. Online, at https://www.icty.org/x/file/About/Reports%20and%20Publications/AnnualReports/annual_report_1994_en.pdf.
International Criminal Tribunal for the former Yugoslavia (1995) Annual Report, A/50/365–S/1995/728. 23 August 1995. Online, at https://www.icty.org/x/file/About/Reports%20and%20Publications/AnnualReports/annual_report_1995_en.pdf.
International Criminal Tribunal for the former Yugoslavia (1996) Annual Report, A/51/292–S/1996/665. 16 August 1996. Online, at https://www.icty.org/x/file/About/Reports%20and%20Publications/AnnualReports/annual_report_1996_en.pdf.
International Criminal Tribunal for the former Yugoslavia (1997) Annual Report, A/52/375–S/1997/729. 18 September 1997. Online, at https://www.icty.org/x/file/About/Reports%20and%20Publications/AnnualReports/annual_report_1997_en.pdf.
International Criminal Tribunal for the former Yugoslavia (1998) Annual Report, A/53/219–S/1998/737. 10 August 1998. Online, at https://www.icty.org/x/file/About/Reports%20and%20Publications/AnnualReports/annual_report_1998_en.pdf.
International Criminal Tribunal for the former Yugoslavia (1999) Annual Report, A/54/187–S/1999/846. 25 August 1999. Online, at https://www.icty.org/x/file/About/Reports%20and%20Publications/AnnualReports/annual_report_1999_en.pdf.
International Criminal Tribunal for the former Yugoslavia (2000) Annual Report, A/55/273–S/2000/777. 7 August 2000. Online, at https://www.icty.org/x/file/About/Reports%20and%20Publications/AnnualReports/annual_report_2000_en.pdf.
International Criminal Tribunal for the former Yugoslavia (2001) Annual Report, A/56/352–S/2001/865. 17 September 2001. Online, at https://www.icty.org/x/file/About/Reports%20and%20Publications/AnnualReports/annual_report_2001_en.pdf.
International Criminal Tribunal for the former Yugoslavia (2002) Annual Report, A/57/379–S/2002/985. 4 September 2002. Online, at https://www.icty.org/x/file/About/Reports%20and%20Publications/AnnualReports/annual_report_2002_en.pdf.
International Criminal Tribunal for the former Yugoslavia (2003) Annual Report, A/58/297–S/2003/829. 20 August 2003. Online, at https://www.icty.org/x/file/About/Reports%20and%20Publications/AnnualReports/annual_report_2003_en.pdf.
International Criminal Tribunal for the former Yugoslavia (2004) Annual Report, A/59/215–S/2004/627. 16 August 2004. Online, at https://www.icty.org/x/file/About/Reports%20and%20Publications/AnnualReports/annual_report_2004_en.pdf.
International Criminal Tribunal for the former Yugoslavia (2005) Annual Report, A/60/267–S/2005/532. 17 August 2005. Online, at https://www.icty.org/x/file/About/Reports%20and%20Publications/AnnualReports/annual_report_2005_en.pdf.

LIST OF ICTY DOCUMENTS 155

International Criminal Tribunal for the former Yugoslavia (2006) Annual Report, A/61/271–S/2006/666. 21 August 2006. Online, at https://www.icty.org/x/file/About/Reports%20and%20Publications/AnnualReports/annual_report_2006_en.pdf.
International Criminal Tribunal for the former Yugoslavia (2007) Annual Report, A/62/172–S/2007/469. 1 August 2007. Online, at https://www.icty.org/x/file/About/Reports%20and%20Publications/AnnualReports/annual_report_2007_en.pdf.
International Criminal Tribunal for the former Yugoslavia (2008) Annual Report, A/63/210–S/2008/515. 4 August 2008. Online, at https://www.icty.org/x/file/About/Reports%20and%20Publications/AnnualReports/annual_report_2008_en.pdf.
International Criminal Tribunal for the former Yugoslavia (2009) Annual Report, A/64/205–S/2009/394. 31 July 2009. Online, at https://www.icty.org/x/file/About/Reports%20and%20Publications/AnnualReports/annual_report_2009_en.pdf.
International Criminal Tribunal for the former Yugoslavia (2010) Annual Report, A/65/205–S/2010/413. 30 July 2010. Online, at https://www.icty.org/x/file/About/Reports%20and%20Publications/AnnualReports/annual_report_2010_en.pdf.
International Criminal Tribunal for the former Yugoslavia (2011) Annual Report, A/66/210–S/2011/473. 31 July 2011. Online, at https://www.icty.org/x/file/About/Reports%20and%20Publications/AnnualReports/annual_report_2011_en.pdf.
International Criminal Tribunal for the former Yugoslavia (2012) Annual Report, A/67/214–S/2012/592. 1 August 2012. Online, at https://www.icty.org/x/file/About/Reports%20and%20Publications/AnnualReports/annual_report_2012_en.pdf.
International Criminal Tribunal for the former Yugoslavia (2013) Annual Report, A/68/255–S/2013/463. 2 August 2013. Online, at https://www.icty.org/x/file/About/Reports%20and%20Publications/AnnualReports/annual_report_2013_en.pdf.
International Criminal Tribunal for the former Yugoslavia (2014) Annual Report, A/69/225–S/2014/556. 1 August 2014. Online, at https://www.icty.org/x/file/About/Reports%20and%20Publications/AnnualReports/annual_report_2014_en.pdf.
International Criminal Tribunal for the former Yugoslavia (2015) Annual Report, A/70/226–S/2015/585. 31 July 2015. Online, at https://www.icty.org/x/file/About/Reports%20and%20Publications/AnnualReports/annual_report_2015_en.pdf.
International Criminal Tribunal for the former Yugoslavia (2016) Annual Report, A/71/263–S/2016/670. 1 August 2016. Online, at https://www.icty.org/x/file/About/Reports%20and%20Publications/AnnualReports/annual_report_2016_en.pdf.
International Criminal Tribunal for the former Yugoslavia (2017) Annual Report, A/72/266–S/2017/662. 1 August 2017. Online, at https://www.icty.org/x/file/About/Reports%20and%20Publications/AnnualReports/annual_report_2017_en.pdf.

ICTY Completion Strategy Reports (n = 30)

International Criminal Tribunal for the former Yugoslavia (2002) Completion Strategy Report, S/2002/678. 19 June 2002. Online, at https://www.icty.org/x/file/About/Reports%20and%20Publications/CompletionStrategy/judicial_status_report_june2002_en.pdf.

International Criminal Tribunal for the former Yugoslavia (2004) Completion Strategy Report, S/2004/420. 24 May 2004. Online, at https://www.icty.org/x/file/About/Reports%20and%20Publications/CompletionStrategy/completion_strategy_24may2004_en.pdf.

International Criminal Tribunal for the former Yugoslavia (2004) Completion Strategy Report, S/2004/897. 23 November 2004. Online, at https://www.icty.org/x/file/About/Reports%20and%20Publications/CompletionStrategy/completion_strategy_23november2004_en.pdf.

International Criminal Tribunal for the former Yugoslavia (2005) Completion Strategy Report, S/2005/343. 25 May 2005. Online, at https://www.icty.org/x/file/About/Reports%20and%20Publications/CompletionStrategy/completion_strategy_25may2005_en.pdf.

International Criminal Tribunal for the former Yugoslavia (2005) Completion Strategy Report, S/2005/781. 14 December 2005. Online, at https://www.icty.org/x/file/About/Reports%20and%20Publications/CompletionStrategy/completion_strategy_14december2005_en.pdf.

International Criminal Tribunal for the former Yugoslavia (2006) Completion Strategy Report, S/2006/353. 31 May 2006. Online, at https://www.icty.org/x/file/About/Reports%20and%20Publications/CompletionStrategy/completion_strategy_31may2006_en.pdf.

International Criminal Tribunal for the former Yugoslavia (2006) Completion Strategy Report, S/2006/898. 15 November 2006. Online, at https://www.icty.org/x/file/About/Reports%20and%20Publications/CompletionStrategy/completion_strategy_15december2006_en.pdf.

International Criminal Tribunal for the former Yugoslavia (2007) Completion Strategy Report, S/2007/283. 16 May 2007. Online, at https://www.icty.org/x/file/About/Reports%20and%20Publications/CompletionStrategy/completion_strategy_16may2007_en.pdf.

International Criminal Tribunal for the former Yugoslavia (2007) Completion Strategy Report, S/2007/663. 12 November 2007. Online, at https://www.icty.org/x/file/About/Reports%20and%20Publications/CompletionStrategy/completion_strategy_12november2007_en.pdf.

International Criminal Tribunal for the former Yugoslavia (2008) Completion Strategy Report, S/2008/326. 14 May 2008. Online, at https://www.icty.org/x/file/About/Reports%20and%20Publications/CompletionStrategy/completion_strategy_#x005F;14may2008_en.pdf.

International Criminal Tribunal for the former Yugoslavia (2008) Completion Strategy Report, S/2008/729. 24 November 2008. Online, at https://www.icty.org/x/file/About/Reports%20and%20Publications/CompletionStrategy/completion_strategy_#x005F;24nov2008_en.pdf.

International Criminal Tribunal for the former Yugoslavia (2009) Completion Strategy Report, S/2009/252. 18 May 2009. Online, at https://www.icty.org/x/file/About/Reports%20and%20Publications/CompletionStrategy/completion_strategy_#x005F;18may2009_en.pdf.

LIST OF ICTY DOCUMENTS 157

International Criminal Tribunal for the former Yugoslavia (2009) Completion Strategy Report, S/2009/258. 21 May 2009. Online, at https://documents-dds-ny.un.org/doc/UNDOC/GEN/N09/333/50/PDF/N0933350.pdf?OpenElement.

International Criminal Tribunal for the former Yugoslavia (2009) Completion Strategy Report, S/2009/589. 13 November 2009. Online, at https://www.icty.org/x/file/About/Reports%20and%20Publications/CompletionStrategy/completion_strategy_#x005F;13nov2009_en.pdf.

International Criminal Tribunal for the former Yugoslavia (2010) Completion Strategy Report, S/2010/270. 1 June 2010. Online, at https://www.icty.org/x/file/About/Reports%20and%20Publications/CompletionStrategy/completion_strategy_#x005F;01june2010_en.pdf.

International Criminal Tribunal for the former Yugoslavia (2010) Completion Strategy Report, S/2010/588. 19 November 2010. Online, at https://www.icty.org/x/file/About/Reports%20and%20Publications/CompletionStrategy/completion_strategy_#x005F;19nov2010_en.pdf.

International Criminal Tribunal for the former Yugoslavia (2011) Completion Strategy Report, S/2011/316. 18 May 2011. Online, at https://www.icty.org/x/file/About/Reports%20and%20Publications/CompletionStrategy/completion_strategy_#x005F;18may2011_en.pdf.

International Criminal Tribunal for the former Yugoslavia (2011) Completion Strategy Report, S/2011/716. 16 November 2011. Online, at https://www.icty.org/x/file/About/Reports%20and%20Publications/CompletionStrategy/completion_strategy_#x005F;16nov2011_en.pdf.

International Criminal Tribunal for the former Yugoslavia (2012) Completion Strategy Report, S/2012/354. 23 May 2012. Online, at https://www.icty.org/x/file/About/Reports%20and%20Publications/CompletionStrategy/completion_strategy_#x005F;23may2012_en.pdf.

International Criminal Tribunal for the former Yugoslavia (2012) Completion Strategy Report, S/2012/847. 16 November 2012. Online, at https://www.icty.org/x/file/About/Reports%20and%20Publications/CompletionStrategy/completion_strategy_#x005F;16november2012_en.pdf.

International Criminal Tribunal for the former Yugoslavia (2013) Completion Strategy Report, S/2013/308. 23 May 2013. Online, at https://www.icty.org/x/file/About/Reports%20and%20Publications/CompletionStrategy/completion_strategy_#x005F;23may2013_en.pdf.

International Criminal Tribunal for the former Yugoslavia (2013) Completion Strategy Report, S/2013/678. 18 November 2013. Online, at https://www.icty.org/x/file/About/Reports%20and%20Publications/CompletionStrategy/completion_strategy_#x005F;18nov2013_en.pdf.

International Criminal Tribunal for the former Yugoslavia (2014) Completion Strategy Report, S/2014/351. 16 May 2014. Online, at https://www.icty.org/x/file/About/Reports%20and%20Publications/CompletionStrategy/completion_strategy_16may2014_en.pdf.

International Criminal Tribunal for the former Yugoslavia (2014) Completion Strategy Report, S/2014/827. 19 November 2014. Online, at https://www.icty.org/x/file/About/Reports%20and%20Publications/CompletionStrategy/completion_strategy_#x005F;19nov2014_en.pdf.

International Criminal Tribunal for the former Yugoslavia (2015) Completion Strategy Report, S/2015/342. 15 May 2015. Online, at https://www.icty.org/x/file/About/Reports%20and%20Publications/CompletionStrategy/completion_strategy_#x005F;15may2015_en.pdf.

International Criminal Tribunal for the former Yugoslavia (2015) Completion Strategy Report, S/2015/874. 16 November 2015. Online, at https://www.icty.org/x/file/About/Reports%20and%20Publications/CompletionStrategy/151116_icty_progress_report_en.pdf.

International Criminal Tribunal for the former Yugoslavia (2016) Completion Strategy Report, S/2016/454. 17 May 2016. Online, at https://www.icty.org/sites/icty.org/files/documents/160517_icty_progress_report_en.pdf.

International Criminal Tribunal for the former Yugoslavia (2016) Completion Strategy Report, S/2016/976. 17 November 2016. Online, at https://www.icty.org/sites/icty.org/files/documents/161117_icty_progress_report_en.pdf.

International Criminal Tribunal for the former Yugoslavia (2017) Completion Strategy Report, S/2017/436. 17 May 2017. Online, at https://www.icty.org/sites/icty.org/files/documents/170517_icty_progress_report_en.pdf.

International Criminal Tribunal for the former Yugoslavia (2017) Completion Strategy Report, S/2017/1001. 29 November 2017. Online, at https://www.icty.org/x/file/About/Reports%20and%20Publications/CompletionStrategy/171129-completion-strategy-report-icty.pdf.

UN Security Council Resolutions (n = 9)

United Nations Security Council (1991) Resolution 713. S/RES/713 (1991). Online, at http://unscr.com/en/resolutions/doc/713.

United Nations Security Council (1992) Resolution 764. S/RES/764 (1992). Online, at http://unscr.com/en/resolutions/doc/764.

United Nations Security Council (1992) Resolution 780. S/RES/780 (1992). Online, at http://unscr.com/en/resolutions/doc/780.

United Nations Security Council (1993) Resolution 808. S/RES/808 (1993). Online, at https://www.icty.org/x/file/Legal%20Library/Statute/statute_808_1993_en.pdf.

United Nations Security Council (1993) Resolution 827. S/RES/827 (1993). Online, at https://www.icty.org/x/file/Legal%20Library/Statute/statute_827_1993_en.pdf.

United Nations Security Council (2010) Resolution 1931. S/RES/1931 (2010). Online, at https://www.icty.org/x/file/Legal%20Library/Statute/statute_1931_2010_en.pdf.

United Nations Security Council (2010) Resolution 1966. S/RES/1966 (2010). Online, at http://unscr.com/en/resolutions/doc/1966.

United Nations Security Council (2011) Resolution 1993. S/RES/1993 (2011). Online, at https://www.icty.org/x/file/Legal%20Library/Statute/statute_1993_2011_en.pdf.

United Nations Security Council (2016) Resolution 2306. S/RES/2306 (2016). Online, at https://www.icty.org/x/file/Legal%20Library/Statute/statute_2306_2016_en.pdf.

ICTY Indictments (n = 20)

Prosecutor v. Duško Tadić, Case No. IT-94-1 (1995), Initial Indictment. 13 February 1995. Online, at https://www.icty.org/x/cases/tadic/ind/en/tad-ii950213e.pdf.

Prosecutor v. Miroslav Kvočka et al., Case No. IT-98-30/1 (1995), Initial Indictment. 13 February 1995. Online, at https://www.icty.org/x/cases/kvocka/ind/en/950213.pdf.

Prosecutor v. Duško Tadić, Case No. IT-94-1 (1995), First Amended Indictment. 1 September 1995. Online, at https://www.icty.org/x/cases/tadic/ind/en/tad-1ai950901e.pdf.

Prosecutor v. Duško Tadić, Case No. IT-94-1 (1995), Second Amended Indictment. 14 December 1995. Online, at https://www.icty.org/x/cases/tadic/ind/en/tad-2ai951214e.pdf.

Prosecutor v. Zdravko Mucić et al., Case No. IT-96-21 (1996), Initial Indictment. 19 March 1996. Online, at https://www.icty.org/x/cases/mucic/ind/en/cel-ii960321e.pdf.

Prosecutor v. Zdravko Mucić et al., Case No. IT-96-21 (1996), Amended Indictment. 30 October 1996. Online, at http://icr.icty.org/.

Prosecutor v. Miroslav Kvočka et al., Case No. IT-98-30/1 (1998), Amended Indictment. 9 November 1998. Online, at https://www.icty.org/x/cases/kvocka/ind/en/kvo-1ai981109e.pdf.

Prosecutor v. Radoslav Brdanin, Case No. IT-99-36 (1999), Initial Indictment. 14 March 1999. Online, at https://www.icty.org/x/cases/brdanin/ind/en/brd-ii990314e.pdf.

Prosecutor v. Radoslav Brdanin, Case No. IT-99-36 (1999), Amended Indictment. 16 December 1999. Online, at https://www.icty.org/x/cases/brdanin/ind/en/brd-1ai991216e.pdf.

Prosecutor v. Miroslav Kvočka et al., Case No. IT-98-30/1 (1999), Second Amended Indictment. 31 May 1999. Online, at https://www.icty.org/x/cases/kvocka/ind/en/kvo-2ai990531e.pdf.

Prosecutor v. Miroslav Kvočka et al., Case No. IT-98-30/1 (2000), Amended Indictment. 26 October 2000. Online, at https://www.icty.org/x/cases/kvocka/ind/en/kvo-ai001026e.pdf.

Prosecutor v. Radoslav Brdanin, Case No. IT-99-36 (2001), New Amended Indictment. 9 March 2001. Online, at https://www.icty.org/x/cases/brdanin/ind/en/brd-2ai100312e.pdf.

Prosecutor v. Radoslav Brdanin, Case No. IT-99-36 (2001), Third Amended Indictment. 16 July 2001. Online, at https://www.icty.org/x/cases/brdanin/ind/en/brd-3ai010716e.pdf.

Prosecutor v. Radoslav Brdanin, Case No. IT-99-36 (2001), Fourth Amended Indictment. 10 December 2001. Online, at https://www.icty.org/x/cases/brdanin/ind/en/brd-4ai011210e.pdf.

Prosecutor v. Radoslav Brdanin, Case No. IT-99-36 (2002), Fifth Amended Indictment. 7 October 2002. Online, at https://www.icty.org/x/cases/brdanin/ind/en/brd-5ai021007e.pdf.

Prosecutor v. Radoslav Brdanin, Case No. IT-99-36 (2003), Sixth Amended Indictment. 9 December 2003. Online, at https://www.icty.org/x/cases/brdanin/ind/en/brd-6ai031209e.pdf.

Prosecutor v. Rasim Delić, Case No. IT-04-83 (2005), Initial Indictment. 17 March 2005. Online, at https://www.icty.org/x/cases/delic/ind/en/delic_050317_indictment_en.pdf.

Prosecutor v. Rasim Delić, Case No. IT-04-83 (2006), Second Amended Indictment. 18 April 2006. Online, at http://icr.icty.org/.

Prosecutor v. Rasim Delić, Case No. IT-04-83 (2006), Consolidated Amended Indictment. 8 May 2006. Online, at http://icr.icty.org/.

Prosecutor v. Rasim Delić, Case No. IT-04-83 (2006), Amended Indictment. 14 July 2006. Online, at https://www.icty.org/x/cases/delic/ind/en/del-ind060714e.pdf.

ICTY Judgments (n = 5)

Prosecutor v. Duško Tadić, Case No. IT-94-1 (1997), Trial Judgment. 7 May 1997. Online, at https://www.icty.org/x/cases/tadic/tjug/en/tad-tsj70507JT2-e.pdf.

Prosecutor v. Zdravko Mucić et al., Case No. IT-96-21 (1998), Trial Judgment. 16 November 1998. Online, at https://www.icty.org/x/cases/mucic/tjug/en/981116_judg_en.pdf.

Prosecutor v. Miroslav Kvočka et al., Case No. IT-98-30/1 (2001), Trial Judgment. 2 November 2001. Online, at https://www.icty.org/x/cases/kvocka/tjug/en/kvo-tj011002e.pdf.

Prosecutor v. Radoslav Brdanin, Case No. IT-99-36 (2004), Trial Judgment. 1 September 2004. Online, at https://www.icty.org/x/cases/brdanin/tjug/en/brd-tj040901e.pdf.

Prosecutor v. Rasim Delić, Case No. IT-04-83 (2008), Trial Judgment. 15 September 2008. Online, at https://www.icty.org/x/cases/delic/tjug/en/080915.pdf.

ICTY Trial Hearings (n = 138)

Prosecutor v. Duško Tadić, Case No. IT-94-1 (1996), Trial hearing. 19 June 1996. Online, at https://www.icty.org/x/cases/tadic/trans/en/960619IT.htm.

Prosecutor v. Duško Tadić, Case No. IT-94-1 (1996), Trial hearing. 21 June 1996. Online, at https://www.icty.org/x/cases/tadic/trans/en/960621ed.htm.

Prosecutor v. Duško Tadić, Case No. IT-94-1 (1996), Trial hearing. 18 July 1996. Online, at https://www.icty.org/x/cases/tadic/trans/en/960718IT.htm.

Prosecutor v. Duško Tadić, Case No. IT-94-1 (1996), Trial hearing. 19 July 1996. Online, at https://www.icty.org/x/cases/tadic/trans/en/960719ed.htm.
Prosecutor v. Duško Tadić, Case No. IT-94-1 (1996), Trial hearing. 23 July 1996. Online, at https://www.icty.org/x/cases/tadic/trans/en/960723ed.htm.
Prosecutor v. Duško Tadić, Case No. IT-94-1 (1996), Trial hearing. 24 July 1996. Online, at https://www.icty.org/x/cases/tadic/trans/en/960724IT.htm.
Prosecutor v. Duško Tadić, Case No. IT-94-1 (1996), Trial hearing. 26 July 1996. Online, at https://www.icty.org/x/cases/tadic/trans/en/960726ed.htm.
Prosecutor v. Duško Tadić, Case No. IT-94-1 (1996), Trial hearing. 30 July 1996. Online, at https://www.icty.org/x/cases/tadic/trans/en/960730IT.htm.
Prosecutor v. Duško Tadić, Case No. IT-94-1 (1996), Trial hearing. 6 November 1996. Online, at https://www.icty.org/x/cases/tadic/trans/en/961106ED.htm.
Prosecutor v. Duško Tadić, Case No. IT-94-1 (1996), Trial hearing. 25 November 1996. Online, at https://www.icty.org/x/cases/tadic/trans/en/961125IT.htm.
Prosecutor v. Duško Tadić, Case No. IT-94-1 (1996), Trial hearing. 26 November 1996. Online, at https://www.icty.org/x/cases/tadic/trans/en/961126ED.htm.
Prosecutor v. Zdravko Mucić et al., Case No. IT-96-21 (1997), Trial hearing. 12 March 1997. Online, at https://www.icty.org/x/cases/mucic/trans/en/970312ed.htm.
Prosecutor v. Zdravko Mucić et al., Case No. IT-96-21 (1997), Trial hearing. 17 March 1997. Online, at https://www.icty.org/x/cases/mucic/trans/en/970317IT.htm.
Prosecutor v. Zdravko Mucić et al., Case No. IT-96-21 (1997), Trial hearing. 18 March 1997. Online, at https://www.icty.org/x/cases/mucic/trans/en/970318ED.htm.
Prosecutor v. Zdravko Mucić et al., Case No. IT-96-21 (1997), Trial hearing. 24 March 1997. Online, at https://www.icty.org/x/cases/mucic/trans/en/970324IT.htm.
Prosecutor v. Zdravko Mucić et al., Case No. IT-96-21 (1997), Trial hearing. 25 March 1997. Online, at https://www.icty.org/x/cases/mucic/trans/en/970325ED.htm.
Prosecutor v. Zdravko Mucić et al., Case No. IT-96-21 (1997), Trial hearing. 26 March 1997. Online, at https://www.icty.org/x/cases/mucic/trans/en/970326it.htm.
Prosecutor v. Zdravko Mucić et al., Case No. IT-96-21 (1997), Trial hearing. 27 March 1997. Online, at https://www.icty.org/x/cases/mucic/trans/en/970327ed.htm.
Prosecutor v. Zdravko Mucić et al., Case No. IT-96-21 (1997), Trial hearing. 2 April 1997. Online, at https://www.icty.org/x/cases/mucic/trans/en/970402IT.htm.
Prosecutor v. Zdravko Mucić et al., Case No. IT-96-21 (1997), Trial hearing. 3 April 1997. Online, at https://www.icty.org/x/cases/mucic/trans/en/970403ed.htm.
Prosecutor v. Zdravko Mucić et al., Case No. IT-96-21 (1997), Trial hearing. 14 April 1997. Online, at https://www.icty.org/x/cases/mucic/trans/en/970414ed.htm.
Prosecutor v. Zdravko Mucić et al., Case No. IT-96-21 (1997), Trial hearing. 22 April 1997. Online, at https://www.icty.org/x/cases/mucic/trans/en/970422ED.htm.
Prosecutor v. Zdravko Mucić et al., Case No. IT-96-21 (1997), Trial hearing. 5 May 1997. Online, at https://www.icty.org/x/cases/mucic/trans/en/970505ED.htm.
Prosecutor v. Zdravko Mucić et al., Case No. IT-96-21 (1997), Trial hearing. 6 May 1997. Online, at https://www.icty.org/x/cases/mucic/trans/en/970506IT.htm.
Prosecutor v. Zdravko Mucić et al., Case No. IT-96-21 (1997), Trial hearing. 7 May 1997. Online, at https://www.icty.org/x/cases/mucic/trans/en/970507ed.htm.

Prosecutor v. Zdravko Mucić et al., Case No. IT-96-21 (1997), Trial hearing. 16 June 1997. Online, at https://www.icty.org/x/cases/mucic/trans/en/970616IT.htm.
Prosecutor v. Zdravko Mucić et al., Case No. IT-96-21 (1997), Trial hearing. 7 July 1997. Online, at https://www.icty.org/x/cases/mucic/trans/en/970707ED.htm.
Prosecutor v. Zdravko Mucić et al., Case No. IT-96-21 (1997), Trial hearing. 8 July 1997. Online, at https://www.icty.org/x/cases/mucic/trans/en/970708IT.htm.
Prosecutor v. Zdravko Mucić et al., Case No. IT-96-21 (1997), Trial hearing. 15 July 1997. Online, at https://www.icty.org/x/cases/mucic/trans/en/970715ED.htm.
Prosecutor v. Zdravko Mucić et al., Case No. IT-96-21 (1997), Trial hearing. 4 August 1997. Online, at https://www.icty.org/x/cases/mucic/trans/en/970804IT.htm.
Prosecutor v. Zdravko Mucić et al., Case No. IT-96-21 (1997), Trial hearing. 7 August 1997. Online, at https://www.icty.org/x/cases/mucic/trans/en/970807ED.htm.
Prosecutor v. Zdravko Mucić et al., Case No. IT-96-21 (1997), Trial hearing. 4 September 1997. Online, at https://www.icty.org/x/cases/mucic/trans/en/970904ED.htm.
Prosecutor v. Zdravko Mucić et al., Case No. IT-96-21 (1997), Trial hearing. 13 October 1997. Online, at https://www.icty.org/x/cases/mucic/trans/en/971013ed.htm.
Prosecutor v. Zdravko Mucić et al., Case No. IT-96-21 (1997), Trial hearing. 14 October 1997. Online, at https://www.icty.org/x/cases/mucic/trans/en/971014ed.htm.
Prosecutor v. Miroslav Kvočka et al., Case No. IT-98-30/1 (2000), Trial hearing. 29 February 2000. Online, at https://www.icty.org/x/cases/kvocka/trans/en/000229it.htm.
Prosecutor v. Miroslav Kvočka et al., Case No. IT-98-30/1 (2000), Trial hearing. 6 March 2000. Online, at https://www.icty.org/x/cases/kvocka/trans/en/000306it.htm.
Prosecutor v. Miroslav Kvočka et al., Case No. IT-98-30/1 (2000), Trial hearing. 4 May 2000. Online, at https://www.icty.org/x/cases/kvocka/trans/en/000504ed.htm.
Prosecutor v. Miroslav Kvočka et al., Case No. IT-98-30/1 (2000), Trial hearing. 8 May 2000. Online, at http://icr.icty.org/.
Prosecutor v. Miroslav Kvočka et al., Case No. IT-98-30/1 (2000), Trial hearing. 15 May 2000. Online, at https://www.icty.org/x/cases/kvocka/trans/en/000515ed.htm.
Prosecutor v. Miroslav Kvočka et al., Case No. IT-98-30/1 (2000), Trial hearing. 17 May 2000. Online, at https://www.icty.org/x/cases/kvocka/trans/en/000517ed.htm.
Prosecutor v. Miroslav Kvočka et al., Case No. IT-98-30/1 (2000), Trial hearing. 19 May 2000. Online, at https://www.icty.org/x/cases/kvocka/trans/en/000519ed.htm.
Prosecutor v. Miroslav Kvočka et al., Case No. IT-98-30/1 (2000), Trial hearing. 5 June 2000. Online, at https://www.icty.org/x/cases/kvocka/trans/en/000605ed.htm.
Prosecutor v. Miroslav Kvočka et al., Case No. IT-98-30/1 (2000), Trial hearing. 13 June 2000. Online, at https://www.icty.org/x/cases/kvocka/trans/en/000613ed.htm.
Prosecutor v. Miroslav Kvočka et al., Case No. IT-98-30/1 (2000), Trial hearing. 3 July 2000. Online, at https://www.icty.org/x/cases/kvocka/trans/en/000703it.htm.
Prosecutor v. Miroslav Kvočka et al., Case No. IT-98-30/1 (2000), Trial hearing. 5 July 2000. Online, at https://www.icty.org/x/cases/kvocka/trans/en/000705ed.htm.
Prosecutor v. Miroslav Kvočka et al., Case No. IT-98-30/1 (2000), Trial hearing. 6 July 2000. Online, at https://www.icty.org/x/cases/kvocka/trans/en/000706ed.htm.

Prosecutor v. Miroslav Kvočka et al., Case No. IT-98-30/1 (2000), Trial hearing. 7 July 2000. Online, at https://www.icty.org/x/cases/kvocka/trans/en/000707ed.htm.

Prosecutor v. Miroslav Kvočka et al., Case No. IT-98-30/1 (2000), Trial hearing. 10 July 2000. Online, at https://www.icty.org/x/cases/kvocka/trans/en/000710ed.htm.

Prosecutor v. Miroslav Kvočka et al., Case No. IT-98-30/1 (2000), Trial hearing. 29 August 2000. Online, at https://www.icty.org/x/cases/kvocka/trans/en/000829ed.htm; https://www.icty.org/x/cases/kvocka/trans/en/000829se.htm.

Prosecutor v. Miroslav Kvočka et al., Case No. IT-98-30/1 (2000), Trial hearing. 30 August 2000. Online, at https://www.icty.org/x/cases/kvocka/trans/en/000830ed.htm.

Prosecutor v. Miroslav Kvočka et al., Case No. IT-98-30/1 (2000), Trial hearing. 31 August 2000. Online, at https://www.icty.org/x/cases/kvocka/trans/en/000831ed.htm;https://www.icty.org/x/cases/kvocka/trans/en/000831SC.htm.

Prosecutor v. Miroslav Kvočka et al., Case No. IT-98-30/1 (2000), Trial hearing. 1 September 2000. Online, at https://www.icty.org/x/cases/kvocka/trans/en/000901it.htm.

Prosecutor v. Miroslav Kvočka et al., Case No. IT-98-30/1 (2000), Trial hearing. 5 September 2000. Online, at https://www.icty.org/x/cases/kvocka/trans/en/000905ed.htm.

Prosecutor v. Miroslav Kvočka et al., Case No. IT-98-30/1 (2000), Trial hearing. 12 September 2000. Online, at https://www.icty.org/x/cases/kvocka/trans/en/000912ed.htm.

Prosecutor v. Miroslav Kvočka et al., Case No. IT-98-30/1 (2000), Trial hearing. 25 September 2000. Online, at https://www.icty.org/x/cases/kvocka/trans/en/000925ed.htm.

Prosecutor v. Miroslav Kvočka et al., Case No. IT-98-30/1 (2000), Trial hearing. 26 September 2000. Online, at https://www.icty.org/x/cases/kvocka/trans/en/000926ed.htm.

Prosecutor v. Miroslav Kvočka et al., Case No. IT-98-30/1 (2000), Trial hearing. 28 September 2000. Online, at https://www.icty.org/x/cases/kvocka/trans/en/000928ed.htm.

Prosecutor v. Miroslav Kvočka et al., Case No. IT-98-30/1 (2000), Trial hearing. 3 October 2000. Online, at https://www.icty.org/x/cases/kvocka/trans/en/001003ed.htm.

Prosecutor v. Miroslav Kvočka et al., Case No. IT-98-30/1 (2001), Trial hearing. 8 February 2001. Online, at https://www.icty.org/x/cases/kvocka/trans/en/010208ed.htm.

Prosecutor v. Miroslav Kvočka et al., Case No. IT-98-30/1 (2001), Trial hearing. 12 February 2001. Online, at https://www.icty.org/x/cases/kvocka/trans/en/010212ed.htm.

Prosecutor v. Miroslav Kvočka et al., Case No. IT-98-30/1 (2001), Trial hearing. 13 February 2001. Online, at http://icr.icty.org/.

Prosecutor v. Miroslav Kvočka et al., Case No. IT-98-30/1 (2001), Trial hearing. 15 February 2001. Online, at https://www.icty.org/x/cases/kvocka/trans/en/010215ed.htm.

Prosecutor v. Miroslav Kvočka et al., Case No. IT-98-30/1 (2001), Trial hearing. 7 March 2001. Online, at https://www.icty.org/x/cases/kvocka/trans/en/010307ed.htm.

Prosecutor v. Miroslav Kvočka et al., Case No. IT-98-30/1 (2001), Trial hearing. 8 March 2001. Online, at https://www.icty.org/x/cases/kvocka/trans/en/010308ed.htm.

Prosecutor v. Miroslav Kvočka et al., Case No. IT-98-30/1 (2001), Trial hearing. 8 May 2001. Online, at https://www.icty.org/x/cases/kvocka/trans/en/010508ed.htm.

Prosecutor v. Miroslav Kvočka et al., Case No. IT-98-30/1 (2001), Trial hearing. 11 May 2001. Online, at https://www.icty.org/x/cases/kvocka/trans/en/010511ed.htm.

Prosecutor v. Radoslav Brdanin, Case No. IT-99-36 (2002), Trial hearing. 25 February 2002. Online, at https://www.icty.org/x/cases/brdanin/trans/en/020225IT.htm.

Prosecutor v. Radoslav Brdanin, Case No. IT-99-36 (2002), Trial hearing. 26 February 2002. Online, at https://www.icty.org/x/cases/brdanin/trans/en/020226IT.htm.

Prosecutor v. Radoslav Brdanin, Case No. IT-99-36 (2002), Trial hearing. 27 February 2002. Online, at https://www.icty.org/x/cases/brdanin/trans/en/020227IT.htm.

Prosecutor v. Radoslav Brdanin, Case No. IT-99-36 (2002), Trial hearing. 16 April 2002. Online, at https://www.icty.org/x/cases/brdanin/trans/en/020416ED.htm.

Prosecutor v. Radoslav Brdanin, Case No. IT-99-36 (2002), Trial hearing. 25 April 2002. Online, at https://www.icty.org/x/cases/brdanin/trans/en/020425IT.htm.

Prosecutor v. Radoslav Brdanin, Case No. IT-99-36 (2002), Trial hearing. 26 April 2002. Online, at https://www.icty.org/x/cases/brdanin/trans/en/020426MH.htm; https://www.icty.org/x/cases/brdanin/trans/en/020426IT.htm.

Prosecutor v. Radoslav Brdanin, Case No. IT-99-36 (2002), Trial hearing. 28 May 2002. Online, at https://www.icty.org/x/cases/brdanin/trans/en/020528IT.htm.

Prosecutor v. Radoslav Brdanin, Case No. IT-99-36 (2002), Trial hearing. 31 May 2002. Online, at https://www.icty.org/x/cases/brdanin/trans/en/020531ED.htm.

Prosecutor v. Radoslav Brdanin, Case No. IT-99-36 (2002), Trial hearing. 3 June 2002. Online, at https://www.icty.org/x/cases/brdanin/trans/en/020603IT.htm.

Prosecutor v. Radoslav Brdanin, Case No. IT-99-36 (2002), Trial hearing. 4 June 2002. Online, at https://www.icty.org/x/cases/brdanin/trans/en/020604IT.htm.

Prosecutor v. Radoslav Brdanin, Case No. IT-99-36 (2002), Trial hearing. 7 June 2002. Online, at https://www.icty.org/x/cases/brdanin/trans/en/020607IT.htm.

Prosecutor v. Radoslav Brdanin, Case No. IT-99-36 (2002), Trial hearing. 17 June 2002. Online, at https://www.icty.org/x/cases/brdanin/trans/en/020617IT.htm.

Prosecutor v. Radoslav Brdanin, Case No. IT-99-36 (2002), Trial hearing. 18 June 2002. Online, at https://www.icty.org/x/cases/brdanin/trans/en/020618IT.htm.

Prosecutor v. Radoslav Brdanin, Case No. IT-99-36 (2002), Trial hearing. 19 June 2002. Online, at https://www.icty.org/x/cases/brdanin/trans/en/020619IT.htm.

Prosecutor v. Radoslav Brdanin, Case No. IT-99-36 (2002), Trial hearing. 21 June 2002. Online, at https://www.icty.org/x/cases/brdanin/trans/en/020621ED.htm.

Prosecutor v. Radoslav Brdanin, Case No. IT-99-36 (2002), Trial hearing. 4 July 2002. Online, at https://www.icty.org/x/cases/brdanin/trans/en/020704IT.htm.

Prosecutor v. Radoslav Brdanin, Case No. IT-99-36 (2002), Trial hearing. 8 July 2002. Online, at https://www.icty.org/x/cases/brdanin/trans/en/020708IT.htm.

Prosecutor v. Radoslav Brdanin, Case No. IT-99-36 (2002), Trial hearing. 4 September 2002. Online, at https://www.icty.org/x/cases/brdanin/trans/en/020904IT.htm.

Prosecutor v. Radoslav Brdanin, Case No. IT-99-36 (2002), Trial hearing. 5 September 2002. Online, at https://www.icty.org/x/cases/brdanin/trans/en/020905IT.htm; https://www.icty.org/x/cases/brdanin/trans/en/020905ED.htm.

Prosecutor v. Radoslav Brdanin, Case No. IT-99-36 (2002), Trial hearing. 9 October 2002. Online, at https://www.icty.org/x/cases/brdanin/trans/en/021009IT.htm.
Prosecutor v. Radoslav Brdanin, Case No. IT-99-36 (2002), Trial hearing. 10 October 2002. Online, at https://www.icty.org/x/cases/brdanin/trans/en/021010ED.htm.
Prosecutor v. Radoslav Brdanin, Case No. IT-99-36 (2002), Trial hearing. 14 October 2002. Online, at https://www.icty.org/x/cases/brdanin/trans/en/021014IT.htm.
Prosecutor v. Radoslav Brdanin, Case No. IT-99-36 (2002), Trial hearing. 15 October 2002. Online, at https://www.icty.org/x/cases/brdanin/trans/en/021015IT.htm.
Prosecutor v. Radoslav Brdanin, Case No. IT-99-36 (2002), Trial hearing. 16 October 2002. Online, at https://www.icty.org/x/cases/brdanin/trans/en/021016IT.htm.
Prosecutor v. Radoslav Brdanin, Case No. IT-99-36 (2002), Trial hearing. 20 November 2002. Online, at https://www.icty.org/x/cases/brdanin/trans/en/021120ED.htm.
Prosecutor v. Radoslav Brdanin, Case No. IT-99-36 (2002), Trial hearing. 4 December 2002. Online, at https://www.icty.org/x/cases/brdanin/trans/en/021204ED.htm.
Prosecutor v. Radoslav Brdanin, Case No. IT-99-36 (2002), Trial hearing. 12 December 2002. Online, at https://www.icty.org/x/cases/brdanin/trans/en/021212ED.htm.
Prosecutor v. Radoslav Brdanin, Case No. IT-99-36 (2003), Trial hearing. 13 January 2003. Online, at https://www.icty.org/x/cases/brdanin/trans/en/030113ED.htm.
Prosecutor v. Radoslav Brdanin, Case No. IT-99-36 (2003), Trial hearing. 27 January 2003. Online, at https://www.icty.org/x/cases/brdanin/trans/en/030127ED.htm.
Prosecutor v. Radoslav Brdanin, Case No. IT-99-36 (2003), Trial hearing. 28 January 2003. Online, at https://www.icty.org/x/cases/brdanin/trans/en/030128ED.htm.
Prosecutor v. Radoslav Brdanin, Case No. IT-99-36 (2003), Trial hearing. 31 January 2003. Online, at https://www.icty.org/x/cases/brdanin/trans/en/030131ED.htm.
Prosecutor v. Radoslav Brdanin, Case No. IT-99-36 (2003), Trial hearing. 6 February 2003. Online, at https://www.icty.org/x/cases/brdanin/trans/en/030206ED.htm.
Prosecutor v. Radoslav Brdanin, Case No. IT-99-36 (2003), Trial hearing. 26 February 2003. Online, at https://www.icty.org/x/cases/brdanin/trans/en/030226ED.htm.
Prosecutor v. Radoslav Brdanin, Case No. IT-99-36 (2003), Trial hearing. 2 June 2003. Online, at https://www.icty.org/x/cases/brdanin/trans/en/030602ED.htm.
Prosecutor v. Radoslav Brdanin, Case No. IT-99-36 (2003), Trial hearing. 3 June 2003. Online, at https://www.icty.org/x/cases/brdanin/trans/en/030603ED.htm.
Prosecutor v. Radoslav Brdanin, Case No. IT-99-36 (2003), Trial hearing. 4 June 2003. Online, at https://www.icty.org/x/cases/brdanin/trans/en/030604ED.htm.
Prosecutor v. Radoslav Brdanin, Case No. IT-99-36 (2003), Trial hearing. 12 June 2003. Online, at https://www.icty.org/x/cases/brdanin/trans/en/030612ED.htm.
Prosecutor v. Radoslav Brdanin, Case No. IT-99-36 (2003), Trial hearing. 13 June 2003. Online, at https://www.icty.org/x/cases/brdanin/trans/en/030613ED.htm.
Prosecutor v. Radoslav Brdanin, Case No. IT-99-36 (2003), Trial hearing. 20 June 2003. Online, at https://www.icty.org/x/cases/brdanin/trans/en/030620ED.htm.
Prosecutor v. Radoslav Brdanin, Case No. IT-99-36 (2003), Trial hearing. 23 June 2003. Online, at https://www.icty.org/x/cases/brdanin/trans/en/030623ED.htm.
Prosecutor v. Radoslav Brdanin, Case No. IT-99-36 (2003), Trial hearing. 25 June 2003. Online, at https://www.icty.org/x/cases/brdanin/trans/en/030625ED.htm.

Prosecutor v. Rasim Delić, Case No. IT-04-83 (2007), Trial hearing. 10 July 2007. Online, at https://www.icty.org/x/cases/delic/trans/en/070710IT.htm.
Prosecutor v. Rasim Delić, Case No. IT-04-83 (2007), Trial hearing. 11 July 2007. Online, at https://www.icty.org/x/cases/delic/trans/en/070711IT.htm.
Prosecutor v. Rasim Delić, Case No. IT-04-83 (2007), Trial hearing. 12 July 2007. Online, at https://www.icty.org/x/cases/delic/trans/en/070712IT.htm.
Prosecutor v. Rasim Delić, Case No. IT-04-83 (2007), Trial hearing. 13 July 2007. Online, at https://www.icty.org/x/cases/delic/trans/en/070713ED.htm.
Prosecutor v. Rasim Delić, Case No. IT-04-83 (2007), Trial hearing. 16 July 2007. Online, at https://www.icty.org/x/cases/delic/trans/en/070716IT.htm.
Prosecutor v. Rasim Delić, Case No. IT-04-83 (2007), Trial hearing. 17 July 2007. Online, at https://www.icty.org/x/cases/delic/trans/en/070717ED.htm.
Prosecutor v. Rasim Delić, Case No. IT-04-83 (2007), Trial hearing. 18 July 2007. Online, at https://www.icty.org/x/cases/delic/trans/en/070718ED.htm.
Prosecutor v. Rasim Delić, Case No. IT-04-83 (2007), Trial hearing. 19 July 2007. Online, at https://www.icty.org/x/cases/delic/trans/en/070719ED.htm.
Prosecutor v. Rasim Delić, Case No. IT-04-83 (2007), Trial hearing. 20 July 2007. Online, at https://www.icty.org/x/cases/delic/trans/en/070720ED.htm.
Prosecutor v. Rasim Delić, Case No. IT-04-83 (2007), Trial hearing. 23 July 2007. Online, at https://www.icty.org/x/cases/delic/trans/en/070723ED.htm.
Prosecutor v. Rasim Delić, Case No. IT-04-83 (2007), Trial hearing. 30 August 2007. Online, at https://www.icty.org/x/cases/delic/trans/en/070830ED.htm.
Prosecutor v. Rasim Delić, Case No. IT-04-83 (2007), Trial hearing. 7 September 2007. Online, at https://www.icty.org/x/cases/delic/trans/en/070907IT.htm.
Prosecutor v. Rasim Delić, Case No. IT-04-83 (2007), Trial hearing. 8 September 2007. Online, at https://www.icty.org/x/cases/delic/trans/en/070908IT.htm.
Prosecutor v. Rasim Delić, Case No. IT-04-83 (2007), Trial hearing. 27 September 2007. Online, at https://www.icty.org/x/cases/delic/trans/en/070927IT.htm.
Prosecutor v. Rasim Delić, Case No. IT-04-83 (2007), Trial hearing. 3 October 2007. Online, at https://www.icty.org/x/cases/delic/trans/en/071003IT.htm.
Prosecutor v. Rasim Delić, Case No. IT-04-83 (2007), Trial hearing. 4 October 2007. Online, at https://www.icty.org/x/cases/delic/trans/en/071004IT.htm.
Prosecutor v. Rasim Delić, Case No. IT-04-83 (2007), Trial hearing. 5 October 2007. Online, at https://www.icty.org/x/cases/delic/trans/en/071005IT.htm.
Prosecutor v. Rasim Delić, Case No. IT-04-83 (2007), Trial hearing. 8 October 2007. Online, at https://www.icty.org/x/cases/delic/trans/en/071008IT.htm.
Prosecutor v. Rasim Delić, Case No. IT-04-83 (2007), Trial hearing. 15 October 2007. Online, at https://www.icty.org/x/cases/delic/trans/en/071015ED.htm.
Prosecutor v. Rasim Delić, Case No. IT-04-83 (2007), Trial hearing. 5 November 2007. Online, at https://www.icty.org/x/cases/delic/trans/en/071105IT.htm.
Prosecutor v. Rasim Delić, Case No. IT-04-83 (2007), Trial hearing. 9 November 2007. Online, at https://www.icty.org/x/cases/delic/trans/en/071109IT.htm.
Prosecutor v. Rasim Delić, Case No. IT-04-83 (2007), Trial hearing. 13 November 2007. Online, at https://www.icty.org/x/cases/delic/trans/en/071113IT.htm.
Prosecutor v. Rasim Delić, Case No. IT-04-83 (2007), Trial hearing. 21 November 2007. Online, at https://www.icty.org/x/cases/delic/trans/en/071121ED.htm.

Prosecutor v. Rasim Delić, Case No. IT-04-83 (2007), Trial hearing. 22 November 2007. Online, at https://www.icty.org/x/cases/delic/trans/en/071122ED.htm.
Prosecutor v. Rasim Delić, Case No. IT-04-83 (2007), Trial hearing. 5 December 2007. Online, at https://www.icty.org/x/cases/delic/trans/en/071205ED.htm.
Prosecutor v. Rasim Delić, Case No. IT-04-83 (2008), Trial hearing. 11 March 2008. Online, at https://www.icty.org/x/cases/delic/trans/en/080311IT.htm.
Prosecutor v. Rasim Delić, Case No. IT-04-83 (2008), Trial hearing. 12 March 2008. Online, at https://www.icty.org/x/cases/delic/trans/en/080312ED.htm.
Prosecutor v. Rasim Delić, Case No. IT-04-83 (2008), Trial hearing. 13 March 2008. Online, at https://www.icty.org/x/cases/delic/trans/en/080313IT.htm.
Prosecutor v. Rasim Delić, Case No. IT-04-83 (2008), Trial hearing. 17 April 2008. Online, at https://www.icty.org/x/cases/delic/trans/en/080417ED.htm.
Prosecutor v. Rasim Delić, Case No. IT-04-83 (2008), Trial hearing. 10 June 2008. Online, at https://www.icty.org/x/cases/delic/trans/en/080610ED.htm.
Prosecutor v. Rasim Delić, Case No. IT-04-83 (2008), Trial hearing. 11 June 2008. Online, at https://www.icty.org/x/cases/delic/trans/en/080611ED.htm.

Other Documents (n = 39)

Kozarski Vjesnik (1992) "Krajina representatives in Prijedor," War Edition. 17 July 1992. English translation. Online, at http://icr.icty.org/.
1 PWO Milinfosum (1993) No. 059. 27 June 1993, Online, at http://icr.icty.org/.
United Nations Security Council (1993) Report of the Secretary-General Pursuant to Paragraph 2 of Security Council Resolution 808 (1993), S/25704. 3 May 1993. Online, at https://www.icty.org/x/file/Legal%20Library/Statute/statute_re808_1993_en.pdf.
United Nations Security Council (1993) Provisional Verbatim Record of the Three Thousand Two Hundred and Seventeenth Meeting, S/PV.3217. 25 May 1993. Online, at https://www.icty.org/x/file/Legal%20Library/Statute/930525-unsc-verbatim-record.pdf.
International Criminal Tribunal for the former Yugoslavia (1994) Rules of Procedure and Evidence, IT/32. 11 February 1994. Online, at https://www.icty.org/x/file/Legal%20Library/Rules_procedure_evidence/IT032_original_en.pdf.
Republic of Bosnia and Herzegovina Ministry of Defence Security Administration (1994) Defence of Republic Military Secret Bulletin, No. 162. 14 August 1994. English translation. Online, at http://icr.icty.org/.
Republic of Bosnia and Herzegovina Ministry of Defence Security Administration (1994) Defence of Republic Military Secret Bulletin, No. 163. 15 August 1994. English translation. Online, at http://icr.icty.org/.
Republic of Bosnia and Herzegovina Ministry of Defence Security Administration (1994) Defence of Republic Military Secret Bulletin, No. 211. 15 October 1994. English translation. Online, at http://icr.icty.org/.

Republic of Bosnia and Herzegovina Ministry of Defence Military Security Administration (1995) Defence of Republic Military Secret Bulletin, No. 7. 10 January 1995. English translation. Online, at http://icr.icty.org/.

Republic of Bosnia and Herzegovina Ministry of Defence Military Security Administration (1995) Defence of Republic Military Secret Bulletin, No. 29. 20 February 1995. English translation. Online, at http://icr.icty.org/.

Republic of Bosnia and Herzegovina Ministry of Defence Security Services Department (1995) Report: Behaviour of Members of the *Asim Čandžić* Unit of the 328th bbr/Mountain Brigade, 03/1-225/195. 6 March 1995. English translation. Online, at http://icr.icty.org/.

Republic of Bosnia and Herzegovina Ministry of Defence Military Security Administration (1995) Defence of Republic Military Secret Bulletin, No. 38. 12 March 1995. English translation. Online, at http://icr.icty.org/.

Republic of Bosnia and Herzegovina Ministry of Defence Military Security Service Administration (1995) Defence of Republic Military Secret Bulletin, 7-3/29-245. 12 April 1995. English translation. Online, at http://icr.icty.org/.

Republic of Bosnia and Herzegovina Ministry of Defence Military Security Service Administration (1995) Defence of Republic Military Secret Bulletin, No. 78. 15 May 1995. English translation. Online, at http://icr.icty.org/.

Republic of Bosnia and Herzegovina Ministry of Defence Military Security Service Administration (1995) Defence of Republic Military Secret Bulletin, No. 81. 18 May 1995. English translation. Online, at http://icr.icty.org/.

Republic of Bosnia and Herzegovina Ministry of Defence Military Security Service Administration (1995) Defence of Republic Military Secret Bulletin, No. 85. 23 May 1995. English translation. Online, at http://icr.icty.org/.

Republic of Bosnia and Herzegovina Ministry of Defence Security Service Section (1995) Defence of Republic Military Secret, Operation "Vranduk" "El Mudžahid" Detachment Delivering Report, 04/8250-1. 9 June 1995. English translation. Online, at http://icr.icty.org/.

Republic of Bosnia and Herzegovina Ministry of Defence Security Service Section (1995) Defence of Republic Military Secret, Information on *El Mudžahedin*, 03-1-174-125. 15 June 1995. English translation. Online, at http://icr.icty.org/.

Republic of Bosnia and Herzegovina Ministry of Defence Military Security Service Administration (1995) Defence of Republic Military Secret Bulletin, No. 125. 10 July 1995. English translation. Online, at http://icr.icty.org/.

Republic of Bosnia and Herzegovina Ministry of Defence Military Security Service Administration (1995) Defence of Republic Military Secret Bulletin, No. 130. 15 July 1995. English translation. Online, at http://icr.icty.org/.

Republic of Bosnia and Herzegovina Ministry of Defence Military Security Service Administration (1995) Defence of Republic Military Secret Bulletin, No. 149. 4 August 1995. English translation. Online, at http://icr.icty.org/.

Republic of Bosnia and Herzegovina Ministry of Defence Department of the Security Service (1995) Defence of Republic Military Secret, Information Relations in the 35th Land Forces Division, 03/1-295-311. 12 August 1995. English translation. Online, at http://icr.icty.org/.

LIST OF ICTY DOCUMENTS 169

Republic of Bosnia and Herzegovina Ministry of Defence Department of the Security Service (1995) Defence of Republic Military Secret, Situation in the *Asim Čamdžić* IDČ Report, 03/1-47-55. 24 October 1995. English translation. Online, at http://icr.icty.org/.

International Criminal Tribunal for the former Yugoslavia (2001) Amendment to Statement and Witness Statement of Mirsad Palić. 31 July 2001. Online, at http://icr.icty.org/.

International Criminal Tribunal for the former Yugoslavia (2002) Witness: Jusuf Arifagić (Open Session), Examined by Mr. Waidyaratne. 28 August 2002 Online, at http://icr.icty.org/.

International Criminal Tribunal for the former Yugoslavia (2002) Disclosure of Additional Relevant Information Provided to the Office of the Prosecutor by Atiz Dzafic, Supplemental Information Sheet. 17 October 2002. Online, at http://icr.icty.org/.

International Criminal Tribunal for the former Yugoslavia (2003) Witness Statement of Alija Verem. 3 March 2003. Online, at http://icr.icty.org/.

International Criminal Tribunal for the former Yugoslavia (2003) Witness Statement of Safet Bibić. 3 March 2003. Online, at http://icr.icty.org/.

International Criminal Tribunal for the former Yugoslavia (2003) Witness Statement of Zijad Ramić. 15 May 2003. Online, at http://icr.icty.org/.

International Criminal Tribunal for the former Yugoslavia (2003) Witness Statement of Ferid Mahalbašić. 28 May 2003. Online, at http://icr.icty.org/.

International Criminal Tribunal for the former Yugoslavia (2003) Witness Statement of Fikret Djikic. 7 July 2003. Online, at http://icr.icty.org/.

International Criminal Tribunal for the former Yugoslavia (2006) Witness Statement of Muhamed Omerašević. 24 October 2006. Online, at http://icr.icty.org/.

International Criminal Tribunal for the former Yugoslavia (2007) Transcript of Conversation between Andrew Hogg (Journalist) and Abdel Aziz. 10 July 2007. Online, at http://icr.icty.org/.

International Criminal Tribunal for the former Yugoslavia (2007) Witness Statement of Branko Šikanić. 19 October 2007. Online, at http://icr.icty.org/.

International Criminal Tribunal for the former Yugoslavia (2007) Witness Statement of Enes Malićbegović. 21 October 2007. Online, at http://icr.icty.org/.

International Criminal Tribunal for the former Yugoslavia (2009) Updated Statute of the International Criminal Tribunal for the former Yugoslavia. September 2009. Online, at https://www.icty.org/x/file/Legal%20Library/Statute/statute_sept09_en.pdf.

International Criminal Tribunal for the former Yugoslavia (2015) Amendments to the Rules of Procedure and Evidence, IT/282. 10 July 2015. Online, at https://www.icty.org/x/file/Legal%20Library/Rules_procedure_evidence/IT032Rev50_en.pdf.

International Criminal Tribunal for the former Yugoslavia (2015) Rules of Procedure and Evidence, IT/32/Rev.50. 8 July 2015. Online, at https://www.icty.org/x/file/Legal%20Library/Rules_procedure_evidence/150710-it-282-en.pdf.

International Criminal Tribunal for the former Yugoslavia (2000) Interview with Drago Prcać at the ICTY, 3/167A. 27-28 April 2000. Online, at http://icr.icty.org/.

Notes

Chapter 1

1. I follow Melanie Richter-Montpetit's lead by using "cis-" in parentheses throughout this book to describe detainees and guards "to indicate that while the public discourse presume[s] that torturers and victims were non-trans∗, we cannot actually know whether they identify as cisgender" (2016, 108).

Chapter 2

1. This project also analyzes the key legal and operational texts of the ICTY: the Statute, UNSC resolutions pertaining to the ICTY, Rules of Procedure and Evidence, annual reports, and completion strategy reports. While the ICTY texts under analysis are all made available in English, there are difficulties related to my positionality and my analysis of the texts. In many instances, testimonies of witnesses or defendants are originally in Serb/Bosnian/Croat, and then translated into English. The process of translation means that any expression may be transformed or altered from its "intended" form (see Perrin 2016, 275–76). Furthermore, my understanding of terms or phrases that are untranslatable or specific to the Balkan languages is also limited by my cultural, national, and ethnic identity.

Chapter 3

1. The conflicts in the former Yugoslavia stemmed from Slovenian, Bosnian, Croatian, and Kosovar declarations of independence. The conflicts were characterized by crimes of ethnic cleansing, particularly by ethnic Serbs against Bosnian Muslims and Albanian Kosovars, but atrocities were also committed by Croats, Bosnian Muslims, and Albanian Kosovars against Serb populations. The conflict in Bosnia and Herzegovina was the deadliest in the region, resulting in at least 100,000 people dead and two million Bosnians displaced. For a more detailed summary of the conflicts in the former Yugoslavia, see ICTY (n.d.).
2. For a critical feminist critique of these radical feminist perspectives, see Engle (2005, 2020).
3. John Reynolds and Sujith Xavier argue that "from a Third World perspective . . . [the ICTR was] seen as a tokenistic corollary" in contrast to the ICTY, as the ICTR's "creation had been rendered unavoidable only by the immediate Yugoslav precedent and belated western guilt over the Rwandan genocide" (2016, 963). Western media attention at the time of the Rwandan genocide and the Yugoslav conflicts tended to focus on the latter. David Patrick argues this was because of the former Yugoslavia's "geographical proximity to the West" (2016, 140). Bridget Robison quotes two peacekeepers who went to Bosnia, encapsulating the racist discourses underpinning intervention: "Bosnia was important because it was Europe. On the doorstep—white Europeans like us being killed. Much worse things were happening in parts of Africa and Asia but they were not considered as important as the Balkans" (2004, 386).
4. As Ba et al. remark, this Nuremberg narrative is both deeply racialized and has racial/racist effects, contributing to the whiteness of international (criminal) law: "To situate Nuremberg as an epochal moment demanding singular and unprecedented redress is to imagine that the

500 years of colonial harm, genocide, war crimes, occupations, and crimes against humanity are somehow lesser horrors" (2023, 3).
5. "The Balkans" and "Balkanism" should be understood as plural and polysemic (M. Todorova 1997, 22), rather than a homogeneous category of classification or analysis. For example, what constitutes Balkan identity is arguably different from a Western or European gaze, in contrast to how Balkan populations view themselves.
6. On the question of religion, ethnic and religious identities are often fused together or interchangeable in the Yugoslav context, so that being Muslim, for example, can be considered a core part of one's ethnic identity (Ognjenović and Jozelić 2014, 3; see Chapter 5): "Religion [in Bosnia] is more than a set of beliefs. It is part of a person's cultural identity, whether or not one is a believer" (Bringa 1995, 86, quoted in Ognjenović and Jozelić 2014, 186).

Chapter 4

1. See also "victiming" (Elander 2018a, 11).
2. *Balija* is an ethnic slur against Bosnian Muslims.
3. See also *Delić* 2005, Initial Indictment, para 30; *Delić* 2007, Trial hearing 3 October; *Delić* 2007, Trial hearing 19 October.
4. Analyzing a different context—UK humanitarian intervention discourse—Patrick Vernon similarly observes a "paradox through which ISIL terrorists are framed as queer subjects and a threat to queers, due to their sexual and civilisational barbarism" (2024, 162).
5. See also in *Delić* where "a foreign Mujahedin forcibly lifted DRW-1's shirt, took down her pants, and touched her breasts and other private parts" (*Delić* 2008, Trial Judgment, para 318).

Chapter 5

1. The discussions here pertain to survivors subverting violence through an analysis of court testimonies and within the broader juridical context of the Tribunal. While I found evidence of witnesses and survivors engaging in acts of resistance before the widespread outbreak of conflict in Bosnia—such as a doctor issuing medical certificates so men could be exempt from conscription (*Brdanin* 2002, Trial hearing 3 June)—these practices are not the focus of my queer reading.
2. See, for example, *Kvočka et al.* 2001, Trial Judgment, para 592; *Mucić et al.* 1997, Trial hearing 18 March; *Mucić et al.* 1997, Trial hearing 25 March; *Brdanin* 2002, Trial hearing 3 June.

Chapter 6

1. Ardi Imseis has characterized international law's relationship with Palestine as one that relegates the latter to "international legal subalternity" (2023).

References

Abazi, Enika, and Albert Doja (2016) "International representations of Balkan wars: A socio-anthropological approach in international relations perspective," *Cambridge Review of International Relations* 29(2): 581–610.

Abazi, Enika, and Albert Doja (2017) "The past in the present: Time and narrative of Balkan wars in media industry and international politics," *Third World Quarterly* 38(4): 1012–1042.

Ackerly, Brooke, and Jacqui True (2008) "Reflexivity in practice: Power and ethics in feminist research on international relations," *International Studies Review* 10(4): 693–707.

Agathangelou, Anna M. (2013) "Neoliberal geopolitical order and value: Queerness as a speculative economy and anti-blackness as terror," *International Feminist Journal of Politics* 15(4): 453–476.

Åhall, Linda (2018) "Affect as methodology: Feminism and the politics of emotion," *International Political Sociology* 12(1): 36–52.

Ahmed, Sara (2014) *The Cultural Politics of Emotion*. New York: Routledge.

Anderson, Kjell (2020) "The perpetrator imaginary: Representing perpetrators of genocide," in Kjell Anderson and Erin Jessee (eds.) *Researching Perpetrators of Genocide*. Madison: University of Wisconsin Press, 23–48.

Anderson, Kjell, and Erin Jessee (2020) "Introduction," in Kjell Anderson and Erin Jessee (eds.) *Researching Perpetrators of Genocide*. Madison: University of Wisconsin Press, 3–22.

Andrić-Ružičić, Duska (2003) "War rape and the political manipulation of survivors," in Wenona Giles, Malathi de Alwis, Edith Klein, and Neluka Silva (co-eds.) with Maja Korač, Djuedja Knežević, and Žarana Papić (ad. eds.) *Feminists under Fire: Exchanges across War Zones*. Ontario: Between the Lines Books, 103–113.

Arendt, Hannah (1963) *Eichmann in Jerusalem: A Report on the Banality of Evil*. New York: Viking Press.

Askin, Kelly D. (1997) *War Crimes against Women: Prosecution in International War Crimes Tribunals*. The Hague: M. Nijhoff Publishers.

Askin, Kelly D. (2003) "Omarska camp, Bosnia: Broken promises of 'never again,'" *Human Rights* 30(1): 12–14.

Atanasoski, Neda (2018) "'Seeing justice to be done': The documentaries of the ICTY and the visual politics of European value(s)," *Transnational Cinemas* 9(1): 68–85.

Ba, Oumar (2021) "Global justice and race," *International Politics Reviews* 9(2): 375–389.

Ba, Oumar, Kelly-Jo Bluen, and Owiso Owiso (2023) "The geopolitics of race, empire, and expertise at the ICC," *Oxford Research Encyclopedia of International Studies*, https://doi.org/10.1093/acrefore/9780190846626.013.717.

Baars, Grietje (2019) "Queer cases unmake gendered law, or, Fucking law's gendering function," *Australian Feminist Law Journal* 45(1): 15–62.

Bacic, Goran (2017) "Concentration camp rituals: Narratives of former Bosnian detainees," *Humanity and Society* 41(1): 73–94.

Baker, Catherine (2018a) "Postcoloniality without race? Racial exceptionalism and Southeast European cultural studies," *Interventions* 20(6): 759–784.

Baker, Catherine (2018b) *Race and the Yugoslav Region*. Manchester: Manchester University Press.

Bakić-Hayden, Milica (1995) "Nesting orientalisms: The case of former Yugoslavia," *Slavic Review* 54(4): 917–931.

Bakić-Hayden, Milica, and Robert M. Hayden (1992) "Orientalist variations on the theme "Balkans": Symbolic geography in recent Yugoslav cultural politics," *Slavic Review* 51(1): 1–15.

Basham, Victoria M., and Sarah Bulmer (2017) "Critical military studies as method: An approach to studying gender and the military," in Rachel Woodward and Claire Duncanson (eds.) *The Palgrave International Handbook of Gender and the Military*. London: Palgrave Macmillan UK, 59–71.

Batinic, Jelena (2001) "Feminism, nationalism, and war: The 'Yugoslav case' in feminist texts," *Journal of International Women's Studies* 3(1): 1–23.

Belloni, Roberto (2007) "The trouble with humanitarianism," *Review of International Studies* 33(3): 451–474.

Berggren, Kalle (2014) "Sticky masculinity: Post-structuralism, phenomenology and subjectivity in critical studies on men," *Men and Masculinities* 17(3): 231–252.

Berlant, Lauren, and Michael Warner (1998) "Sex in public," *Critical Inquiry* 24(2): 547–566.

Biddolph, Caitlin (2020) "Queering temporalities of international criminal justice: Srebrenica remembrance and the International Criminal Tribunal for the former Yugoslavia (ICTY)," *Griffith Law Review* 29(3): 401–424.

Biddolph, Caitlin (2021) "Queering crimes of torture: A (re)imagining of torture in International Criminal Tribunal for the former Yugoslavia jurisprudence," *Australian Journal of Human Rights* 27(2): 382–391.

Biddolph, Caitlin (2024a) "Death, grief, and mourning in an ICTY film: Exploring relational and non/living worlds," *International Studies Quarterly* 68(2): squae076.

Biddolph, Caitlin (2024b)"Haunting justice: Queer bodies, ghosts, and the International Criminal Tribunal for the former Yugoslavia," *International Feminist Journal of Politics* 26(2): 216–239.

Biddolph, Caitlin (2024c) "Queering the global governance of transitional justice: Tensions and (im)possibilities," *International Journal of Transitional Justice* 18(2): 281–298.

Boas, Gideon (2012) "What is international criminal justice?," in Michael Scharf and William Schabas (eds.) *International Criminal Justice: Legitimacy and Coherence*. Cheltenham and Northampton: Edward Elgar Publishing, 1–24.

Boesten, Jelke, and Polly Wilding (2015) "Transformative gender justice: Setting an agenda," *Women's Studies International Forum* 51:75–80.

Bosia, Michael J. (2018) "Do queer visions trouble human security?," in Caron E. Gentry, Laura J. Shepherd, and Laura Sjoberg (eds.) *The Routledge Handbook of Gender and Security*. London and New York: Routledge, 94–105.

Bracewell, Wendy (2000) "Rape in Kosovo: Masculinity and Serbian nationalism," *Nations and Nationalism* 6(4): 563–590.

Brammertz, Serge, and Michelle Jarvis (2010) "Lessons learned in prosecuting gender crimes under international law: Experiences from the ICTY," in Chile Eboe-Osuji (ed.) *Protecting Humanity: Essays in International Law and Policy in Honour of Navanethem Pillay*. Brill Online, https://brill.com/edcollbook/title/18293?language=en, 93–118.

Bringa, Tone (1995) *Being Muslim the Bosnian Way*. Princeton, NJ: Princeton University Press.

Buchan, Russell (2015) "Developing democracy through liberal international law," *Cambridge Journal of International and Comparative Law* 4(2): 319–343.

Bueno-Hansen, Pascha (2018) "The emerging LGBTI rights challenge to transitional justice in Latin America," *International Journal of Transitional Justice* 12(1): 126–145.

Burgis-Kasthala, Michelle, and Barrie Sander (2024) "Contemporary international criminal law after critique: Towards decolonial and abolitionist (dis-)engagement in an era of anti-impunity," *Journal of International Criminal Justice* 22: 127-150.

Buss, Doris (1998) "Women at the borders: Rape and nationalism in international law," *Feminist Legal Studies* 6(2): 171–203.

Buss, Doris (2007) "The curious visibility of wartime rape: Gender and ethnicity in international criminal law," *Windsor Yearbook of Access to Justice* 25(1): 3–22.

Buss, Doris, and Blair Rutherford (2018) "'Dangerous desires': Illegality, sexuality and the global governance of artisanal mining," in Dianne Otto (ed.) *Queering International Law: Possibilities, Alliances, Complicities, Risks*. Abingdon and New York: Routledge, 35–52.

Butler, Judith (1986) "Sex and gender in Simone de Beauvoir's Second Sex," *Yale French Studies* 72:35–49.

Butler, Judith (1988) "Performative acts and gender constitution: An essay in phenomenology and feminist theory," *Theatre Journal* 40(4): 591–531.

Butler, Judith (1995) "Contingent foundations," in Nancy Fraser (ed.) *Feminist Contentions: A Philosophical Exchange*. New York and London: Routledge, 35–58.

Butler, Judith (1999) *Gender Trouble*, 10th ed. New York: Routledge.

Butler, Judith (2014) *Bodies That Matter: On the Discursive Limits of "Sex."* New York: Routledge.

Campbell, David (2002a) "Atrocity, memory, photography: Imaging the concentration camps of Bosnia—the case of ITN versus Living Marxism, Part 1," *Journal of Human Rights* 1(1): 1–33.

Campbell, David (2002b) "Atrocity, memory, photography: Imaging the concentration camps of Bosnia—the case of ITN versus Living Marxism, Part 2," *Journal of Human Rights* 1(2): 143–172.

Campbell, David (2007) "Poststructuralism," in Tim Dunne, Milja Kurki, and Steve Smith (eds.) *International Relations Theories: Discipline and Diversity*. Oxford: Oxford University Press, 203–228.

Campbell, Kirsten (2002) "Legal memories: Sexual assault, memory, and international humanitarian law," *Signs: Journal of Women in Culture and Society* 28(1): 149–178.

Campbell, Kirsten, Elma Demir, and Maria O'Reilly (2019) "Understanding conflict-related sexual violence and the 'everyday' experience of conflict through witness testimonies," *Cooperation and Conflict* 54(2): 254–277.

Carlson, Åsa (2010) "Gender and sex: What are they? Sally Haslanger's debunking social constructivism," *Distinktion: Journal of Social Theory* 11(1): 61–72.

Cetinkaya, Hasret (2023) "The coloniality of contemporary human rights discourses on 'honour' in and around the United Nations," *Feminist Legal Studies* 31:343–367.

Chadwick, Rachelle (2023) "The question of feminist critique," *Feminist Theory*, https://journals.sagepub.com/doi/10.1177/14647001231186526.

Charlesworth, Hilary (1999) "Feminist methods in international law," *The American Journal of International Law* 93(2): 379–394.

Charlesworth, Hilary, and Christine Chinkin (2000) *The Boundaries of International Law: A Feminist Analysis*. Manchester: Manchester University Press.

Charrett, Catherine (2019) "Diplomacy in drag and queer IR art: Reflections on the performance, 'Sipping Toffee with Hamas in Brussels,'" *Review of International Studies* 45(2): 280–299.

Chow, Rey (2002) "The interruption of referentiality: Poststructuralism and the conundrum of critical multiculturalism," *South Atlantic Quarterly* 101(1): 171–186.

Chowdhry, Geeta, and L.H.M. Ling (2017) "Race(ing) international relations: A critical overview of postcolonial feminism in international relations," in Robert A. Denemark and Renée Marlin-Bennett (eds.) *The International Studies Encyclopedia*. Wiley-Blackwell, 10.1093/acref/9780191842665.001.0001, n.p.

Civil Rights Congress (1951) *We Charge Genocide: The Historic Petition to the United Nations for Relief from a Crime of the United States Government against the Negro People*, edited by William L. Patterson. New York: Civil Rights Congress.

Clark, Lindsay C. (2019) *Gender and Drone Warfare: A Hauntological Perspective*. London and New York: Routledge.

Clarke, Kamari (2019) *Affective Justice: The International Criminal Court and the Pan-Africanist Pushback*. Durham, NC: Duke University Press.

Cohen, Cathy J. (1997) "Punks, bulldaggers, and welfare queens: The radical potential of queer politics?," *GLQ: A Journal of Lesbian and Gay Studies* 3:437–465.

Cohn, Carol (1993) "Wars, wimps, and women: Talking gender and thinking war," in Miriam Cooke and Angela Woollacott (eds.) *Gendering War Talk*. Princeton, NJ: Princeton University Press, 227–246.

Coles, Kimberley (2007) "Ambivalent builders: Europeanisation, the production of difference and internationals in Bosnia-Herzegovina," in Xavier Bouragel, Elissa Helms, and Ger Duijzings (eds.) *The New Bosnian Mosaic: Identities, Memories and Moral Claims in a Post-War Society*. Aldershot and Burlington, VT: Ashgate, 255–272.

Copelon, Rhonda (2000) "Gender crimes as war crimes: Integrating crimes against women into international criminal law," *McGill Law Journal* 46: 217–240.

Cunha, Leonam Lucas Nogueira (2023) "Queer methodologies in the study of law: Notes about queering methods," *Australian Feminist Law Journal*, https://www.tandfonline.com/doi/full/10.1080/13200968.2023.2196819.

Dauphinée, Elizabeth (2007) *The Ethics of Researching War: Looking for Bosnia*. Manchester: Manchester University Press.

Dauphinée, Elizabeth (2008) "War crimes and the ruin of law," *Millennium: Journal of International Studies* 37(1): 49–67.

Dauphinée, Elizabeth (2016) "Narrative engagement and the creative practices of international relations," in Jack L. Amoureux and Brent J. Steele (eds.) *Reflexivity and International Relations: Positionality, Critique, and Practice*. London and New York: Routledge, 44–60.

Davis, Angela Y. (2003) *Are Prisons Obsolete?* New York: Seven Stories Press.

De Beauvoir, Simone (2010) [1949] *The Second Sex*, translated by Constance Borde and Sheila Malovany-Chevallier. New York: Alfred A. Knopf.

De Lauretis, Teresa (1997) "The violence of rhetoric: On representation and gender," in Roger N. Lancaster and Micaela di Leonardo (eds.) *The Gender Sexuality Reader: Culture, History, Political Economy*. New York and London: Routledge, 265–278.

Dembour, Marie-Bénédicte, and Emily Haslam (2004) "Silencing hearings? Victim-witnesses at war crimes trials," *European Journal of International Law* 15(1): 151–177.

Derrida, Jacques (1978) *Writing and Difference*. London: Routledge.

Derrida, Jacques (1988) "Signature event context," in Jacques Derrida, Samuel Weber, and Jeffrey Mehlman (trans.) *Limited Inc*. Evanston: Northwestern University Press, 1–24.

Detamore, Mathias (2010) "Queer(y)ing the ethics of research methods: Toward a politics of intimacy in researcher/researched relations," in Kath Browne and Catherine J. Nash (eds.) *Queer Methods and Methodologies: Intersecting Queer Theories and Social Science Research*. London and New York: Routledge, 167–182.

Deutsch, Nancy L. (2004) "Positionality and the pen: Reflections on the process of becoming a feminist researcher and writer," *Qualitative Inquiry* 10(6): 885–902.

Doty, Roxanne Lyn (1993) "Foreign policy as social construction: A post-positivist analysis of U.S. counterinsurgency in the Philippines," *International Studies Quarterly* 37:297–320.

Doty, Roxanne Lyn (1996) *Imperial Encounters: The Politics of Representation in North-South Relations*. Minneapolis: University of Minnesota Press.

Drumond, Paula (2019) "Sex, violence, and heteronormativity: Revisiting performances of sexual violence against men in former Yugoslavia," in Marysia Zalewski, Paula Drumond, Elisabeth Prügl, and Maria Stern (eds.) *Sexual Violence against Men in Global Politics*. Abingdon and New York: Routledge, 152–166.

Duffy, Sandra (2021) "Contested subjects of human rights: Trans- and gender-variant subjects of international human rights law," *The Modern Law Review* 84(5): 1041–1065.

Dumaničić, Marko, and Krešimir Krolo (2017) "Dehexing postwar West Balkan masculinities: The case of Bosnia, Croatia, and Serbia, 1998 to 2015," *Men and Masculinities* 20(2): 154–180.

Edelbi, Souheir (2020) "Making race speakable in international criminal law: Review of Lingaas' The Concept of Race in International Criminal Law," *Third World Approaches to International Law Review* 16:1-8.

Edkins, Jenny (1999) *Poststructuralism and International Relations: Bringing the Political Back In*. Boulder, CO, and London: Lynne Rienne Publishers.

Edkins, Jenny (2007) "Poststructuralism," in Martin Griffiths (ed.) *International Relations Theory for the Twenty-First Century: An Introduction*. London: Routledge, 88-98.

Eichert, David (2021) "Expanding the gender of genocidal sexual violence: Towards the inclusion of men, transgender women, and people outside the binary," *UCLA Journal of International Law and Foreign Affairs* 25(2): 157-201.

Elander, Maria (2013) "The victim's address: Expressivism and the victim at the Extraordinary Chambers in the Courts of Cambodia," *International Journal of Transitional Justice* 7(1): 95-115.

Elander, Maria (2018a) *Figuring Victims in International Criminal Justice: The Case of the Khmer Rouge Tribunal*. Abingdon and New York: Routledge.

Elander, Maria (2018b) "In spite: Testifying to sexual and gender-based violence during the Khmer Rouge period," in Dianne Otto (ed.) *Queering International Law: Possibilities, Alliances, Complicities, Risks*. Abingdon and New York: Routledge, 110-127.

Engle, Karen (2005) "Feminism and its (dis)contents: Criminalizing wartime rape in Bosnia and Herzegovina," *The American Journal of International Law* 99(4): 778-816.

Engle, Karen (2015) "Anti-impunity and the turn to criminal law in human rights," *Cornell Law Review* 100(5): 1069-1128.

Engle, Karen (2016) "Feminist legacies," in "*Symposium on the International Criminal Tribunals for the former Yugoslavia and Rwanda: Broadening the Debate*," special issue, *AJIL Unbound* 110:220-225.

Engle, Karen (2017) "A genealogy of the centrality of sexual violence to gender and conflict," in Fionnuala Ní Aoláin, Naomi Cahn, Dina Francesca Haynes, and Nahla Valji (eds.) *The Oxford Handbook of Gender and Conflict*. Oxford: Oxford University Press, 132-144.

Engle, Karen (2020) *The Grip of Sexual Violence in Conflict: Feminist Interventions in International Law*. Stanford, CA: Stanford University Press.

Erakat, Noura, and John Reynolds (2021) "We charge apartheid? Palestine and the International Criminal Court," *Third World Approaches to International Law Review* 33:1-11.

Fobear, Katherine (2014) "Queering truth commissions," *Journal of Human Rights Practice* 6(1): 51-68.

Foucault, Michel (1976) *The History of Sexuality: The Will to Knowledge*, translated by Robert Hurley. London: Penguin Books.

Freccero, Carla (2017) "Les chats de Derrida," in Christian Hite (ed.) *Derrida and Queer Theory*. Earth: Punctum Books, 132-163.

Gaillard, Chloé, and Marion Pineau (2015) "Mothers of Srebrenica: The fight for truth and justice," *Peace Insight*, June 15. Available at https://www.peaceinsight.org/en/articles/mothers-of-srebrenica-the-fight-for-truth-and-justice/?location=western-balkans&theme= (accessed July 25, 2023).

Gal, Susan, and Gail Kligman (2000) *The Politics of Gender after Socialism.* Princeton, NJ: Princeton University Press.

Gani, Jasmine K., and Rabea M. Khan (2024) "Positionality statements as a function of coloniality: Interrogating reflexive methodologies," *International Studies Quarterly* 68(2): squae038.

Gannon, Susanne, and Bronwyn Davies (2012) "Postmodern, post-structural, and critical theories," in Sharlene Nagy Hesse-Biber (ed.) *Handbook of Feminist Research: Theory and Praxis.* Thousand Oaks, CA: Sage Publications, 65–91.

Garbett, Claire (2016) "From passive objects to active agents: A comparative study of conceptions of victim identities at the ICTY and ICC," *Journal of Human Rights* 15(1): 40–59.

Gentry, Caron E. (2016) "Chechen political violence as desperation," in Annick T.R. Wibben (ed.) *Researching War: Feminist Methods, Ethics and Politics.* London: Routledge, 33–45.

Ghazal, Farah (2022) "Towards anti-carceral feminist justice in Egypt," *Alternative Policy Solutions*, January 31. Available at https://aps.aucegypt.edu/en/articles/764/towards-anti-carceral-feminist-justice-in-egypt (accessed July 26, 2023).

Giffney, Noreen (2009) "Introduction: The 'q' word," in Noreen Giffney and Michael O'Rourke (eds.) *The Ashgate Research Companion to Queer Theory.* London: Routledge, 1–13.

Gonzalez-Salzberg, Damian (2022) "Queering reparations under international law: Damages, suffering, and (heteronormative) kinship," *AJIL Unbound* 116:5–9.

Goodman, Hannah (2021) "Anti-carceral futures: A comparative perspective of restorative and transformative justice practices in the United States and New Zealand," *Fordham International Law Journal* 44(5): 1215–1266.

Grady, Kate (2021) "Towards a carceral geography of international law," in Shane Chalmers and Sundhya Pahuja (eds.) *Routledge Handbook of International Law and the Humanities.* London: Routledge, 357–368.

Griffin, Penny (2007) "Sexing the economy in a neo-liberal world order: Neo-liberal discourse and the (re)production of heteronormative heterosexuality," *The British Journal of International Relations* 9(2): 220–238.

Griffin, Penny (2009) *Gendering the World Bank: Neoliberalism and the Gendered Foundations of Global Governance.* Basingstoke: Palgrave Macmillan.

Griffin, Penny (2011) "Sexuality, power and global social justice," in Heather Widdows and Nicola J. Smith (eds.) *Global Social Justice.* Abingdon: Routledge, 138–150.

Griffin, Penny (2013) "Deconstruction as 'anti-method,'" in Laura J. Shepherd (ed.) *Critical Approaches to Security.* London: Routledge, 208–222.

Griffin, Penny (2015) *Popular Culture, Political Economy and the Death of Feminism: Why Women Are in Refrigerators and Other Stories.* London: Routledge.

Griffin, Penny (2016) "Gender, finance, and embodiments of crisis," in Aida A. Hozić and Jacqui True (eds.) *Scandalous Economies: Gender and the Politics of Financial Crises.* New York: Oxford University Press, 179–200.

Grosz, Elizabeth (1995) *Space, Time, and Perversion: Essays on the Politics of Bodies.* New York and London: Routledge.

Haddeland, Hanna B., and Katja Franko (2021) "Between legality and legitimacy: The courtroom as a site of resistance in the criminalisation of migration," *Punishment and Society*, https://doi.org/10.1177/1462474521996815.

Hamzić, Vanja (2018) "International law as violence: Competing absences of the other," in Dianne Otto (ed.) *Queering International Law: Possibilities, Alliances, Complicities, Risks*. Abingdon and New York: Routledge, 77–90.

Hansen, Lene (2000) "Gender, nation, rape: Bosnia and the construction of security," *International Feminist Journal of Politics* 3(1): 55–75.

Hansen, Lene (2006) *Security as Practice: Discourse Analysis and the Bosnian War*. Abingdon and New York: Routledge.

Haritaworn, Jin (2008) "Shifting positionalities: Empirical reflections on a queer/trans of colour methodology," *Sociological Research Online* 13(1): 162–173.

Haslanger, Sally (1995) "Ontology and social construction," *Philosophical Topics* 23(2): 95–125.

Haslanger, Sally (2000) "Gender and race: (What) are they? (What) do we want them to be?," *Noûs* 34(1): 31–55.

Hatzopoulos, Pavlos (2003) "'All that is, is nationalist': Western imaginings of the Balkans since the Yugoslav wars," *Journal of Southern Europe and the Balkans* 5(1): 25–38.

Heathcote, Gina (2005) "Article 51 self-defense as a narrative: Spectators and heroes in international law," *Texas Wesleyan Law Review* 12(1): 131–154.

Heathcote, Gina (2011) *The Law on the Use of Force: A Feminist Analysis*. Abingdon and New York: Routledge.

Heathcote, Gina (2017) "Humanitarian intervention and gender dynamics," in Fionnuala Ní Aoláin, Naomi Cahn, Dina Francesca Haynes, and Nahla Valji (eds.) *The Oxford Handbook of Gender and Conflict*. Oxford: Oxford University Press, 199–210.

Heathcote, Gina (2018a) "On feminist legal methodologies: Split, plural and speaking subjects," *feminists@law* 8(2): 1–20.

Heathcote, Gina (2018b) "War's perpetuity: Disabled bodies of war and the exoskeleton of equality," *Australian Feminist Law Journal* 44(1): 71–91.

Heathcote, Gina (2019) *Feminist Dialogues on International Law*. Oxford: Oxford University Press.

Heathcote, Gina, and Lucia Kula (2023) "Abandoning the idealized white subject of legal feminism: A manifesto for silence in a Lusophone register," *Global Constitutionalism* 12(3): 469–494.

Helms, Elissa (2008) "East and west kiss: Gender, orientalism, and Balkanism in Muslim-majority Bosnia-Herzegovina," *Slavic Review* 67(1): 88–119.

Henry, Marsha (2003) "'Where are you really from?' Representation, identity and power in the fieldwork experiences of a South Asian diasporic," *Qualitative Research* 3(2): 229–242.

Henry, Marsha (2007) "If the shoe fits: Authenticity, authority and agency feminist diasporic research," *Women's Studies International Forum* 30(1): 70–80.

Henry, Nicola (2014) "The fixation on wartime rape: Feminist critique and international criminal law," *Social and Legal Studies* 23(1): 93–111.

Hernandez-Truyol, Berta Esperanza (2011) "Unsex CEDAW—No—Super-sex it," *Columbia Journal of Gender and Law* 20(2): 195–223.

Holzer, Lena, Bérénice K. Schramm, Juliana Santos de Carvalho, and Manon Beury (2023) "An introduction to international law dis/oriented: Sparking queer futures in international law," *Australian Feminist Law Journal* 49(1): 1–15.

Howarth, David (2000) *Discourse*. Buckingham: Open University Press.

Imre, Anikó (2014) "Postcolonial media studies in postsocialist Europe," *boundary 2* 41(1): 113–134.

Imseis, Ardi (2023) *The United Nations and the Question of Palestine: Rule by Law and the Structure of International Legal Subalternity*. Cambridge: Cambridge University Press.

International Criminal Tribunal for the former Yugoslavia (2013) "Crimes before the ICTY: Prijedor," *United Nations International Criminal Tribunal for the former Yugoslavia*, https://www.icty.org/en/sid/11341 (accessed November 8, 2024).

International Criminal Tribunal for the former Yugoslavia (n.d.) "The conflicts,' *United Nations International Criminal Tribunal for the former Yugoslavia*, https://www.icty.org/en/about/what-former-yugoslavia/conflicts (accessed May 12, 2019).

International Criminal Tribunal for the former Yugoslavia (2003) "Miroslav Kvocka granted provisional release pending the hearing of his appeal,' press release, *United Nations International Criminal Tribunal for the former Yugoslavia*, December 19, https://www.icty.org/en/press/miroslav-kvocka-granted-provisional-release-pending-hearing-his-appeal (accessed October 3, 2021).

International Criminal Tribunal for the former Yugoslavia (2009) "Updated Statute of the International Criminal Tribunal for the former Yugoslavia," September 2009. Online, at https://www.icty.org/x/file/Legal%20Library/Statute/statute_sept09_en.pdf.

Jacobs, Janet (2017) "The memorial at Srebrenica: Gender and the social meanings of collective memory in Bosnia-Herzegovina," *Memory Studies* 10(4): 423–439.

Jiggins, Robert (2018) "Bosnian war," in Alexander Mikaberidze (ed.) *Behind Barbed Wire: An Encyclopedia of Concentration and Prisoner-of-War Camps*. Santa Barbara, CA: ABC-CLIO, 39–40.

Jones, Emily (2023) *Feminist Theory and International Law: Posthuman Perspectives*. London: Routledge.

Kantola, Johanna (2007) "The gendered reproduction of the state in international relations," *The British Journal of Politics and International Relations* 9(2): 270–283.

Kapur, Ratna (2015) "Precarious desires and ungrievable lives: Human rights and postcolonial critiques of legal justice," *London Review of International Law* 3(2): 267–294.

Kapur, Ratna (2018) "The (im)possibility of queering international human rights law," in Dianne Otto (ed.) *Queering International Law: Possibilities, Alliances, Complicities, Risks*. Abingdon and New York: Routledge, 131–147.

Kaye, David (2014) "Archiving justice: Conceptualising the archives of the United Nations International Criminal Tribunal for the former Yugoslavia," *Archival Science* 14(3–4): 381–396.

Kerr, Rachel (2007) "Peace through justice? The International Criminal Tribunal for the former Yugoslavia," *Southeast European and Black Sea Studies* 7(3): 373–385.

Khalid, Maryam (2017) *Gender, Orientalism, and the "War on Terror": Representation, Discourse, and Intervention in Global Politics*. London: Routledge.

Kim, Jihyun, Caitlin Biddolph, and Laura J. Shepherd (2024) "Care ethics and critical friends: Feminist research practice as an insider/outsider," *European Journal of Politics and Gender*, 1–23.

Kinsella, Helen M. (2004) "Securing the civilian: Sex and gender in the laws of war," in Michael Barnett and Raymond Duvall (eds.) *Power in Global Governance*. Cambridge: Cambridge University Press, 249–272.

Koomen, Jonneke (2014) "Language work at international criminal courts," *International Feminist Journal of Politics* 16(4): 581–600.

Kovačević, Nataša (2008) *Narrating Post/Communism: Colonial Discourse and Europe's Borderline Civilisation*. London and New York: Routledge.

Krystalli, Roxani (2023) "Teaching and learning reflexivity in the world politics classroom," *International Political Sociology* 17(4): olad018.

Kumarakulasingam, Narendran (2014) "Bloody translations: The politics of international compassion and horror," *Journal of Narrative Politics* 1(1): 61–75.

Labuda, Patryk I. (2024) "Countering imperialism in international law: The Special Tribunal for Aggression against Ukraine through a post-colonial Eastern European lens," *Yale Journal of International Law* 49: 272-310.

Laclau, Ernesto, and Chantal Mouffe (1985) *Hegemony and Socialist Strategy: Towards a Radical Democratic Politics*. London and New York: Verso.

Lai, Daniela (2020) *Socioeconomic Justice: International Intervention and Transition in Post-War Bosnia and Herzegovina*. Cambridge: Cambridge University Press.

Lambevski, Sasho A. (1999) "Suck my nation—Masculinity, ethnicity and the politics of (homo)sex," *Sexualities* 2(4): 397–419.

Lee, Po-Han (2021) "A pluralist approach to 'the international' and human rights for sexual and gender minorities," *Feminist Review* 128(1): 79–95.

Lee, Po-Han (2022) "Struggle for recognition: Theorising sexual/gender minorities as rights-holders in international law," *Feminist Legal Studies* 30(1): 73–95.

Loenen, Titia (1994) "Rethinking sex equality as a human right," *Netherlands Quarterly of Human Rights* 12(3): 253–270.

MacKinnon, Catharine A. (1994) "Rape, genocide, and women's human rights," *Harvard Women's Law Journal* 17:5–16.

MacKinnon, Catharine A. (2013) "Creating international law: Gender as leading edge," *Harvard Journal of Law and Gender* 36:105–123.

Mahdavi, Mojtaba (2015) "A postcolonial critique of responsibility to protect in the Middle East," *Perceptions* 20(1): 7–36.

Maier, Nicole (2020) "Queering Colombia's peace process: A case study of LGBTI inclusion," *The International Journal of Human Rights* 24(4): 377–392.

Manchanda, Nivi (2015) "Queering the Pashtun: Afghan sexuality in the homo-nationalist imaginary," *Third World Quarterly* 36(1): 130–146.

Mazel, Odette (2022) "Queer jurisprudence: Reparative practice in international law," *AJIL Unbound* 116:10–15.

Mazel, Odette (2023) "The texture of 'lives lived with law': Methods for queering international law," *Australian Feminist Law Journal*, https://www.tandfonline.com/doi/full/10.1080/13200968.2023.2188690.

McLeod, Laura (2016) *Gender Politics and Security Discourse: Personal-Political Imaginations and Feminism in "Post-Conflict" Serbia*. London and New York: Routledge.

McNeilly, Kathryn (2019) "Sex/gender is fluid, what now for feminism and international human rights law? A call to queer the foundations," in Susan Harris Rimmer and Kate Ogg (eds.) *Research Handbook on Feminist Engagement with International Law*. Cheltenham: Edward Elgar, 430–444.

Mehler, Daniela (2017) "The last 'never again'? Srebrenica and the making of a memory imperative," *European Review of History* 24(4): 606–630.

Meiches, Benjamin (2019) "The charge of genocide: Racial hierarchy, political discourse, and the evolution of international institutions," *International Political Sociology* 13(1): 20–36.

Mertens, Charlotte, Stéphanie Perazzone, and David Mwambari (2022) "Fatal misconceptions: Colonial durabilities, violence and epistemicide in Africa's Great Lakes region," *Critical African Studies* 14(1): 2-18.

Mertus, Julie (2004) "Shouting from the bottom of the well: The impact of international trials for wartime rape on women's agency," *International Feminist Journal of Politics* 6(1): 110–128.

Mibenge, Chiseche Salome (2013) *Sex and International Tribunals: The Erasure of Gender from the War Narrative*. Philadelphia: University of Pennsylvania Press.

Milliken, Jennifer (1999) "The study of discourse in international relations," *European Journal of International Relations* 5(2): 225–254.

Morgan, Wayne (2000) "Queering international human rights law," in Carl Stychin and Didi Herman (eds.) *Sexuality in the Legal Arena*. London: The Athlone Press, 208–225.

Moyo, Khanyisela (2015) "Mimicry, transitional justice and the land question in racially divided former settler colonies," *International Journal of Transitional Justice* 9(1): 70–89.

Munhazim, Ahmad Qais (2024) "'Imperial solidarity': Do queer and trans Afghan Muslims need 'saving?,'" *International Feminist Journal of Politics* 26(2): 286–305.

Murdock, Esme G. (2018) "Storied with land: 'Transitional justice' on Indigenous lands," *Journal of Global Ethics* 14(2): 232–239.

Muslimovic, Admir (2017) "Bosnian widow spends last days between sons' graves," *Balkan Insight*, May 25. Available at https://balkaninsight.com/2017/05/25/bosnian-widow-spends-last-days-between-sons-graves-05-25-2017-1/#:~:text=The%20life%20of%20Nura%20Alispahic,1992%2D5%20war%20in%20Bosnia (accessed July 25, 2023).

Mutua, Makau (2001) "Savages, victims, and saviours: The metaphor of human rights," *Harvard International Law Journal* 42(1): 201–245.

Myrttinen, Henri (2018) "Languages of castration—Male genital mutilation in conflict and its embedded messages," in Marysia Zalewski, Paula Drumond, Elisabeth Prügl, and Maria Stern (eds.) *Sexual Violence against Men in Global Politics*. Abingdon and New York: Routledge, 71–88.

Nadj, Daniela (2011) "The culturalization of identity in an age of 'ethnic conflict'—Depoliticised gender in ICTY wartime sexual violence jurisprudence," *The International Journal of Human Rights* 15(5): 647–663.

Nadj, Daniela (2018) *International Criminal Law and Sexual Violence against Women: The Interpretation of Gender in the Contemporary International Criminal Trial.* Abingdon and New York: Routledge.

Nagy, Rosemary (2022) "Transformative justice in a settler colonial transition: Implementing the UN Declaration on the Rights of Indigenous Peoples in Canada," *The International Journal of Human Rights* 26(2): 191–216.

Namaste, Ki (1994) "The politics of inside/out: Queer theory, poststructuralism, and a sociological approach to sexuality," *Sociological Theory* 12(2): 220–231.

Nash, Catherine J. (2010) "Queer conversations: Old-time lesbians, transmen and the politics of queer research," in Kath Browne and Catherine J. Nash (eds.) *Queer Methods and Methodologies: Intersecting Queer Theories and Social Science Research.* Farnham and Burlington, VT: Ashgate, 129–142.

Nelaeva, Galina (2011) "Establishment of the International Criminal Tribunal in the former Yugoslavia (ICTY): Dealing with the 'war raging at the heart of Europe'," *Romanian Journal of European Affairs* 11(1): 100–108.

Nesiah, Vasuki (2019) "Crimes against humanity: Racialized subjects and deracialized histories," in Immi Tallgren and Thomas Skouteris (eds.) *The New Histories of International Criminal Law: Retrials.* Oxford: Oxford University Press, 167–188.

Neu, Joyce (2012) "Pursuing justice in the midst of war: The International Criminal Tribunal for the former Yugoslavia," *Negotiation and Conflict Management* 5(1): 72–95.

Norris, David A. (2006) "Cinema and the national narrative: Whose 'war and peace' in the Balkan conflict?," in Cristina Demaria and Colin Wright (eds.) *Post-Conflict Futures: Rituals of Representation.* London: Zolius Press, 98–109.

Nouwen, Sarah M.H., and Wouter G. Werner (2015) "Monopolizing global justice: International criminal law as challenge to human diversity," *Journal of International Criminal Justice* 13(1): 157–176.

O'Hara, Claerwen (2022) "Consensus and diversity in the World Trade Organization: A queer perspective," *AJIL Unbound* 116:32–37.

O'Hara, Claerwen (2023) "In search of a queerer law: Two people's tribunals in 1976," *Australian Feminist Law Journal,* https://www.tandfonline.com/doi/full/10.1080/13200968.2023.2184449.

Omerovic, Azra Husaric (2021) "Srebrenica mothers' last wish: To see Ratko Mladic convicted," *Balkan Insight,* June 2. Available at https://balkaninsight.com/2021/06/02/srebrenica-mothers-last-wish-to-see-ratko-mladic-convicted/ (accessed July 25, 2023).

Oosterveld, Valerie (2005) "The definition of 'gender' in the Rome Statute of the International Criminal Court: A step forward or back for international criminal justice?" *Harvard Human Rights Journal* 18:55–84.

O'Reilly, Maria (2012) "Muscular interventionism: Gender, power and liberal peacebuilding in post-conflict Bosnia-Herzegovina," *International Feminist Journal of Politics* 14(4): 529–548.

O'Reilly, Maria (2016) "Peace and justice through a feminist lens: Gender justice and the Women's Court for the former Yugoslavia," *Journal of Intervention and Statebuilding* 10(3): 419–445.

O'Reilly, Maria (2018) *Gendered Agency in War and Peace: Gender Justice and Women's Activism in Post-Conflict Bosnia-Herzegovina*. London: Palgrave Macmillan.

Ognjenović, Gorna, and Jasna Jozelić (2014) "Introduction: The power of symbolism," in Gorna Ognjenović and Jasna Jozelić (eds.) *Politicization of Religion, the Power of Symbolism: The Case of the Former Yugoslavia and Its Successor States*. New York: Palgrave Macmillan, 1–6.

Orentlicher, Diane (2018) *Some Kind of Justice: The ICTY's Impact in Bosnia and Serbia*. New York: Oxford University Press.

Otto, Dianne (2007) "'Taking a break' from 'normal': Thinking queer in the context of international law," *Proceedings of the American Society of International Law Annual Meeting* 101:119–122.

Otto, Dianne (2013) "Transnational homo-assemblages: Reading 'gender' in counter-terrorism discourses," *Jindal Global Law Review* 4(2): 79–97.

Otto, Dianne (2015) "Queering gender [identity] in international law," *Nordic Journal of Human Rights* 33(4): 299–318.

Otto, Dianne (2016) "Impunity in a different register: People's tribunals and questions of judgment, law, and responsibility," in Karen Engle, Zinaida Miller, and D.M. Davis (eds.) *Anti-Impunity and the Human Rights Agenda*. Cambridge: Cambridge University Press, 291–328.

Otto, Dianne (2017) "Beyond legal justice: Some personal reflections on people's tribunals, listening and responsibility," *London Review of International Law* 5(2): 225–249.

Otto, Dianne (2018a) "Introduction: Embracing queer curiosity," in Dianne Otto (ed.) *Queering International Law: Possibilities, Alliances, Complicities, Risks*. Abingdon and New York: Routledge, 1–11.

Otto, Dianne (2018b) "Resisting the heteronormative imaginary of the nation-state: Rethinking kinship and border protection," in Dianne Otto (ed.) *Queering International Law: Possibilities, Alliances, Complicities, Risks*. Abingdon and New York: Routledge, 236–257.

Otto, Dianne (2020) "Rethinking 'peace' in international law and politics from a queer feminist perspective," *Feminist Review* 126(1): 19–38.

Otto, Dianne (2022a) "Is international criminal law particularly impervious to feminist reconstruction? Legally authorized resistances to feminist judging," in Indira Rosenthal, Valerie Oosterveld, and Susana Sácouto (eds.) *Gender and International Criminal Law*. Oxford: Oxford University Press, 387–414.

Otto, Dianne (2022b) "Queerly troubling international law's vision of 'peace,'" *AJIL Unbound* 116:22–26.

Owczarzak, Jill (2009) "Introduction: Postcolonial studies and postsocialism in Eastern Europe," *Focaal—European Journal of Anthropology* 53:3–19.

Paige, Tamsin Phillipa (2018) "The maintenance of international peace and security heteronormativity," in Dianne Otto (ed.) *Queering International Law: Possibilities, Alliances, Complicities, Risks.* Abingdon and New York: Routledge, 91–109.

Parashar, Swati (2013) "What wars and 'war bodies' know about international relations," *Cambridge Review of International Affairs* 26(4): 615–630.

Parashar, Swati (2016) "Feminism and postcolonialism: (En)gendering encounters," *Postcolonial Studies* 19(4): 371–377.

Patrick, David (2016) "A concern for humanity? Anglo-American press coverage of Bosnia and Rwanda, 1992–1995," *International Politics* 53(1): 138–153.

Pavlović, Tatjana (1999) "Women in Croatia: Feminists, nationalists and homosexuals," in Sabrina P. Ramet (ed.) *Gender Politics in the Western Balkans: Women and Society in Yugoslavia and the Yugoslav Successor States.* University Park: Pennsylvania State University Press, 131–152.

Peet, Jessica L., and Laura Sjoberg (2019) *Gender and Civilian Victimisation in War.* Abingdon and New York: Routledge.

Perrin, Kristen (2016) "Memory at the International Criminal Tribunal for the former Yugoslavia (ICTY): Discussions on remembering and forgetting within victim testimonies," *East European Politics and Societies* 30(2): 270–287.

Peterson, V. Spike (1992) "Introduction," in V. Spike Peterson (ed.) *Gendered States: Feminist (Re)Visions of International Relations Theory.* Boulder, CO, and London: Lynne Rienner Publishers, 1–30.

Peterson, V. Spike (1999) "Political identities/nationalism as heterosexism," *International Feminist Journal of Politics* 1(1): 34–65.

Philipose, Elizabeth (2002) "Prosecuting violence, performing sovereignty: The trial of Dusko Tadic," *International Journal for the Semiotics of Law* 15(2): 159–184.

Phillips, Anne (2010) "What's wrong with essentialism?," *Distinktion: Journal of Social Theory* 11(1): 47–60.

Pinto, Mattia (2021) "Of sex and war: Carceral feminism and its anti-carceral critique," *London Review of International Law* 8(2): 351–364.

Popovski, Vesselin (2002) "The UN Security Council approach to the conflicts in the former Yugoslavia," *Southeast European and Black Sea Studies* 2(3): 39–62.

Power, Samantha (2002) *A Problem from Hell: America and the Age of Genocide.* New York: Basic Books.

Puar, Jasbir (2005) "Queer times, queer assemblages," *Social Text* 23(3–4): 121–139.

Puar, Jasbir (2007) *Terrorist Assemblages: Homonationalism in Queer Times.* Durham, NC: Duke University Press.

Puar, Jasbir, and Amit Rai (2002) "Monster, terrorist, fag: The war on terrorism and the production of docile patriots," *Social Text* 20(3): 117–148.

Pupavac, Vanessa (2004) "International therapeutic peace and justice in Bosnia," *Social and Legal Studies* 13(3): 377–401.

Quindlen, Anna (1993) "Public & private; gynocide," *New York Times*, March 10.

Rajagopal, Balakrishnan (2003) "International law and third world resistance: A theoretical inquiry," in Antony Anghie, Bhupinder Chimni, Karin Mickelson, and Obiora C. Okafor (eds.) *The Third World and International Order.* Leiden: Brill, 145–172.

Rao, Rahul (2010) *Third World Protest: Between Home and the World*. New York: Oxford University Press.
Rao, Rahul (2018) "A tale of two atonements," in Dianne Otto (ed.) *Queering International Law: Possibilities, Alliances, Complicities, Risks*. Abingdon and New York: Routledge, 15–34.
Rao, Rahul (2020) *Out of Time: The Queer Politics of Postcoloniality*. New York: Oxford University Press.
Rexhepi, Piro (2023) *White Enclosures: Racial Capitalism and Coloniality along the Balkan Route*. Durham, NC: Duke University Press.
Reynolds, John, and Sujith Xavier (2016) "'The dark corners of the world': TWAIL and international criminal justice," *Journal of International Criminal Justice* 14: 959–983.
Richter-Montpetit, Melanie (2016) "Militarised masculinities, women torturers, and the limits of gender analysis at Abu Ghraib," in Annick T.R. Wibben (ed.) *Researching War: Feminist Methods, Ethics and Politics*. London: Routledge, 83–100.
Richter-Montpetit, Melanie (2017) "Everything you always wanted to know about sex (in IR) but were afraid to ask: The 'queer turn' in international relations," *Millennium: Journal of International Studies* 46(2): 220–240.
Rigney, Sophie (2024) "Building an abolition movement for international criminal law?," *Journal of International Criminal Justice*, 22(1): 211-233.
Robison, Bridget (2004) "Putting Bosnia in its place: Critical geopolitics and the representation of Bosnia in the British print media," *Geopolitics* 9(2): 378–401.
Rome Statute for the International Criminal Court (1998) UN Doc. A/Conf.183/9.
Rosenfeld, Gavriel D. (2009) "A looming crash or a soft landing? Forecasting the future of the memory 'industry,'" *The Journal of Modern History* 81(1): 122–158.
Rudling, Adriana (2019) "'I'm not that chained-up little person': Four paragons of victimhood in transitional justice discourse," *Human Rights Quarterly* 41(2): 421–440.
Ruskola, Teemu (2010) "Raping like a state," *UCLA Law Review* 57:1477–1536.
Ruskola, Teemu (2013) *Legal Orientalism: China, the United States, and Modern Law*. Cambridge, MA: Harvard University Press.
Rydén, Johanna Bergqvist (2018) "When bereaved of everything: Objects from the concentration camp of Ravensbrück as expressions of resistance, memory, and identity," *International Journal of Historical Archaeology* 22(3): 511–530.
Sagan, Ann (2010) "African criminals/African victims: The institutionalised production of cultural narratives in international criminal law," *Millennium: Journal of International Studies* 39(1): 3–21.
Said, Edward (1978) *Orientalism*. London and New York: Penguin.
Santos de Carvalho, Juliana (2022) "The powers of silence: Making sense of the non-definition of gender in international criminal law," *Leiden Journal of International Law*, https://doi.org/10.1017/S0922156522000541.
Schabas, William (2012) *Unimaginable Atrocities: Justice, Politics, and Rights at the War Crimes Tribunals*. Oxford: Oxford University Press.
Schwöbel-Patel, Christine (2021) *Marketing Global Justice: The Political Economy of International Criminal Law*. Cambridge: Cambridge University Press.
Scott, James C. (1989) "Everyday forms of resistance," *The Copenhagen Journal of Asian Studies* 4(1): 33–62.

Sedgwick, Eve Kosofsky (1993) *Tendencies*. Durham, NC: Duke University Press.
Sedgwick, Eve Kosofsky (1994) *Epistemology of the Closet*. London: Penguin.
Sedgwick, Eve Kosofsky (2003) *Touching Feeling: Affect, Pedagogy, Performativity*. Durham, NC, and London: Duke University Press.
Serano, Julia (2009) *Whipping Girl: A Transsexual Woman on Sexism and the Scapegoating of Femininity*. Emery: Seal Press.
Sesay, Mohamed (2022) "Decolonization of postcolonial Africa: A structural justice project more radical than transitional justice," *International Journal of Transitional Justice* 16(2): 254–271.
Shapiro, Michael (1988) *The Politics of Representation: Writing Practices in Biography, Photography, and Policy Analysis*. Madison: University of Wisconsin Press.
Shepherd, Laura J. (2008a) *Gender, Violence and Security*. London: Zed Books.
Shepherd, Laura J. (2008b) "Power and authority in the production of United Nations Security Council 1325," *International Studies Quarterly* 52(2): 383–404.
Shepherd, Laura J. (2012) *Gender, Violence and Popular Culture: Telling Stories*. London: Routledge.
Shepherd, Laura J. (2013) "Feminist security studies," in Laura J. Shepherd (ed.) *Critical Approaches to Security: An Introduction to Theories and Methods*. Abingdon and New York: Routledge, 11–23.
Shepherd, Laura J. (2015) "Constructing civil society: Gender, power and legitimacy in United Nations peacebuilding discourse," *European Journal of International Relations* 21(4): 887–910.
Shepherd, Laura J. (2016) "Research as gendered intervention: Feminist research ethics and the self in the research encounter," *Critica Contemporànea* 6: 1–15.
Shepherd, Laura J. (2017) *Gender, UN Peacebuilding, and the Politics of Space: Locating Legitimacy*. Oxford: Oxford University Press.
Shepherd, Laura J. (2021) *Narrating the Women, Peace and Security Agenda: Logics of Global Governance*. Oxford: Oxford University Press.
Shepherd, Laura J., and Laura Sjoberg (2012) "Trans-bodies in/of war(s): Cisprivilege and contemporary security strategy," *Feminist Review* 101:5–23.
Shotwell, Alexis, and Trevor Sangrey (2008) "Resisting definition: Gendering through interaction and relational selfhood," *Hypatia* 24(3): 56–76.
Simić, Olivera (2012) "Challenging Bosnian women's identity as rape victims, as unending victims: The 'other' sex in times of war," *Journal of International Women's Studies* 13(4): 129–142.
Simić, Olivera (2014) "Memorial culture in the former Yugoslavia: Mothers of Srebrenica and the destruction of artefacts by the ICTY," in Peter D. Rush and Olivera Simić (eds.) *The Arts of Transitional Justice*. New York: Springer, 155–172.
Simm, Gabrielle (2018) "Peoples' tribunals, women's courts and international crimes of sexual violence," in Andrew Byrnes and Gabrielle Simm (eds.) *Peoples' Tribunals and International Law*. Cambridge: Cambridge University Press, 61–83.
Simm, Gabrielle (2020) "Queering CEDAW? Sexual orientation, gender identity and expression and sex characteristics (SGIESC) in international human rights law," *Griffith Law Review* 29(3): 374–400.

Sirleaf, Matiangai V.S. (2024) "Palestine as a litmus test for transitional justice," *International Journal of Transitional Justice* 18(1): 162–188.

Sjoberg, Laura (2010a) "Women and the genocidal rape of women: The gender dynamics of gendered war crimes," in Debra Bergoffen, Paula Ruth Gilbert, Tamara Harvey, and Connie L. McNeely (eds.) *Confronting Global Gender Justice: Women's Lives, Human Rights*. London: Routledge, 21–34.

Sjoberg, Laura (2010b) "Women fighters and the 'beautiful soul' narrative," *International Review of the Red Cross* 92(877): 53–68.

Sjoberg, Laura (2012) "Towards trans-gendering international relations?," *International Political Sociology* 6(4): 337–354.

Sjoberg, Laura (2015) "Seeing sex, gender, and sexuality in international security," *International Journal* 70(3): 435–453.

Sjoberg, Laura (2016) "Centering security studies around felt, gendered insecurities," *Journal of Global Security Studies* 1(1): 51–63.

Sjoberg, Laura (2017a) "Queering IR constructivism," in Harry D. Gould (ed.) *The Art of World-Making: Nicholas Greenwood Onuf and His Critics*. Abingdon and New York: Routledge, 68–79.

Sjoberg, Laura (2017b) *Women as Wartime Rapists: Beyond Sensation and Stereotyping*. New York: New York University Press.

Sjoberg, Laura (2018) "War families and the Iraq wars," *Journal of Women of the Middle East and the Islamic World* 16:236–265.

Sjoberg, Laura (2020) "Trans∗ theorising for ethics in international relations," in Birgit Schippers (ed.) *The Routledge Handbook to Rethinking Ethics in International Relations*. Abingdon and New York: Routledge, 80–90.

Sjoberg, Laura, and Caron E. Gentry (2007) *Mothers, Monsters, Whores: Women's Violence in Global Politics*. London and New York: Zed Books.

Slootmaeckers, Koen (2023) *Coming In: Sexual Politics and EU Accession in Serbia*. Manchester: Manchester University Press.

Smart, Carol (1990) "Law's power, the sexed body, and feminist discourse," *Journal of Law and Society* 17:194–210.

Smith, Nicola, and Donna Lee (2015) "What's queer about political science?," *The British Journal of International Relations* 17(1): 49–63.

Solomon, Ty (2015) "Embodiment, emotions, and materialism in international relations," in Linda Åhall and Thomas Gregory (eds.) *Emotions, Politics and War*. London: Routledge, 58–70.

Soreanu, Raluca (2010) "Feminist creativities and the disciplinary imaginary of international relations," *International Political Sociology* 4(4): 380–400.

Sørlie, Anniken (2018) "Governing (trans)parenthood: The tenacious hold of biological connection and heterosexuality," in Dianne Otto (ed.) *Queering International Law: Possibilities, Alliances, Complicities, Risks*. Abingdon and New York: Routledge, 171–190.

Spade, Dean (2011) *Normal Life: Administrative Violence, Critical Trans Politics and the Limits of Law*. Brooklyn: South End Press.

Spivak, Gayatri Chakravorty (1988) "Can the subaltern speak?," in Cary Nelson and Larry Grossberg (eds.) *Marxism and the Interpretation of Culture*. Urbana: University of Illinois Press, 66–111.

Spivak, Gayatri Chakravorty (2004) "Terror: A speech after 9-11," *boundary 2* 31(2): 81–111.

Spoerri, Marlene, and Annette Freyberg-Inan (2008) "From prosecution to persecution: Perceptions of the International Criminal Tribunal for the former Yugoslavia (ICTY) in Serbian domestic politics," *Journal of International Relations and Development* 11(4): 350–384.

Stanley, Penny (1999) "Reporting of mass rape in the Balkans: Plus ça change, plus c'est la même chose? From Bosnia to Kosovo," *Civil Wars* 2(2): 74–110.

Steinweis, Alan E. (2005) "The Auschwitz analogy: Holocaust memory and American debates over intervention in Bosnia and Kosovo in the 1990s," *Holocaust and Genocide Studies* 19(2): 276–289.

Subotić, Jelena (2021) "Ethics of archival research on political violence," *Journal of Peace Research* 58(3): 342–354.

Suhr, Valérie V. (2022) *Rainbow Jurisdiction at the International Criminal Court: Protection of Sexual and Gender Minorities under the Rome Statute*. The Hague: TMC Asser Press.

Swimelar, Safia (2019) "LGBT rights in Bosnia: The challenge of nationalism in the context of Europeanisation," *Nationalities Papers* 48(4):768-790.

The Yugoslawomen + Collective (2020) "The tale of 'good' migrants and 'dangerous' refugees," *The Disorder of Things*, July 19, https://thedisorderofthings.com/2020/07/19/17977/ (accessed July 14, 2021).

Todorova, Maria (1997) *Imagining the Balkans*. New York and Oxford: Oxford University Press.

Todorova, Miglena S. (2018) "Race and women of colour in socialist/postsocialist transnational feminisms in central and southeastern Europe," *Meridians* 16(1): 114–141.

Touquet, Heleen, and Philipp Schulz (2020) "Navigating vulnerabilities and masculinities: How gendered contexts shape the agency of male sexual violence survivors," *Security Dialogue* 52(3): 213-230.

United Nations Security Council (1993) Resolution 827. S/RES/827 (1993). Online, at https://www.icty.org/x/file/Legal%20Library/Statute/statute_827_1993_en.pdf.

United States Holocaust Memorial Museum (2019) "Documenting numbers of victims of the Holocaust and Nazi persecution," *Holocaust Encyclopedia*, https://encyclopedia.ushmm.org/content/en/article/documenting-numbers-of-victims-of-the-holocaust-and-nazi-persecution (accessed November 12, 2020).

Veličković, Marina (2024) "Ethical challenges of using trial transcripts for research purposes: A case study of the International Criminal Tribunal for the Former Yugoslavia," *London Review of International Law* 11(3): 381–404.

Veličković, Vedrana (2012) "Belated alliances? Tracing the intersections between postcolonialism and postcommunism," *Journal of Postcolonial Writing* 48(2): 164–175.

Venzke, Ingo (2021) "Cognitive biases and international law: What's the point of critique?," in Andrea Bianchi and Moshe Hirsch (eds.) *International Law's Invisible Frames*. Oxford: Oxford University Press, 55–71.

Vernon, Patrick (2024) *The Coloniality of Humanitarian Intervention*. Abingdon & New York: Routledge.

Wagner, Sarah (2019) "Identifying Srebrenica's missing: The 'shaky balance' of universalism and particularism," in Alexander Laban Hinton (ed.) *Transitional Justice: Global Mechanisms and Local Realities after Genocide and Mass Violence*. New Brunswick, NJ: Rutgers University Press, 25–48.

Watson, Irene (2014) *Aboriginal Peoples, Colonialism and International Law: Raw Law*. London: Routledge.

Weber, Cynthia (2016) *Queer International Relations*. Oxford: Oxford University Press.

Weber, Cynthia (2017) "'The terrorist': The out-of-place and on-the-move 'perverse homosexual' in international relations," *Critical Studies on Terrorism* 10(2): 240–252.

Weedon, Chris (1997) *Feminist Practice and Poststructuralist Theory*. 2nd ed. Oxford and Cambridge: Blackwell.

Weerawardhana, Chamindra (2018) "Profoundly decolonising? Reflections on a transfeminist perspective of international relations," *Meridians* 16(1): 184–213.

Wilcox, Lauren (2014) "Queer theory and the 'proper objects' of international relations," *International Studies Review* 16(4): 612–615.

Wilcox, Lauren (2015) *Bodies of Violence: Theorising Embodied Subjects in International Relations*. Oxford: Oxford University Press.

Women's Court (2012) *Women's Court—Feminist Approach to Justice*, http://www.zenskisud.org/en/.

Zalewski, Marysia (2017) "What's the problem with the concept of military masculinities?," *Critical Military Studies* 3(2): 200–205.

Zalnieriute, Monika (2018) "The anatomy of neoliberal internet governance: A queer critical political economy perspective," in Dianne Otto (ed.) *Queering International Law: Possibilities, Alliances, Complicities, Risks*. Abingdon and New York: Routledge, 53–73.

Zarkov, Dubravka (2007) *The Body of War: Media, Ethnicity, and Gender in the Break-Up of Yugoslavia*. Durham, NC, and London: Duke University Press.

Zarkov, Dubravka (2012) "Towards a new theorising of women, gender, and war," in Kathy Davis, Mary S. Evans, and Judith Lorber (eds.) *Handbook of Gender and Women's Studies*. London: Sage Publications, 214–233.

Zarkov, Dubravka (2014) "Ontologies of international humanitarian and criminal law: 'Locals' and 'internationals' in discourses and practices of justice," in Dubravka Zarkov and Marlies Glasius (eds.) *Narratives of Justice in and out of the Courtroom*. Cham: Springer, 3–21.

Zarkov, Dubravka (2017) "From women and war to gender and conflict?," in Fionnuala Ní Aoláin, Naomi Cahn, Dina Francesca Haynes, and Nahla Valji (eds.) *The Oxford Handbook of Gender and Conflict*. Oxford: Oxford University Press, 17–34.

Index

For the benefit of digital users, indexed terms that span two pages (e.g., 52–53) may, on occasion, appear on only one of those pages.

Abolition *see also* anticarceral
   Of slavery 138–139, 143–144
   Prison 149
Adjudication 21, 87–88, 96–99
Adjudicators 21, 44–45, 69–70, 72–73, 99–107, 141–142
Agency 10–13, 108–109, 112, 114–117, 118–121
Agents of violence 2–3, 21, 44, 57, 72–73, 81–84, 87, 91–92, 102, 107, 122, 128, 133, 145
Assemblages 35–36
Atanasoski, Neda 67–68

Baars, Grietje 136, 145
Balkanism 18–19, 50–51, 62–71, 75
Banality of evil 125–126
Butler, Judith 30–31, 33, 44

Carceral 5, 17–18, 36–38, 57–58, 59–60, 102, 107, 140–141, 144–145, 149–151
   Anti- 17–18, 140–141, 149
Chetniks 90, 128–130
Cisgender 1–3, 9, 170 n.1
Cis-heteronormativity 3, 9
Cis-normativity 9
Colonialism *see also* coloniality 14–15, 52–53, 64–65, 138–139, 143–144, 170 n.4
Coloniality *see also* colonialism 4–5, 14–15, 65–66, 68, 71, 77, 90, 143–144
Compassion *see* kindness 109–110, 123–124, 130–132
Criminality 4–6, 8–9, 35, 37–38, 44–45, 47–48, 72, 75–76, 98, 124, 126, 131–132, 139–140
Criminalization 17–18, 81–82, 141–142
Criminals 11, 21, 44, 49–51, 67, 72–73, 123, 126, 132, 147–148

Defendants 85, 86–88, 118–119, 128
Defense attorneys 11–12, 83–86, 98, 110–111, 121–122

Denunciation 19–20, 68–69, 72–73, 87–101
Detention camps in Bosnia 17–18, 51–52, 54–57, 67, 74, 80–82, 90, 92–93, 95–96, 112–113, 117, 120–121, 128, 133
Discourse 11, 23–27

Embodiment 10–13, 25, 30–31, 34–36, 98–99, 106–107
Engle, Karen 17–18, 53–54, 170 n.2
Ethnoreligious nationalism 42, 68
Eurocentrism 4–6, 16, 50–51, 52–53, 64, 67, 71, 90, 92–94, 150
Evil 54, 66–67, 70, 80–81, 90, 103–104, 132

Feminist new materialism 35
Former Yugoslavia 17, 50–51, 54–55, 62–70
Foucault, Michel 31, 111–112

Gender
   Biological essentialist theory of 32–34
   Poststructural theory of 34–36
   Social constructivist theory of 32–34

Healing 52–53, 81–82, 123–124
Heathcote, Gina 9, 29–30, 39–40, 101–102, 123
Heteronormativity 8–9
Heterosexuality 8–9
Holocaust 51–52, 53–55, 66
Homonationalism 14–15
Homophobia 9–10
Homosexuality 8–10
Hyper-heteromasculinity 10, 37, 49–50, 65, 69, 82–83, 90, 95, 123, 141, 147

ICC *see* International Criminal Court
Imprisonment 2, 13, 17–19, 45–46, 49–50, 72–73, 79–80, 87–89, 99–100, 105, 126, 135–136, 138, 140–142, 149
ICTR *see* International Criminal Tribunal for Rwanda

ICTY *see* International Criminal Tribunal for the former Yugoslavia
ICTY cases
   Brdanin 46–47, 53, 76–77, 85, 91–92, 95, 112–114, 115–116, 119–120, 122, 127–129, 132
   Delić 46–47, 89, 90–91, 92–93, 95, 116, 127, 128
   Kvočka et al. 46–47, 74, 80–81, 86–87, 90, 114–115, 117–119, 124–126, 127–128
   Mucić et al. 46–47, 77, 80–81, 82–84, 89, 90–92, 95–96, 97–98, 114–117, 119–120, 127
   Prlić 98
   Tadić 46–47, 80, 91, 94, 115–116
Infantilization 2, 49–50, 54, 58–59, 65–66, 70, 99–100, 101–102, 105–106
Innocence 16, 47–48, 75–76, 86–87, 110–111, 125–126
International Criminal Court *see* ICC 4–5, 33–34, 49–50, 55–56, 59, 138–139, 143–144
International criminal law *see* international criminal justice 4–5, 17–18, 61, 77, 138, 140–141, 149
International criminal justice *see* international criminal law
International Criminal Tribunal for Rwanda *see* ICTR 61, 170 n.3
International Criminal Tribunal for the former Yugoslavia *see* ICTY
   Creation 17, 49–53, 54–55, 56–57, 58–62, 64–65, 96–97, 136–137, 170 n.3
   Documentary films 56–57, 67–68
   Office of the Prosecutor *see also* prosecutors 11–12, 75–76, 81–82, 147
   Organizational structure 11–12
   Origin stories 51–62, 64, 66–67, 75, 100–101, 104–105, 147
   Presidents 11–12, 61–62, 64, 69–70, 75–76, 100–101, 103, 118–119
   Statute 55–56, 105–106
International humanitarian law
   Crimes against humanity 43, 60–61, 96–97, 104–105, 125–126
   Crimes of genocide 17, 60–61
   Grave breaches of the Geneva Conventions of 1949 2, 17
   War crimes 17, 60–61, 96–97, 105–106, 147–148, 170 n.4
International law scholarship
   Feminist 3–4, 17–18, 69–70

   Queer 5–6, 16
   Postcolonial or TWAIL 4–5, 138, 143–144
Intervention
   Economic 51, 66–67, 72
   Legal 20, 83, 141–142
   Humanitarian 14–15, 57–58, 59–60, 64–65, 171 n.3
   Military 13, 36–37, 51, 57–58, 59–60, 66–67, 72, 77, 142–143

Judges 11–12, 14, 46–47, 61–62, 69–70, 74–75, 80–81, 82–87, 90–93, 95, 98–99, 100–101, 103, 110–111, 119–120, 125–126, 128
Justice
   Community-based 17–18
   Gender 55–56
   Human 83–84, 92, 109–111, 116, 118–120, 122, 135–136, 146–147, 151–152
   Legal 15, 137, 140, 144–145, 146–147
   Procedural 92, 109–110, 111–112, 118–119, 122
   Retributive 85–86, 102, 137–138, 140–141, 149
   Transformative 149
   Transitional 5, 59–61, 150

Kapur, Ratna 15, 78, 140–141, 144–145, 151–152
Kindness *see* compassion

Legality 6, 47–48, 72, 75–76, 121–122, 136
LGBTQIA+
   People 5, 19, 79
   Rights *see* queer rights 5, 14
Logics
   And/or 7, 19–20, 28–30, 66–67, 114–115, 122–124, 128, 130–131
   Balkanist *see* Balkanism
   Civilizational 2, 14–15, 19–20, 53–54, 62–70, 75–77, 99–100, 135–136, 140–143, 150, 152
   Queer 4, 22, 27–30, 109–110, 136, 145, 149–150
   Racial 5, 49–50, 53–54, 140–141, 143

Mujahedin 92–93, 128, 171 n.4
Muslim women 55–56, 65–66, 69–70, 75–76, 95

NATO *see* North Atlantic Treaty Organization 59–60, 70, 104
"Never Again" 51–55, 66–67

Normal *vs.* perverse 6, 28, 32–33, 37–38, 87–88, 94, 127
North Atlantic Treaty Organization *see* NATO

Oppressed groups 2–3, 15, 112, 135–136, 138–141, 150–151
Orientalism 14–15, 18–19, 50–51, 63–65, 69–70, 90, 92–93
   Legal 50–51
   Nesting 68–69
Otto, Dianne 3–4, 16, 144–145, 148

Palestine 117, 138–140, 171 n.1
Paternalism
   Lawful adjudicators 76, 82, 100–102
   The only civilized alternative 2, 59, 72–73, 82, 102–107, 122
Performativity 30–32, 33–34, 47–48, 73–74, 76–77, 87–89, 96–97
Perpetrators
   Balkan 19–20, 28, 68–69, 89, 91–92, 94, 96–97, 98–102, 105, 130
   Complex 21, 24–25, 109–110, 123–133
   Homophobic 10, 14, 69, 90, 93–94, 98–99
   Homosexual 10, 68–69, 90, 94
   Hyper-heteromasculine 19–21, 34, 36–37, 49–51, 55–56, 61–63, 65, 69–71, 75, 83, 87–88, 90, 95, 99–100, 123, 142–143, 147–148
   Kind 109–110, 123, 124–126, 127–129, 133–134
   Monstrous 14–15, 70–71, 90, 93, 98–99, 125–126, 130–133
   Perverse *see* queer
   Queer *see* perverse 69, 87–88, 93, 141, 146
   Racialized 14–15, 21, 49–50, 99–100
   Sadistic 5, 11, 13, 31, 43–44, 69–70, 72–73, 87–95, 103–104, 123, 126, 130, 141
   Women 91–92
Poststructuralism
   Feminist 23, 25, 30–31, 33–34
Poststructural discourse analysis 23–25, 41–47
Prosecutors *see also* Office of the Prosecutor 76–77, 80–81, 83–84, 86, 97–99, 100–101, 103, 107, 109, 118–120, 142–143
Protection 21, 31, 49–50, 70, 72–73, 79–80, 82–83, 99–100, 101–102, 103–104, 143–144
Puar, Jasbir 14, 35–36

Queer critique 145–152
Queer (governance) mechanism 6–8

Queer postcolonial scholarship in international relations 14–15
Queer poststructural discourse analysis 25–27, 41–47
Queer rights *see* LGBTQIA+ rights
Queer theories of governance 8–10

Race, ethnicity, and religion 18–19, 34, 65–66, 119
Racism 5–6, 14–15, 58–59, 63, 66, 68, 138–139, 143–144
Reflexivity 38–41
Representation 23–27
(Re)productive power 30–32
Resistance 2–3, 7, 109–110, 111–113, 115–118, 120–122, 133, 139–140, 151
Reynolds, John 138, 140, 149–150, 170 n.3
Rule of law 59, 101–102, 105–106

Saviors 5, 14–15, 64–65, 70, 143–144
Sexual violence
   Against LGBTQIA+ people 45–46
   Against men *see also* homophobic violence 11–12, 98
   Against women *see* rape victims
   Fate-worse-than-death 77
Sexuality 33–35, 36–37
Shepherd, Laura 27–28, 36
Sjoberg, Laura 24–25, 36, 45, 132
Spivak, Gayatri 117, 140–141, 151
Split subject 29, 115–116, 123–124, 130–131, 145
Srebrenica genocide 53, 56–57, 112, 138, 147
Straightness *see also* heteronormativity 9, 32, 79, 87–88
Suicide 115–116, 117–118
Noisy survivors 12–13, 109–122, 128–129, 133

Therapeutic governance 58–59, 103
Todorova, Maria 65–67, 68–69
Transphobia 6, 9
Trans-theorising 9
Tribunals
   International criminal 13, 68, 81–82, 86–87, 121–122
   People's 121–122, 148–149
   War crimes or postwar 51–54, 57, 59–61, 70–71, 100–101, 104–105, 143

UN *see* United Nations
United Nations *see* UN 52, 54, 57–59, 64–65, 99–101, 103–105, 140, 146–147

Secretary-general 11–12, 60–61
UNSC *see* United Nations Security Council
United Nations Security Council *see* UNSC 11–12, 17, 49–50, 55, 58–59, 60–61, 64–65, 104–105

Vernon, Patrick 27, 171 n.3
Victimization 36–37, 72–87, 107, 109–110, 114, 143, 147
Victimhood 8–9, 35, 43, 44–45, 73–74, 80–82, 83–84, 101, 114, 116, 139–140
Victims
  Balkan 64–65, 73–74, 79–80, 100–101
  Dead 67, 70, 80
  Feminized 2, 5, 21, 36–37, 43, 49–50, 70, 72–73, 74–77, 87, 99–100, 111, 141–143, 146
  Homogenous 72–73, 80–83, 87, 107, 109–111, 114, 118, 143–144
  Iconic 56, 75–76
  Legitimate 79–80, 87
  Maimed 70, 80–83
  Passive 28, 36–37, 43, 73–74, 86, 112–113, 114–133
  Racialized 21, 49–50, 99–100
  Rape *see* sexual violence against women 74–77, 78–79, 86–87, 95–96, 103, 115

Silenced 72–73, 83–87, 107, 116, 118, 135–136, 146–147
Violence
  Homophobic *see also* sexual violence against men 36, 97–99
  Legal 13, 36–37, 72–74, 75–76, 81–82, 86, 87–88, 106–107, 135–136, 148, 152
  Legitimate 14–15, 83, 96, 104–105, 147
  Nonsexual 45–47, 76–77, 98–99
  Sexual 42–43, 45–46, 55–56, 74–76, 77–79, 90–91, 97, 101–102, 115

War on Terror 14–15, 35–36, 93
Weber, Cynthia 29–30, 38–39
Western gaze 14–16, 51–53, 55, 64–65, 68–69, 120, 170 n.3, 171 n.5
Whiteness 4–5, 14–15, 64–66, 68, 143–144, 170 n.4
World War II 51–53, 65–67

Xavier, Sujith 138, 140, 149–150, 170 n.3

Yugoslav conflicts of the 1990s 54, 58–61, 69–70, 170 n.1

Zarkov, Dubravka 77, 86